POWER AND PARTICIPATORY DEVELOPMENT

Power and Participatory Development

Theory and Practice

edited by
NICI NELSON and SUSAN WRIGHT

INTERMEDIATE TECHNOLOGY PUBLICATIONS

Intermediate Technology Publications
103/105 Southampton Row, London WC1B 4HH, UK

Reprinted 1997, 2000

British Library Cataloguing in Publication Data

Power and Participatory Development:
Theory and Practice
I. Wright, Susan   II. Nelson, Nici
307.14

ISBN 1-85339-241-3

Typeset by Dorwyn Ltd, Rowlands Castle, Hants
Printed by SRP Exeter

Contents

PART FOUR: 'COMMUNITY' AND 'USER' PARTICIPATION: NEGOTIATING LOCAL AND BUREAUCRATIC POWER

PART FIVE: 'PARTICIPATION' IN THE LANGUAGE AND PRACTICE OF GOVERNMENTAL AND NON-GOVERNMENTAL ORGANIZATIONS

Notes on contributors

Fatima Akilu is reading for a PhD in Psychology at Reading University on young homelessness. After taking a degree in the USA she became interested in this field whilst carrying out an MSc project on research methods. She has written on different aspects of homelessness including a chapter in P. Kennett (ed.) *New Approaches to Homelessness* SAUS Working Paper No. 104 (1992).

Robert Chambers is a Fellow of the Institute of Development Studies at the University of Sussex. He has worked on rural development in sub-Saharan Africa and south Asia and is currently concentrating on the development and spread of the approaches and methods of participatory rural appraisal. He is the author of *Rural Development: Putting the Last First* (Harlow: Longman 1983).

Donald Curtis, PhD, is Director of the Development Administration Group at the University of Birmingham. His research and practice interests are in nonformal organization for common benefit, reflected in *Beyond Government* (Macmillan 1991); NGO and private roles in rural development; the enabling role of the state; management and organizational development.

Rosalind Eyben, PhD, trained as a social anthropologist and since then worked in development assistance for a variety of aid agencies. Currently she is Principal Social Development Adviser at the Overseas Development Administration.

Jane C.V. Gronow has a BSc in Forestry and MA in Rural Social Development. She is currently employed by Overseas Development Administration as a Technical Co-operation Officer on loan to the Government of Ghana, working with the staff of the Ghana Forestry Department to explore and develop the potential for professional foresters and local institutions to collaborate on the management of the tropical high forest of southern Ghana. Prior to working in Ghana, she worked for eight years in the middle hills of Nepal with the professional foresters of the Nepalese Forestry Department on the development of community forest management.

Karim Hussein is a Research Assistant at the Institute of Development Studies at the University of Sussex. He has a Masters in Rural Development from Sussex University. His main research interests include: how to encourage participatory development strategies; appropriate methods to measure the poverty reduction effects of development interventions; famine early warning and response mechanisms in the Sahel and eastern Africa; food aid and the organization of material relief for refugees, especially Mozambiquan refugees in Malawi.

Sarah Ladbury, PhD, is a freelance social development consultant who has worked extensively for the Overseas Development Administration and other aid agencies in south east Asia and Africa across a range of sectors. Her current interests include training national consultants to undertake consultancy work more effectively for multilateral and bilateral agencies. She is a tutor on the Wye External Programme course 'Gender Relations and Agrarian Change' at Wye College, University of London, and is an Honorary Research Fellow in the Department of Anthropology, University of Kent.

Jacqueline Lane has a degree in Economics (Cambridge, 1990) and studied Rural Development at the University of Sussex. Since October 1991 she has been the Research Assistant in the Research and Statistics Unit at Charities Aid Foundation, which carries out a wide programme of qualitative and quantitative research into the size and scope of the voluntary sector in the UK. Recent publications include chapters on resourcing and corporate support for the voluntary sector in *Researching the Voluntary Sector* (Charities Aid Foundation).

Vanessa Maher (PhD Cantab) is Associate Professor of Cultural Anthropology at the University of Turin. Author of books and articles in English and Italian on social life in Morocco and in Italy, her interests include the anthropology of gender, urban anthropology, ethnicity and emigration. She worked between 1988 and 1991 with a research team of immigrants on a study of immigration to Italy and has since been involved in various practical applications of this research.

Alex Mavrocordatos is a theatre worker by profession. Since 1992, he has been working through Oxfam with RISE, a Namibian non-governmental organization, training their field workers to use theatre techniques in work with farmers, and women's and youth associations. He is interested in the use of theatre as a vehicle for empowerment and has pioneered 'listening theatre' which concentrates on groups of community volunteers who use interactive theatre performances that explore problems rather than instructing on solutions. He has also worked with Oxfam and World Neighbors in Mali and is writing a book on the evolution of theatre for development approaches.

Pathika Martin has a Master's degree in the field of non-formal education and many years' experience in the health sector. She has worked on the SOS Sahel Oral History Project and in Mali on an environmental project where she was responsible for co-ordinating training, extension and women's activities. More recently, she has carried out research into methods of participatory evaluation and general factors which influence the degree of local participation in development projects. Currently, she is rearing a small son.

Kevin Meethan has a DPhil. in Social Anthropology (Sussex) and his current post is Senior Lecturer in Urban Studies, University of Humberside. His fieldwork on community care was undertaken while he was Research

Fellow at the Social Policy Research Unit, University of York, and was funded by the Joseph Rowntree Foundation. His current research interests include urban policy and urban regeneration.

David Mosse has a DPhil. in Social Anthropology (Oxford) and is at the Centre for Development Studies, University College Swansea. He is engaged in teaching, research and consultancy, focusing on natural resources development in south Asia. He has lived and worked in India frequently since 1978. He has provided consultancy support to participatory development projects in India, Sri Lanka, Bangladesh, Nepal and Tanzania, worked as Oxfam Representative for south India in Bangalore (1987–91) and in the ODA Social Development Unit (1986–7). He is the author of several articles on social organization, popular religion and rural development in India.

Nici Nelson, PhD, is Lecturer in Social Anthropology at Goldsmiths College, University of London. She combines interest in action anthropology with her academic interest in gender, urbanization and development in Africa, with a specific focus on East Africa and the Horn. She carries out short term consultancies with various non-government organizations, such as ERA and ACORD.

Jules N. Pretty is Director of the Sustainable Agriculture Programme of the International Institute for Environment and Development. The programme is engaged in policy research, development of and training in participatory methods and approaches, and capacity support with groups in the South. His current research interests focus on the linkages between local and community-level action for regenerative agriculture, soil and water conservation, and other resource management issues. He is co-author of the book *Unwelcome Harvest: Agriculture and Pollution*, (Earthscan, London 1991) and sole author of the book *Regenerating Agriculture: Policies and Practice for Sustainable Growth and Self-Reliance*, (Earthscan, 1994).

Joke Schrijvers, PhD, is Professor of Development Studies at the Institute of Development Research Amsterdam (InDRA), The Netherlands. In 1976 she helped in establishing the Research and Documentation Centre on Women and Autonomy at the University of Leiden, followed by anthropological action-research in Sri Lanka in 1977–8 on the effects of planned and unplanned changes in the lives of peasant women. She has supervised research projects in Sri Lanka, Indonesia, Egypt, Mexico and Bangladesh. She has published works on Sri Lanka and feminist anthropology, and her current research interests include displacement and violence (*The Violence of Development*, 1993).

Ian Scoones is a research associate in the Sustainable Agriculture and Drylands Programmes of the International Institute for Environment and Development. He holds a doctorate in applied ecology from the University of London. His current research interests focus on the management of natural resources in dryland Africa, particularly drawing on land-users' perspectives on resource management issues. He is co-editor of the book *Beyond Farmer First: rural people's knowledge, agricultural research and extension practice*, (Intermediate Technology Publications, London, 1994).

Parmesh Shah is a DPhil. student at the Institute of Development Studies, University of Sussex. Previously he was Senior Programme Executive with the Aga Khan Rural Support Programme, India. He is an agricultural engineer with a postgraduate degree in Agricultural Management. Currently he is assessing the impact of participatory development and local institution-building on natural resource management in India. He is co-ordinating an international research programme on Economic and Environmental Impact of Participatory Watershed Management and is facilitating training programmes on Participatory Rural Appraisal in India, East Africa and Vietnam.

Janet Townsend, DPhil. (Oxford), has been a Lecturer in Geography at the University of Durham since 1970. Since 1965, she has been working with people making farms out of the rainforest in Latin America, especially in Colombia and Mexico. Since 1984, she has been working more with the women in these farm families. She co-edited with Janet Momsen *Geography of Gender in the Third World* (Hutchinson, London 1987), and edited *Indigenous Peoples: A Field Guide to Development* by John Beauclerc and Jeremy Narby (Oxfam, Oxford 1988). Forthcoming are Janet Townsend, Ursula Arrevillaga, Socorro Cancino, Silvana Pacheco and Elia Perez, *Voces Femeninas de las Selvas* (Montecillo: Colegio de Postgraduados) and in collaboration with Jennie Bain, Socorro Cancino, Susan F. Frenk, Silvana Pacheco and Elia Perez, *Women's Voices from the Rainforest* (Routledge, London).

Susan Wright is a lecturer in social anthropology at Sussex University. Her doctoral research was on tribal responses to modernizing state policies in Iran. Since then she has worked on relations between people and the state in Britain, doing participant observation as a community worker, and studying a participatory development programme in a declining market town, community arts, and an attempt by a county council to develop an 'enabling' local state. She is the editor of *Anthropology of Organizations* (Routledge, 1994).

Preface

In July 1992, on behalf of GAPP (Group for Anthropology in Policy and Practice) we organized a conference to explore participatory development in theory and practice. The papers from that conference formed the basis of this volume.

We would like to express our appreciation to the institutions and individuals whose help made this volume possible. Firstly, we would like to thank the British Overseas Development Administration (ODA) and the German Gesellschaft fur Technische Zusammenarbeit (GTZ) for grants which made it possible to hold the conference. Goldsmiths College was the venue for the conference. Our thanks go to Simon Cohn and Susan Greenwood for very efficient administration of the event. The participants at the conference not only provided interesting papers but also generated discussion during the experimental participatory sessions which stimulated the interest in having the proceedings published.

We would like to thank the contributors to this volume for their good-natured and prompt responses to our requests and deadlines over the two years it has taken to complete the editing. Without the efficient and dedicated help of Katie Sollohub, the final preparation of the manuscript would have been a very difficult task indeed. Janice Baker's generosity with time and ideas far exceeded her official role as publisher's sub-editor and we are very grateful for her help. We wish to thank *Anthropology in Action* for releasing funds which assisted with costs incurred in the preparation of the manuscript. Finally we would like to express our appreciation to the Overseas Development Administration for the grant to disseminate the results of the conference which was used to reduce the cover price of this book.

SUSAN WRIGHT
Cultural and Community Studies
University of Sussex

NICI NELSON
Goldsmiths College
University of London

July 1994

1. Participation and power

NICI NELSON and SUSAN WRIGHT

The theme of this book arose from a three-day conference organized by GAPP (Group for Anthropology in Policy and Practice) to explore critically the theories and practices of participatory development. The issue that emerged most strongly from the conference was that 'participation', if it is to be more than a palliative, involves shifts in power. These occur within communities, between 'people' and policy-making and resource-holding institutions, and within the structure of those organizations. Shifts in power therefore became the theme of this book. This immediately raised questions about the meanings of participation and power and in this introduction these two concepts will be discussed in turn.[1]

Agencies and individuals use the term participatory development in a variety of ways. One of the most common distinctions made by many of the authors in this volume is that of participation as a *means* (to accomplish the aims of a project more efficiently, effectively or cheaply) as opposed to participation as an *end* (where the community or group sets up a process to control its own development). Both types of participation imply the possibility of very different power relationships between members of a community as well as between them and the state and agency institutions. Simply put, the extent of empowerment and involvement of the local population is more limited in the first approach than it is in the second.

Establishing an ideal definition is not the end of the matter. First, the word participation has historically accumulated certain meanings and these are all available to be drawn upon, with the possibility of slippage from one to another. Second, where, with the best of intentions, 'participation' is used to mean 'empowering the weakest and poorest', institutional procedures may work out in other ways. Third, in any contemporary context, participation is imbued with different ideologies or given particular meanings by people situated differently within any organization. In other words, the ideal definition of participation is only the start to exploring what meanings are attached to it in any context, how they are contested and deployed, and who gains and who loses in the process. We argue that those who are trying to shift the development apparatus to enable women and marginalized people 'to determine choices in life and to influence the direction of change' (Moser 1989: 1815) need critical analyses of ethnographic contexts to see how the discourse and procedures of participation actually

1

work in practice. Such analyses draw on new theoretical and methodological developments, discussed in the first two sections of the book. The context that needs to be studied is a vertical slice (Nader 1980) stretching from people in villages and towns, through in-country agencies and governments to international development agencies, represented in the later sections of the book.

'Participation' in policy: accumulated meanings

Participation, like community, is a 'warmly persuasive word' which 'seems never to be used unfavourably, and never to be given any positive opposing or distinguishing term' (Williams 1976: 76). Yet it can be attached to very different sets of relations, often seemingly by its 'warmness' distracting close attention from the nature of those relations. For example, in Britain in the 1960s and 1970s 'popular participation' or 'political participation' – or the lack thereof – was of great academic and political concern (Parry 1972). It had become evident that local government was not fulfilling its role as a democratic means of organizing local affairs (Lumb 1980: 105). Popular participation meant only how a larger number of people could be persuaded to get involved in public decision-making. Participatory procedures were to bring newly formed tenants' associations, pressure groups and protest campaigns into contact with those making decisions about them but without them. Such groups were not necessarily asked to share in making actual decisions; more often they were to be consulted on policy proposals or asked to help implement them. At a time when housing, town centres and road networks were being modernized, planning was seen to have the most important impact on people's lives. A national report (Skeffington 1969) resulted in 'participation' being essential for the legitimacy of new Structure Plans and Local Plans. Councils invited letters, used questionnaires and held public meetings, usually to ask 'the public' which of a number of pre-determined options in a draft plan they preferred. Even the small numbers who participated felt disillusioned (Lumb 1980: 110). Local councils determined the terms on which people participated, whilst using participation to check their worst excesses and justify their claims to democratic status (Wright 1990: 52). In this sense, participation was experienced as political co-option.

The policy history of participation in the Third World introduces further meanings. Early post-war models of development were based on the image that capital penetration, commoditization and industrialization would transform a traditionally isolated, subsistence peasantry into participants in a modern economy and in the politics of the nation state (Ferguson 1990: 15,56). This use of participation suggested people were not economically and politically active before development came along. In this construction of people as objects of a national programme of development, their participation in projects often meant contributions in the form of labour, cash or kind. In the 1980s discussions began on why thirty years of conventional, technocratic, top-down forms of development were not working. Initially the failure of many such public programmes was traced to the alienation of 'beneficiaries'. Some researchers highlighted the marginalization of women in the development process. For example, one of the root causes of the decrease in food production in Africa was thought to be the fact that research and implementation had ignored female farming practices (Bryson 1981). This led to ideas about beneficiary involvement.

Others, in a more sweeping critique, took 'development', the agenda of the post-colonial state, to have been a failure. There was an argument for people not to be dependent on the state but through participatory action research (PAR) to define their own development (Fals Borda 1988). In the 1970s, international non-governmental organizations had also argued that development should generate more self-sufficiency rather than depend on top-down state provision of services. They attempted, not often successfully, to design income-generating projects so that people would have the resources to look after their own welfare, either by providing services themselves or by mobilizing to obtain services that they determined from the state. Participation had a corollary in self-sufficiency and self-help, in opposition to, or independence from, the state.

A strange echo of these approaches came in the World Bank's monetarist 'structural adjustment policies' in the 1980s, which moved functions from the state to the private and non-governmental sectors. As well as jointly lobbying for debt relief, international non-governmental organizations produced critiques of structural adjustment policies. For example, a study for UNICEF argued that whilst adjustment policies were necessary, their effect on vulnerable groups, especially children, should be alleviated by maintaining the incomes of the poor, expanding health and education services, and supporting children's nutrition (Cornia, Jolly and Stewart 1989). The response of the World Bank to this, *Adjustment with a Human Face*, appropriated earlier language of the non-governmental organizations about self-sufficiency. This rhetoric was, however, double-edged. Soon the World Bank was arguing that the state should not be omnipresent and 'clients' should be involved in the production of their own services. Structural adjustment policies were accompanied by an emphasis on 'community' and 'family' (i.e. principally women) taking on welfare and service responsibilities formerly ascribed to the state. The crucial difference between this notion of self-sufficiency and the earlier ideas of non-governmental organizations was that this work was unresourced.

In evaluations of the shortcomings of development at the end of the decade, a call for 'participatory development' began. The pressure came partly from Southern organizations. Five hundred representatives of African grassroots organizations at the Arusha Conference in 1990, organized by the

3

United Nation's Economic Commission for Africa, called for 'popular participation and transformation'. The South Commission's 'twenty-nine leading personalities' of the Third World in the same year proposed strategies for making people central to development through economic growth, good government, equity and popular participation. In the North, the results of large programmes to incorporate participation into the practice of UN agencies were being reported. For example, Oakley (1991) analysed participation in practice in 120 projects for the People's Panel on Participation (funded by FAO, ILO, UNIFEM and WHO and founded in 1982). Ideas were spreading in other international agencies. The Development Assistance Committee's Expert Group on Women in Development produced guiding principles which showed how aid design could be more gender aware and shift asymmetrical relations between women and men through participatory development (ODA 1993: 93). In 1991, the OECD's Development Assistance Committee's Chairman's Report had a chapter on participatory development. This was defined as strategies which 'combine effective economic policies, equitable access to basic social and economic services and broader popular participation in decision-making, on the orientation of government policies and programmes' (OECD 1991: 2). Participatory development was beginning to look like a portmanteau concept. It carried baggage from old ideas about participation in national economies (now being restructured) and government decision-making, and about improving the effectiveness of projects by beneficiary involvement. It also contained new ideas about gender equity and good government.

Several European bilateral agencies experimented with definitions and approaches. For example, the German agency GTZ was using participatory methods to generate qualitative understandings of development (Kochendörfer-Lucius and Osner 1991). In 1991 a report was produced based on GTZ's experience of participatory management of projects in Asia. Identifying the aim of development as reaching not the poorest of the poor but those who still had some resources left (GTZ 1991: 5), they defined participation as 'co-determination and power sharing throughout the . . . programme cycle', (ibid: 4). The report detailed procedures for treating poor people as equal partners from the initial definition of the project idea through appraisal and management to evaluation. Participatory methods of appraisal and evaluation were also widely known. By 1990 all the bilateral agencies had policies on participation (Swedish SIDA since 1980; ODA 1993) although the details were still being worked out.

From 1991 this work began to focus on the World Bank, which the bilateral agencies influenced, and by which, as the World Bank's ideas advanced, they were in turn influenced. A Learning Group on Participatory Development had been established in December 1990, drawn from World Bank staff. It was to identify challenges to the Bank in stepping up its efforts to support participation in its operations. SIDA, later joined by

4

GTZ, paid for the research studies it commissioned. In May 1994 a draft report was discussed by 200 Bank staff across both country and central policy departments and by 60 non-Bank participants. The role of the latter was to act as a pressure group to give additional leverage to the internal constituency for change.

The report introduced the idea of 'stakeholders' as 'parties who either affect or are affected by the Bank's actions and policies' (World Bank 1994: 1). Defining the Bank's overriding objective as poverty reduction, the primary stakeholders were unequivocally stated to be the poor and marginalized: those who lack information and power and are excluded from the development process (ibid: 2). The governments of borrowing countries were called 'borrowing stakeholders'. Secondary stakeholders were non-governmental organizations, businesses and professional bodies who had technical expertise and linkages to primary stakeholders. Participation was defined as 'a process through which stakeholders influence and share control over development initiatives, decisions and resources which affect them'. Excluded from this definition were situations where primary stakeholders were involved simply as passive recipients, informants or labourers in a development effort (ibid: 6 – these were included in the OECD report in 1991). The non-Bank participants' addendum added that the goal of participation was to reach and engage primary stakeholders in ways that were transformational, not instrumental. Getting communities to decide on their own priorities was called transformative; getting people to buy into a donor's project was instrumental.

As, at the same time, the World Bank was encouraging borrowing governments and implementing agencies to take greater control of Bank projects, the proposals were for borrowers to develop processes by which primary stakeholders could 'initiate, influence and control development activities'. These included involving more stakeholders in country-wide economic and sector work, ensuring that in all projects stakeholders were systematically identified and involved at all stages, making financial resources more available to the poor, and strengthening the management capacity of primary stakeholders' organizations. The next issue will be to 'mainstream' these approaches in the work procedures and the performance criteria of all staff. To say that this will require 'significant shifts in the Bank's institutional culture and procedures' is an understatement (ibid:1). At the moment 20 per cent of Bank staff are responsible for 70 per cent of participatory projects, and only a very small number of projects have any participatory element (in 1991, 13 per cent of projects in the Africa Region portfolio had primary stakeholder participation). How will these ideas be 'mainstreamed' alongside the Bank's structural adjustment policies (the quintessentially centralized and top-down approach) and in a highly centralized organizational structure, where 80 per cent of bank staff are based at headquarters at Washington? (Hancock 1988: 127).

5

There is considerable enthusiasm in the development community about the World Bank Learning Group's work. Its definition of participation is now ahead of some of the bilateral agencies. The poor are given the status of primary stakeholders. Participation means their active, not passive, involvement and it should be transformative. Participation has, however, positioned people very differently in relation to the development apparatus in the past – as a presence, as objects of a theoretical process of economic and political transformation; as expected 'beneficiaries' of programmes with pre-set parameters; as contributors of casual labour to help a project achieve its ends; as politically co-opted legitimizers of a policy; or as people trying to determine their own choices and direction independent of the state. In any ethnographic context, several of these accumulated meanings may be in play.

Theoretical and ideological bases of 'participation'

Two key words in the World Bank's participation strategy are 'stakeholder' and 'transformative'. Both of these derive from theories about how society is organized and how it can be changed, and are in that sense ideological. Indeed, 'transformation', like 'participation' itself, is often used by people with different ideological positions, who give it very different meanings. Once these words come into everyday use in policy-making organizations, they may appear neutral and 'common sense', yet they still carry their ideological positioning with them (Wright 1994:22). In order to analyse the impact of participatory initiatives in organizational contexts, it is therefore important to denaturalize these words and see their ideological implications.

Chambers associates these changes in the World Bank with the introduction of new ideas from North American organizational management which emphasise 'decentralisation, trust, rapid adaptation, falling forwards, and diversity' (1994).[2] In such organizations the rigidities of Fordism are being eliminated by removing middle management, and 'empowering' workers to operate flexibly in teams, responding to situations as they arise and communicating ideas for improvements directly to senior management. This only appears to be empowerment if a pluralistic view is taken of society as made up of free-floating actors, each with different interests which they pursue by bargaining with each other in interactional space. Then the questions are how to design procedures to bring the parties into contact, how to change the behaviour and attitudes of those who are used to dominating, and how to give 'primary stakeholders' more chance of voicing their view of the world. These are important but not sufficient if a structural view is taken which sees people as positioned within systems of relations through which inequalities are reproduced. From this point of view (from which many of the calls for

6

participation originally came), 'transformation' is structural, not just behavioural.

Ideology is embedded in the meanings and implications of such key words, but in some contexts it is also quite explicit. Turbyne (1994 and forthcoming) has shown that in Guatemala, organizations with political ideologies as far apart as the military and radical popular movements were using the language of participation and empowerment. Different meanings were given to key words, not just between organizations but also within them (ibid). The headquarters staff of one organization adopted participatory approaches and talked about 'local control' in a way which she described as neo-liberal. They had a seemingly apolitical agenda for people to stand on their own feet and get ahead in life. In contrast, the organization's middle management did not use the word 'empowerment', and 'participation', to them, meant self-management to ensure project efficiency and success. At field level, the workers had not heard of either self-management or empowerment, as the use of the term 'beneficiaries' gave 'participation' a functional meaning – they had to participate in the project by building a latrine or roofing a house in order to receive a food parcel.

An organization is therefore not monolithic. Within it there will be multiple meanings of participation. In some cases people will be aware of the different meanings they give to a word and will contest them. In others, people will assume that they understand each other when they use the same word, and implicit ideological differences will not be openly contested. In the case above, communication between the layers of a steeply hierarchical organization seemed so poor that they did not even share the same words, let alone meanings. The ways multiple meanings of key words are (or are not) negotiated between people positioned differently in such hierarchies not only reveal different theoretical and ideological approaches to social organization, they also introduce issues of power.

Power and empowerment

The concept of power and the question of how to analyse it has been a central topic of debate in the social sciences since the 1960s. It was complicated further when, associated with participation, 'empowerment' was introduced, with the idea that some can act on others to give them power or enable them to realize their own potential.

Power is both experienced in encounters in everyday life and as part of systems. For example 'the family' is experienced in personalized, face to face relations within a household, but those experiences are not idiosyncratic; they are systematic, heavily imbued with ideology, with some aspects subject to intervention and control by the state. Equally, access to resources, control of the elements and processes of production, and rights to dispose of products are experienced in face to face relations, but are also part of wider and systematic economic relations. How people stand in relation to each other in these systems is described as power. Power is a description of a relation, not a 'thing' which people 'have'. However, there are three models of power currently being used to analyze different aspects of participation and empowerment. Based on different metaphors, they convey very different ideas about 'what power is and how it works'.

The first model is often called 'power to' and uses a metaphor of human development. This suggests that, like human abilities, power can grow infinitely if you work at it, and 'growth' of one person does not necessarily negatively affect another. The danger with this metaphor is that it can suggest that power is a personal attribute. Hartsock (who avoids this danger) describes this as an energy definition of power which is ever-expanding (1984). It is a generative power, stimulating activity in each other to realize what capacities and knowledge can be developed in a collective way. It is transformative, in the sense that, for those who view the world from its margins, 'The point is to develop an account of the world which treats our perspectives not as subjugated or disruptive knowledges, but as primary and constitutive of a different world' (1990: 171).

Using this model, 'empowerment' starts from an examination of how power is present in multiple and heterogeneous social relations. In these relations individuals are simultaneously undergoing and exercising power; through which they are constituting their subjectivity and participating in each others' oppression (Hartsock 1990: 168). In such everyday encounters, individuals are both reproducing and challenging, or changing, systematic relations. Relations are always structured but never determined. In some models of empowerment, this process of connecting personal experience to systems of hierarchical relations starts with an emotional response to a 'mobilizing event' of personal significance (Kieffer 1984, quoted in Turbyne forthcoming). In other models, this comes from an interaction between, say, a category of women who are sharing details of their everyday experiences, and an outsider who provides a more distanced 'sociological imagination' (Hymes 1972). In the process, both parties question the 'realities' with which they started and both transform their understanding (Freire 1972; Fals Borda 1988). Out of this interaction, the aim is to find 'more spaces of control' (Giddens 1984) where, although never powerless to start with, by developing confidence and changing attitudes and behaviours, they can alter the power differentials in their relationships. Rowlands (1992) argues that this process has three levels. First, the personal level involves developing confidence and abilities (including undoing the effects of internalized oppression). Second, is the ability to negotiate and influence close relationships. The third involves working collectively to have greater impact than each could have alone. This is where 'power to' overlaps with the next model of power.

8

The second model of power has been described as 'power over' and involves gaining access to 'political' decision-making, often in public forums. Following Rowlands, hitherto marginalized people with an expanding sense of their ability to influence ever more aspects of their lives will soon encounter relations where control of resources has been institutionalized, sometimes within the locality, sometimes in more distant councils. The challenge is for the marginalized group to gain treatment as equal partners in a process of development from people in such institutions, so that they have long-term access to resources and decision-making. The expansion of 'power to' to the point where they tackle 'power over' may be described as the second stage of empowerment.

'Power over', however, is based on a different metaphor. In contrast to the images of human growth used to express the ever-expanding 'power to', early studies treated 'power over' as a 'thing' of which there was a finite amount in a closed system. Like the idea of redistributing a closed amount of wealth within a national economy, if one party gained more power, it would be at the expense of others – a zero sum. This model derived from studies of city government in the sixties and seventies (Polsby 1963; Dahl 1961). They started with the premise that power was only found in observable conflicts resulting in 'concrete decisions' where one party prevailed over another and made them do what they would not otherwise have done. This was phrased as 'A has power over B'. A further dimension was introduced by Bachrach and Baratz (1970) who saw power being exercised when one party established barriers (political values and institutional practices) which prevented others from voicing their interests, let alone getting them on the agenda. The result was 'non decision-making' on key issues, and conflict was not visible. This was summarized as 'A affects B in a manner contrary to B's interests'. Lukes (1974) introduced a third dimension, where the interests of the dominant party were taken to be natural or god-given, so that no alternative to the status quo could be imagined. In other words, 'A exercises power over B . . . by influencing, shaping or determining his very wants' (1974: 23). As a result B accepts his (sic) role in the existing order of things (ibid: 24) and no conflict arises. In contrast to the first two, Lukes' third kind of power may not be attributable to a particular individual's behaviour, and is not confined to decision-making within institutions but distributed in society through relations of gender, race and class, imbued with ideology. These analyses of 'power over' viewed power relations as coercive, centred in institutions of government, although spilling over into wider structures of society. They did not explain how power works when the practical and ideological impact of relations are experienced yet they are not visible.

A third, 'decentred' model of power is introduced by Ferguson (1990), following Foucault. Contrary to the previous view, this model asserts that power is not a substance possessed and exercised by any person or institution conceived of as a 'powerful' subject. Power is subjectless and is an apparatus consisting of discourse, institutions, actors and a flow of events. These interact invisibly with a logic that is only apparent afterwards, to draw or tie in more and more relations within the ambit of the state as in a tight knotting in the middle of a tangle of string.

Escobar (1988) analysed how the post-war discourse and practices of development economics and planning were established in international development organizations. He shows how particular ways of knowing the world and defining 'problems' were conferred upon sets of economic and political events, inviting intervention. Ferguson analyses how Lesotho was constructed as a 'less developed country', an object of development.

> In the course of being run through the theoretical machine of 'development', an impoverished labour reserve becomes a 'traditional, subsistence, peasant society'; wage labourers become farmers; the determinations of South African state and capital over the economic life of the Bosotho disappear; and a government of entrenched elites becomes an instrument for empowering the poor (1990: 66).

The design of a technical, large-scale 'integrated rural development project' flowed from this construction. In tracing the history of this project, the 'development system' was not simply explained by this discourse or by plotting the interests of the actors. Systems work through a process of struggle which runs through a stream of events and has startlingly unexpected outcomes. The project failed, as most had done. But the side effects of deploying the development apparatus were two-fold. First was an instrumental effect. Through the project, a wide range of state departments, including the military, established a permanent presence in the area. Referring more and more relations through bureaucratic circuits represented a 'tying together', 'multiplying' and 'knotting' of state power. The second was a conceptual effect. Because the development apparatus consistently represented the state and the project as apolitical and technical, this most sensitive political operation was achieved under a suspension of politics. Thus in the 1970s, projects like this failed in terms of stated intentions, but the side effect of the development apparatus was the expansion of state power. By living within the conceptual parameters of the development apparatus and not taking a distanced, reflexive stance, the project staff did not see the project's political embeddedness. Out of a stream of unplanned events, 'behind the backs' of the project staff, and masked by the visibility of the intentional plan, a silent process with a very different logic took place. Ferguson saw it as an anonymous set of interrelations that only had retrospective coherence.

This way of analysing decentred power raises two questions. First, bilateral and international agencies are developing participatory pro-

10

gramme management with a professed decentring of power in order to try and base development on the realities of marginalized people and non-governmental organizations. Inadvertently, however, and 'behind their backs', will the invisible side-effect logic of the development apparatus be incorporating the marginalized in even more distant clusterings of power, undermining their resistance? Second, if bureaucrats and researchers are embedded in this apparatus, and do not look reflexively at how it is working, how can they 'empower' others? Using the 'power over' and 'power to' models, Rowlands asks a similar question. How can empowerment be initiated by those who have 'power over' others when, as she asserts, 'any notion of empowerment being given by one group to another hides an attempt to keep control' (1992: 52)? She argues that this potentially bottom-up concept can be used to perpetuate and disguise continued top-down attitudes and approaches.

Shifts of power in research processes

This dilemma about how external agencies can intervene in such a way as to engender 'power to' among those subordinated by their own 'power over' faces researchers as much as other actors in the development scene. During the seventies and eighties so-called scientific models of research through which neutral experts elicited objective facts were criticized for turning people into passive objects of knowledge. Surely, it was argued, the aim of research should be the opposite – to enable categories of people traditionally objectified and silenced to be recognized as legitimate 'knowers'; to define themselves, increase their understanding of their circumstances, and act upon that knowledge. These ideas about participatory research came from three directions: from development, feminism and anthropology. The chapters in the first section of this book, by Chambers, Schrijvers, and Wright and Nelson, set out the theoretical developments in each of these three fields. Chambers argues that there is a paradigm shift from externally determined, product-based development, to participatory systems of research and decision-making which prioritize a process in which categories of people hitherto excluded become more powerful. Schrijvers sets out the thinking in feminism which might constitute an epistemological shift. Feminism has been concerned to break down the distance between the subject and object of research, to find ways of taking the 'standpoint' of marginalized people, and to conduct research in the form of a dialogue rather than an extractive process. Wright and Nelson trace the parallel histories of participant observation and participatory research in the social sciences in order to explore the limitations on the 'participatoriness' of participant observation, the central method in anthropology. Each of these chapters raises questions about the role of researchers in the participatory dilemma.

11

Whereas most social science seeks to understand social relations, not change them, the aim of Schrijvers' dialogic approach is to be transformative. Her case study among displaced people in Sri Lanka (this volume) indicates the limits to transformative research in a context of violence and fear. Instead, she acted as an advocate, a role whose empowering possibilities and limitations are further explored in Townsend's account of research among women pioneers in remote forests of Mexico. Townsend's research fulfilled the demands of participatory research in its early stages but she did not have the time or ease of access to take the conclusions of the research back to the women pioneers. She is left with an inability to discuss with them a major difference between the women's desire for homeworking opportunities and her judgement that this would be exploitative and unremunerative, based on her knowledge about the operations of the new international division of labour. Where time and access allows, people involved in research have the opportunity to challenge the knowledge, approach and role of an outside researcher. This is seen in Maher's discussion of work among immigrants in Italy where there was a debate about the primacy of experience over analysis as a source of understanding.

Chambers characterizes the professional and institutional authority of researchers and developers as 'holding the stick' – a symbol for having knowledge and the right to speak. 'Handing over the stick' is a dominant image in his work about legitimizing knowledges of marginalized and hitherto silenced people to whom development efforts are directed. This is a visible transfer of power from salaried research and development 'experts' to those with everyday expert knowledge as farmers, water gatherers, or other managers of scarce resources in contexts of high risk. Shah's chapter details some of the participatory research techniques which have been developed. Farmers mapped their watersheds, established water conservation and carried out technical experiments. They used other participatory methods to evaluate their environmental and economic success and to assess the distribution of benefits to different sectors of society. This involved development of 'power to' in ways similar to those described by Akilu for homeless people in Reading. Members of this most fragmented and stressed population in Britain increased their self-confidence and communication skills, organized themselves and worked together. Farmers in Bangladesh however, have extended this to training not only neighbouring villagers in participatory research techniques but also to training bureaucrats in the styles of behaviour needed for participatory decision-making in the institutions with which they deal. They have used their 'power to' to challenge and negotiate with researchers, programme implementers and bureaucrats who have institutional 'power over' them.

12

Shifts in power within communities

Lane points out that participation is always risky because it will challenge local power structures. The point of participatory research techniques like those described by Shah is to give a voice to those who are not regularly heard in the forums where village issues and decisions are determined. In Shah's case this was not just one-off; research was followed by development of local institutions which gave them continued ability to voice their issues within the village and in negotiations with bureaucrats. He does not indicate how this was achieved without provoking existing power-holders to undermine the institutions or shift the centre of decision-making elsewhere. Mosse's case study demonstrates how the project facilitators sought to promote greater participation by low-caste villagers in the irrigation system without alienating the high-caste villagers. Gronow questions the unexamined assumption of many policy-makers that shifting power is both desirable and unproblematical. Before attempting to shift power in a system it is important that the basis of existing and future institutional arrangements are well understood.

In establishing institutional links between villagers and wider systems, Scoones and Pretty warn against creating a parallel structure to that of the state through what amounts to local non-governmental organizations. Because these may not be elected they would not be accountable; they can be subject to corruption and are unlikely to persist. In addition, they consider that such localized participatory structures can rarely exercise any political clout beyond the local area. They suggest local-level organizations could join together in federations, 'scaling up' to carry greater political influence over state policy and draw on wider expertise than that available locally. Whatever model is adopted, the point is to institutionalize processes whereby those with newly acquired 'power to' can negotiate with those with 'power over' in the community and in agencies in ways which are 'unpickable' and sustainable when the outsider researcher or development worker has left.

Shifts of power within agencies

Several contributors notice how officials who speak the rhetoric of participation exhibit behaviour which is hierarchical. Gronow recounts how the district field staff of the Nepalese Forestry Department were frequently lectured in a top-down and directive manner on how to set up participatory processes and structures in villages. As Gronow points out, it was no wonder that such staff later adopted a pupil-teacher relationship with the villagers, the very antithesis of a participatory dialogic relationship. This seems to be especially the case in health projects where, as Eyben and Ladbury point out, the top levels of the project structure are highly trained men, the middle and lower levels untrained women, and the users mainly

13

poor women. Meethan provides another example of how a top-down authoritarian approach is taken to health care delivery. The Care in the Community policy in Britain intends health-care professionals, specialist voluntary organizations, family and informal carers to be equal partners supporting the person concerned with a combined package of care. Through a detailed case study of procedures, Meethan shows how 'professionals' tried to retain a privileged position and how the person in receipt of care was not 'empowered' by the way the policy operated. The policy language and the procedures were at variance.

There are many middle-level technocrats and bureaucrats who genuinely wish to increase 'power to' at the expense of their own 'power over'. Pretty and Scoones (this volume) describe a relatively successful initiative in Kenya based on a version of participatory methodology referred to as 'adaptive planning'. However, the ability of development workers and bureaucrats to achieve this shift in power often relies not only on their own behaviour in the field, but also on hierarchical organizational structures and decision-making systems, of which they are a part and from which they cannot cushion participants: their interaction is part of the development process.

Our contributors have not been slow to point out ways in which participatory rhetoric of agencies is often at odds with their organizational structures. Hussein examines the paradox of a stated objective of local empowerment held by certain non-governmental organizations while ultimate power is still held by outsiders. He charted the history of a so-called participatory project in Africa where a non-governmental organization, after appropriate and laudable consultation to obtain a local social needs assessment, proceeded to make its own assumptions about social needs from the central office. Local people had asked for an increase in health care. The non-governmental organization's central office planners then set up a fishing project in the area. This leap was justified by reasoning that by introducing an income-generating project, people could engage in self-sufficient development and could buy better health care. Those running the project from outside, and using a rhetoric of participation, finally determined what the people needed, even after hearing the people articulate their needs themselves.

Gaps between institutional rhetoric and practice

There are always differences between what people say and what they do, or, within oganizations, between their rhetoric and practice. A reflexive analysis of this difference may be a useful tool for encouraging organizational change. Several unexamined concepts may be plugging the gap between institutional rhetoric and practice. One is the continued use of 'community' as if it covered a homogeneous, idyllic, unified population with which researcher and developers can interact unproblematically. Eyben and Ladbury say that

14

'community' is a word which generates a good feeling in an observer (also Williams 1976). Too often homogeneity of interests is assumed, whereas an intervention, however 'participatory', will benefit some people while others lose out. Shifts in power between community members engaged in participatory development processes need to be examined carefully and discussed. Mavrocordatos and Martin (this volume) found that regular dramatic performances in a development context in West Africa tapped currents of duplicity and distrust which had surfaced as problems with collective work on environmental projects. All this was under the seemingly harmonious surface of a unified community. Mosse's description of a southern Indian water project demonstrates that participatory implementers were very aware of the potential divisions in communities they worked in. They pursued strategies designed to widen the base of involvement in decision-making and access to resources in a community historically divided by caste. Community is a concept often used by state and other organizations, rather than the people themselves, and it carries connotations of consensus and 'needs' determined within parameters set by outsiders. Curtis (this volume) warns against eliding colonial and post-colonial community development (characterized as facilitation of state intervention) with facilitation of 'development under local control'.

There is an allied issue which is highlighted by feminism. There is a tendency to believe that within a community consensus can be reached. Often different categories of people, like women, young men, low caste, landless and poor people are given separate arenas in participatory research projects to put over their own view of the 'space' in which they are located, how they experience its limitations, and what would be their priorities for change. In a forum they can present their perspective to other categories of people, who might not have heard these views before. A consensus on priorities for action is then needed within categories and between them, in the community as a whole. Feminism however, has been breaking down such categories, seeing that they hide many cross-cutting differences, as Wright and Nelson discuss. Living with difference is not the same as reaching consensus.

Just as writers of projects and documents may use unexamined concepts of community, so they may use vague definitions of 'participation'. Its accumulated meanings which were discussed above are illustrated in several chapters. Its user-friendly feel may disguise less-than-friendly agendas. Participatory methods may aim to transfer project costs from an agency to intended 'beneficiaries'. Mosse contends that the state government transferred the control and management of water tanks to village committees because there were too few resources to do it centrally. Gronow's chapter on forest management in Nepal implies that the government emphasizes local control for reasons of economy. This, despite the fact that analysts such as Cernea have warned that:

15

introducing bottom-up planning is not an operation free of incremental costs. It requires more staff time for the diagnosis phases than conventional top-down planning and costlier logistical means (1992: 58).

Too few have heeded those warnings, as Eyben and Ladbury make clear. The expectation that participants will provide volunteer or cheap labour in the process of participating in health projects may be unrealistic. The opportunity cost for the participants may be too high.

Though none of our contributors put forward such examples, the rhetoric of participation may also be a way of co-opting protest in a programme area as exemplified in Britain in the 1970s (discussed above). While building a wider process of consultation under the guise of participation, vociferous or ambitious members of the community may also become clients of an agency. Mosse fears that a new form of dependency is being created in the tank management project in southern India in terms of inputs and supports. In the project Mavrocordatos and Martin were involved in, the *griots* ('traditional' singers) who were encouraged to join the project in the first year, came to be seen as employees of the project. In subsequent years villagers provided them with less support.

The rhetoric of participation may also mask continued centralization in the name of decentralization. Several of the contributors (Mosse, Hussein, Eyben and Ladbury) have commented on the paradox of aid agencies which exert top-down influence while at the same time desiring to create local capacity for participation and decision-making. Lane demonstrates that Northern non-governmental organizations talk about decentralization, while continuing to direct the development process from the North by controlling funds. Lane calls for a transfer of resources and a devolution of power from the Northern to Southern non-governmental organizations as a way to promote empowerment in their practice. She maintains that Northern non-governmental organizations should concentrate on raising money, consciousness raising and education while leaving the actual 'doing of development' to their counterparts in the South. The Intermediate Technology Development Group (ITDG) is a leader in this field. They decentralized project management and funding to Southern offices in 1991, while the work of the UK office focuses on fundraising, influencing other development agencies, and development education almost exclusively. At present ITDG staff in all offices are aware, however, that the UK-based office could easily try to dominate international policy work which would then be redefined as the central purpose of the organization. To avoid this the directors from each office sit on the executive committee which manages the organization at the international level. Furthermore, efforts are being made to include all the offices in all advocacy work by making international team membership compulsory. Even so, these ideals are still difficult to put into practice while only about half of the staff of ITDG are located in the South (Crewe, personal communication 1994).

16

Finally, a gap between rhetoric and practice may be revealed when appeals are made to participation as an end, which implies a bottom-up process of empowerment. The organization, however, may still revolve around projects, evaluated in terms of externally defined, countable, tangible 'products' (see Marsden and Oakley 1990 for alternative, interpretative systems of evaluation). Many of the contributors record how organizational 'needs' of development agencies place constraints on participatory development. This is especially true at the planning stage if funders require to know what the project's objectives will be, yet funding is needed first to find out what participants want. Then there is a need for concrete results to prove that a project is working. Mavrocordatos and Martin lament that the intangible benefits of theatre activities in empowering village people had to be weighed against the need for tangible results (especially the adoption of technical imputs) for the agency's evaluation teams to measure. As Cernea points out, 'many benefits will remain invisible and do not lend themselves to easy measurement' (1992: 59). The problem goes further than the fact that the benefits defy measurement. Even when benefits occur, participatory development is too slow to fit into the normal funding cycle of most agencies. Eyben and Ladbury comment that there is often pressure in agencies to speed up implementation, which makes it difficult for them to consult adequately with project field staff, much less pursue participatory activities with beneficiaries. In addition, agencies must satisfy their donors and this creates a need to justify expenditure by showing tangible results relatively quickly. For Hussein this explains why agencies concentrate on programmes implementing technical changes.

Conclusion

Most of the participatory approaches used in development at the moment are 'participation as means'. In these types of approaches participants' 'power to', their confidence in themselves, their personal and collective abilities to exercise power within existing structural and institutional constraints, can undoubtedly be enhanced. Some of the project descriptions in this book, however, (Gronow on the Nepalese forestry project, Mosse on tank managment, Akilu on the video and mural projects with homeless people) could conceivably lead on to village residents, women, low-caste members and homeless youth moving beyond their practical needs to contest and challenge or even re-negotiate political relationships and processes.

It is very important that practitioners and researchers involved in participatory projects work with an eye to the future to create a long-lasting process which is difficult to undermine or reverse. All such approaches have to be backed up by institutions committed to participation in more than the print in their policy documents. This is where anthropologists involved in development can make a significant contribution. For many years, one of the rationales for

17

participant observation fieldwork has been that this is the one way in which the gap between the ideal (what people say should be the normative practice) and the real (what actually happens) is most clearly identifiable. It is axiomatic that this difference always exists, but taking a distanced and reflexive stance to try and identify these contradictions between rhetoric and practice may assist in promoting organizational change.

How practitioners and researchers might contribute to participatory development must be the personal judgement of each individual in any particular context. The first way we can promote the aims of participation is to help create these 'unpickable' situations at local level. To obtain changes at higher levels of development organizations, one approach is to work within aid organizations and bureaucracies to identify sympathetic individuals, practices or opportunities to shift top-down development approaches towards a more participatory ideal. The Social Development Advisers of the Overseas Development Administration or the Learning Group on Participatory Development in the World Bank are examples of this kind of working from within.

Another method is to work from without: to be willing to speak out, even if this means jeopardizing one's job. One anthropologist spoke out at the Participatory Development panel organized by Anthropology in Action at the 1993 conference of the Association of Social Anthropologists at Oxford (Fleming 1993). He had refused to continue a project evaluation run by a large agency on the grounds that it was unacceptably top-down and inegalitarian. He convinced the team to pull out with him. If more individuals had this commitment to ideals of egalitarian and locally directed development it would be an additional pressure for agencies to close the gap between their participatory rhetoric and their practice. They cannot 'give' empowerment to their 'beneficiaries', 'targets of development' or 'clients': to be 'participants' people have to be able to use their 'power to' to negotiate and transform those hopefully willing partners who have institutional and structural 'power over'. On the third model of power, however reflexive an approach agency personnel take to their own practice, it perhaps remains for researchers to view the political embeddedness of participatory development programmes from sufficient critical distance to help those involved to see whether their work is being transformative. Does it enable people, traditionally objectified and silenced, to be recognized as legitimate 'knowers', to extend their understanding of power relations, widen their choices and determine their ideas of development? And are such 'people-centred perspectives' transforming the apparatus of development? Or, masked by the visibility of expressed intentions, does the flow of events surrounding participatory development programmes produce side effects which incorporate marginalized people more effectively within a decentred subjectless system of power, working invisibly and 'behind our backs'?

18

2. Participation and Power: a transformative feminist research perspective[1]

JOKE SCHRIJVERS

In the latter half of 1993 I carried out research on internal refugees and resettlement in Sri Lanka. As a result of civil war, since 1983 tens of thousands of Sri Lankans have lost their lives or have been displaced. Due to a fresh outbreak of violence in 1990, new waves of internal refugees have spread over the country. In October 1990 this was aggravated by the Liberation Tigers of Tamil Eelam's sudden expulsion of all Muslims who were living in the north. Official estimates speak of 618 420 persons in 1993 displaced within the country. The actual numbers – including those who without state support were able to take refuge in the houses of relatives or in rented rooms – are much higher.

Exploring the subject, it struck me that little was known about the actual experiences, needs and priorities of the refugees themselves. Relief and rehabilitation work by the state and most non-governmental organizations has been designed and carried out in a top-down manner. I wished to contribute knowledge in support of the interests of refugees themselves, especially women and children. Because of the continuing civil war I was not sure about the political space for action in this field, which made me reflect even more critically on my approach.

In this chapter I will first explore the links between feminist scholarship and the politics of research. Then I will discuss the complexities of taking sides, examining the characteristics of *dialectical* and *dialogical* research within the broader perspective of what I call a *transformative* approach (Schrijvers 1993). Finally I reflect on my current study in the context of a country torn apart by war. To what extent could I practise my own ideals?

A view from below

The idea that social science serves human objectives is as old as the discipline itself. Since Marx, liberation from oppression has been defined by some as the aim of social science. However, what was defined as knowledge and how it was to be researched by the social science profession are now seen to have run counter to those aims. A neo-positivist methodology, adopted from the natural sciences, treated people as objects about whom

19

knowledge was to be collected dispassionately. It tried to deny or nullify the influence of the research process on the researched by making the researcher invisible in the results. The processes of collecting data, analysing and writing it, whilst depending on social interaction and professional authority, were presented as simple and transparent. What was considered 'value free' research is now seen as an obfuscation of the power relationships involved (Schrijvers, 1993: 33–41). First the agenda for research was set by professional social scientists in a way later revealed to be ethno- and androcentric (Rohrlich-Leavitt *et al.* 1975; Schrijvers 1979); second, the researched had no input in defining relevant topics of research; third, they were objectified and disempowered during the research process; and fourth, far from the results being useful for their 'liberation from oppression', they were produced primarily for the academic community and secondarily for use by governments.

From the 1960s, a *view from below* was sought particularly by Latin American scholars, but also by a minority of social scientists in rich countries (Huizer 1979). Feminism added to this view from below the perspectives of women. This transformed the entire approach, as women could not simply be *added:* the theoretical and methodological rules which had excluded women's perspectives had to be changed (Watkins 1983: 87). Feminism changed the perception of the nature of power relations and undermined the credibility of *all* existing theoretical approaches – including those from below (Caplan 1988; Schrijvers 1985: 143–165, 1987; Bell *et al.* 1993).

The politics of research.

Since de Beauvoir, feminist theory has been dealing with subject – object dichotomies and hierarchies. She revealed the dominant construction of the female as 'the other' and began the process of finding ways to constitute and claim ourselves, women, as subjects (Bowles and Duelli Klein 1983; Mascia-Lees 1989: 11). Knowing the feeling of 'otherness', feminist anthropologists consciously tried to mediate between the positions of the subject and object in anthropological research. Hence our extensive writing about the 'self', and about sex and gender in field research (Golde 1970; Whitehead and Conaway 1986; Warren 1988; Bell *et al.* 1993).

The undoubted subject in the total research process, the often implicit 'knower' who studies those to be 'known', is of course a much more problematic category than suggested by academic practice. 'We', the 'learned ones', have long been wrapped in silence. In the words of Said (1989: 142)

This silence is thunderous. . .you will begin perhaps suddenly to note how someone, an authoritative, explorative, elegant, learned voice, speaks and analyses, amasses evidence, theorizes, speculates about everything – except itself. Who speaks? For what and to whom?

Feminist theory and practice, probably more deeply than any other approach, have dealt with the problematic issues of knowledge, power, representation and authority. However, in the majority of cases it has been the learned voices of white women which have theorized – about 'all' women and gender relations, or, especially in the case of feminist anthropology, about 'other' women. Black feminist critiques demonstrated that these power structures were reproduced by the dominant feminist perspective with its all too often universalizing theories of male oppression and female solidarity (Hull et al. 1982; Mohanty 1988, 1991; Mohanty et al. 1991; Steady 1981).

Gradually, it has become clear that ethnic and race relations crosscut gender, as do class, culture, and age. Generalizations have given way to (comparative) studies which stress historically and locally specific contexts. Claims to universal knowledge have come under heavy attack, to make place for partial perspectives. Although I find this development extremely valuable, I also notice that the post-modernist preoccupations with discourses, representations and texts have increasingly undermined the direct link between politics and feminist studies that was so clear in the beginning.

Mascia-Lees et al. (1989) argue that constructing the 'other' entails relations of domination and that the so-called 'new ethnography', with its narrative devices and dialogical experiments which aim to give the 'other' a voice in the text, may 'constitute a masking and empowering of Western bias rather than a diffusion of it' (ibid) (see also Harding 1987; Hartsock 1987; Nencel and Pels 1991: 18; Okely and Callaway 1992). Although postmodernism can contribute to the erosion of dualistic theory and universalistic, totalitarian and ethnocentric paradigms, they conclude that those who wish to confront these power relations 'would do better to turn to feminist theory and practice than to postmodernism' (Mascia-Lees et al. 1989: 32–3; also Bell et al. 1993). Stacey agrees (1988: 26), arguing that acknowledging the partiality of representations is not enough: the ethical issues have to be taken into account. Post-modernism can support an extremely relativistic and amoral attitude, which implicitly embraces a political choice: the liberal, survival-of-the-fittest, and the taken-for-granted attitude which entails taking sides with the more powerful forces in society (Schrijvers 1993).

Feminist theory and methodology have shown the highly problematic nature of the representations of research (whose voices, whose perspectives, whose theories?), the communications (what kind of research interactions?), the texts (whose authority?), and the objectives (in whose interest, for what?). We are still struggling with the complexities of connecting political critique, theory and practice. How can we create more equitable relations during the research process, especially within the context of severe political repression, in Sri Lanka and in many countries today? How can we support the *envoicing* (Harding 1987) of participants

21

whose voices are seldom, if ever, heard and integrate into the research their interests and concerns?

The complexities of taking sides

To my knowledge, Maria Mies (1977) was the first to systematically conceive the methodological criteria for a feminist social science. I quote her first postulate:

> The postulate of *value free research*, of neutrality and indifference towards the research objects, has to be replaced by *conscious partiality*, which is achieved through partial identification with the research objects (Mies 1983: 122).

Conscious partiality is different from mere subjectivism or simple empathy. *Critical consciousness* and *exchange* are crucial elements of this approach. The researcher takes the side of a certain group, partly identifies, and in a conscious process creates space for critical dialogues and reflection on both sides. This enables both research 'subjects' and 'objects' to become more aware of the power differences and dynamics involved, and of distortions of perceptions to be corrected on both sides. Paradoxically, precisely through this process of *partial identification* a critical and *dialectical distance* is created between the researcher and the 'researched' (Mies 1983: 123). Feminist standpoint theory equally emphasizes that, whereas western thought has 'started out' from the lives of dominant men,

> starting thought from women's lives decreases the partiality and distortion in our images of nature and social relations. It creates knowledge. . .that is. . .still partial in both senses of the word, but less distorted than thought originating in the agendas and perspectives of the lives of dominant group men (Harding 1992: 181).

I like to avoid terms like the 'researched', 'informants', 'respondents', and 'interviewees'. We need terms which do not create dichotomous, hierarchical oppositions between an active subject and a passive object. The term participants perhaps best expresses the more egalitarian relations between researcher and those with whom the research takes place (de Josselin de Jong 1977).[2]

'Conscious partiality' may open the way for a socially situated, contextualized knowledge which is more explicitly inter-subjective and dynamic; the result of unique, time- and place-specific dialogues which continuously raise new questions and images of reality in a *dialectical* way. This entails complex ambivalences as feminist researchers continuously struggle with the alternate positions of constructed and experienced 'other'. Being aware of the importance of building on our own experiences as women, there is no typical 'woman's life' from which feminists can start.

22

Informed by women's global and local social movements of tremendous diversity, feminist studies have continued to problematize subject-object hierarchies (see e.g. Jayawardena 1986; Sen and Grown 1988; Jaquette 1989; Shallat 1990; Gandhi and Shah 1992; Khasiani 1992).

This brings us back to the politics of research. If people belong to a socially or economically vulnerable group (as often pertains to women in comparison to men of the same background), there is a good chance that more powerful people, although belonging to the same society, will deny the 'truth' of the interpretations they adopt. A critical, dialectical approach leaves room for interpretations which question the dominant order of things, which are counterpoints (Wertheim 1954, 1964) to the status quo. How to embody these counterpoints in the practice of research?

Theory and practice

Bearing the political and epistemological complexities in mind, it is not surprising that one of the key dilemmas in feminist studies is how to bridge the gap between theory and practice. This dichotomy is a fundamental structural element of positivist social science theory (Mies and Reddock 1982: iv). According to the academic values of distance and detachment, it is commonly accepted that 'good' researchers should not engage in action; at least not during the research itself. Research is considered an intellectual activity, whereas action is classified as social work. The distance between subject and object, ego and alter, expert and target-group, is established and maintained by a rigorous dichotomization of the two parties concerned, and reproduced by the norm that the researcher and the researched should not change places. The hierarchy in this classification is evident – academic work has more prestige and it is paid better than social work. It is precisely this mechanism of hierarchical dichotomization which keeps researchers from feeling responsible for the use of their written products.

For me a way to handle this dilemma has been to distinguish the *dialogical* approach, within the full context of dialectical research, as a specific focus during fieldwork (Schrijvers 1991). If dialogues form the main communication process in this stage, the objects of research become subjects as well. They are conceptualized as social actors who themselves actively participate in the research and therefore co-determine the outcome (see also Torres 1992). They, too, are constructing knowledge and interpreting reality. The researcher is not in a top-down manner projecting her or his own received conceptions, classifications and interpretations of the situation, but does so in dialogue with the other actors. The outcome is intersubjective and negotiated, there is not one 'reality' or 'truth'. The different interpretations are seen as constructs created by many subjects, leading to different, situated knowledges (Haraway 1990: 183–202). This dialogical approach makes room not merely for a plurality of views, but for advocacy

23

and action based on those views which are not part of the dominant discourse. By creating space for (possible) action, the need to analyse power relations during the research becomes even more clear.

On the basis of my own experience I distinguished five characteristics of dialogical communication (Schrijvers 1991: 170). The first is a *dynamic focus on change*. The second is *exchange*: 'researcher' and 'researched' continuously change places as both are subject and object, active and passive and the interpretations of both are open for discussion. The third characteristic is the *ideal of egalitarian relations*. The researcher and all participants in the research become acutely aware of power inequalities that separate them. By verbalizing the differences, the less powerful will sense an increased effort by the more powerful to take a perspective from below. Fourth, *shared objectives* and priorities of research are determined by all participants. The researcher and funding agency lose the prerogative to regulate this stage of the research process. Fifth is a *shared power to define* the image of reality produced by the research. All participants are empowered to construct concepts and categories, discuss results and determine the course and outcome of the research.

Many obstacles are encountered when trying to practice this research ideal. I refer for instance to the stage of *writing* as a major dilemma of representation (c.f. Clifford and Marcus 1986; Bell *et al.* 1993). So long as the researcher remains the one who exclusively carries out this final stage of research, the ultimate 'power to define' will remain with her or him.

Dialogical communication appears plausible with people who are relatively powerless. What about sharing the power to define with the more powerful? In principle, this would imply the envoicing of those who already have the power to shape and define the image of 'reality'. It would thus help to maintain the (conceptual) status quo, and as such run counter to an approach 'from the bottom up'. However, the distinction between 'the powerful' and 'the powerless' is too simple, and too rigid. During research, power relations between the researcher and the other subjects may change continuously (Schrijvers 1991).

If transformation inspired by a critical view from below is the explicit aim of dialectical research, I prefer to speak of a *transformative approach* (Schrijvers 1993: 37–41). Based on a critical conception of knowledge, a transformative approach aims at bridging the gap between theory and practice, and supporting processes of change from the bottom up. The term 'bottom up' is complicated because the 'poor', the 'vulnerable', or the 'oppressed' comprise an extraordinarily heterogeneous category. As a researcher you have opted to be an intellectual intermediary in this transformational process, by trying to enter the perspectives and the interests of those for whom you have chosen within the given context. You interrogate yourself time and again: in whose interests do I make my choice of perspective out of the heterogeneous reality existing in the research situation, and how relevant is the acquired knowledge from *their* perspective? What possibilities do I have for returning the insights gained back to them? There is a great temptation to omit or forget these sorts of questions, because scholarly prestige is not awarded on the basis of judgements made by the people on whom the research is based (Schrijvers 1991, 1993: 37–41).

If a transformative approach includes *direct* action for change, it is usually called *action- or partisan research*. Action-research not merely allows for inter-subjectivity in the construction of situated knowledges. The researcher explicitly takes sides with a certain category or group of people who want to change their situation. Consequently all actors become involved in a combined process of research and action (Huizer 1979: 23). The aim is primarily to create knowledge which directly helps to bring about socio-political change such as desired and defined by the participants in the research. One of the participants is the researcher who acts as a facilitator in the process of change. The decision to take sides with a certain category or group of people does not mean that the researcher, as a *tabula rasa*, passively has to accept the interpretations of the other actors. It means that *all* parties create room to make explicit their points of view so that they can exchange and discuss their interpretations – among which are their images of each other and of the power relations at stake. For security reasons action-researchers, feeling responsible for the use of their written products, often decide not to publish the knowledge created.

Research and transformation

In my earlier research in 1977 and 1978 in a small, Sinhalese village in the North-Central Dry Zone of Sri Lanka, I decided to side with the interests of economically deprived, (semi)landless women. During the last stage of research, on their request I supported their establishing a collective farm. I remained involved for years afterwards (Schrijvers 1985, 1991, 1994). This research contained many elements of what I now call a dialogical, transformative approach. What happened during my current research among refugees in Sri Lanka? To what extent could this be labelled as *transformative*? It is rather confronting to interrogate myself now, right after the first explorative months of research in a country torn apart by war. This time, I feel the space for transformation from below has been quite limited.

First of all, given the overall political crisis and the sensitive nature of the subject, a period of three months was far too short to reach the level of in-depth understanding that is a prerequisite for partial identification and exchange. Also, I could not yet speak Tamil, and not speaking their language was a serious barrier to dialogical communication. Secondly, it was not at all clear to me whose side to take. Internal refugees in Sri Lanka are an extremely heterogeneous population. They can be differentiated

25

according to their socio-economic, regional and ethnic background (Sri Lankan Tamils, Indian Tamils, Muslims,[3] Sinhalese), and according to age, religion, caste and gender. There were refugee camps in the rural areas all along the war frontier from the North-West to the East, as well as in the capital of Colombo. Refugees who were better-off did not live on relief, whereas many who had been officially resettled were still depending on state and non-governmental support. State policy has clearly favoured Sinhalese refugees, but all ethnic groups have experienced extreme, traumatic violence. The future prospects of Tamil and Muslim refugees were most gloomy, and according to some, the Muslims received least attention of all. After two months of research in various locations I found it impossible and even immoral to decide which category of refugees would deserve my conscious partiality most! Even my feminist consciousness did not help me in the beginning. I was not sure whether women refugees were the most downtrodden of all. Inside the camps the women continued the domestic tasks they had had before, although under extremely miserable conditions. Wherever they could they worked for an income, inside or outside the camps, and many of them appeared to have had more inner strength than the men to bear the unbearable. Within the space of the camps the men, hanging around or sleeping, seemed the most displaced of all, especially if the opportunities for earning were minimal. There was a high degree of male alcoholism and violence in the camps. I felt perhaps most empathy for the many children who had grown up in refugee camps and had never known a period of peace.

It was only during the last month, when I had worked more in depth in one location, that I realized why primarily women and girls needed support. In spite of their impressive strengths, within the camps as well as in the outside world they were kept at the very bottom by processes of power that were not neutral but were gendered. Becoming more familiar with them I learned how vulnerable they were when it came to physical autonomy and how confined in their mobility. Their ability to take the lead, to define and change their own situation was very restricted. This experience again taught me that there is no general indicator for deciding beforehand whose interests to support through research activities. My ideal of conscious partiality helped me to analyze the total, heterogeneous context, in which each time new choices have to be made as to for whom, how and for what purpose the research will take place and what power relations are influencing it.

The dilemma of taking sides as a matter of course also complicated the ideal of serving *shared objectives*. Refugees from different ethnic backgrounds had fled from the (often combined) violence of the State Forces, the Indian Peace Keeping Force (IPKF), Security Guards, Death Squads and various militant groups, but they had suffered violence also from 'ordinary' people belonging to other ethnic groups. They had been induced to fear and hate the 'ethnic other' with whom they lived in peace before. This increased their vulnerability in the overall political crisis, and deepened their fear of resettlement even in so-called 'cleared' areas. As the roots of the conflict had not been taken away, people told me time and again that 'all the things that happened may happen again'. Within the context of a complex civil war, a decision to support the interests of one ethnic group of refugees, for instance to obtain more physical and economic security, might endanger the lives of other refugees. The characteristics of transformative research in such a context seem to be a distant ideal. The more I started to understand the depth of the crisis in Sri Lanka, the more powerless and at times ludicrous I felt with my research ideals. However, having acquired more critical distance now, I can also see some encouraging elements.

Although I was worried that direct help did not form part of the research, I was struck by the explicit and repeated appreciation of many refugees for my *immaterial* concern. I was told in different camps: 'You are the only outsider so far who has sat down with us and came back again to listen at length to our stories'. My attitude obviously strengthened their sense of human dignity and identity, which were precisely the qualities that had been taken away from them – first by their traumatic experiences and later by their institutionalization into refugee camps and a system of 'relief and rehabilitation'. To a certain degree, therefore, my approach established a more *egalitarian basis for exchange* than immediate 'help' would have done. By telling their own stories to a complete outsider, they gained some power to conceptualize their own experiences – a first step towards re-defining their identities.

Looking back now I believe that the envoicing of relatively powerless people by the *sharing of defining power* is a decisive element in a transformative approach. It empowers them to co-determine the course and outcome of the research, and thereby guarantees its inherently *dynamic* nature. From the start, my research agenda was set by the concerns of refugees themselves, as I encountered them throughout my fieldwork: their concerns for physical and economic security, and a future for their children. I decided to go to the Eastern Province which had just been declared 'cleared' and safe enough to resettle the refugees. After resettlement the Tamil and Muslim populations were forced to live together again as neighbours, even though the ethnic polarization between these communities very recently had led to extremes of violence. Gradually I understood more about the role of both the Sri Lankan state and the leaders of militant groups in this process of ethnic polarization. Concepts of masculinity and femininity appeared to be crucial elements in the construction of ethnicity and violence; the power mechanisms at work were highly gendered. This view helped me to *partly identify* with the women in both communities, which also opened my eyes to the different barriers to increasing their sense of security. On the one hand the Muslim community compared to the Tamils offered their women, and especially widows, more support. On the other hand the non-governmental sector was predominantly favouring the Tamil community, which had already resulted in the formation of tens of 'widow's groups' – a doubtful construct in face of the social stigma attached to Hindu Tamil widows. We started dialogues with groups of Tamil village women, in which we encouraged widows to exchange their views and feelings with women whose husbands were still alive.[4]

One of the ways I sought to use this information in a process of change from the bottom up was through advocacy. In the offices in Colombo, I exchanged views with several key bureaucrats, foreign agents and non-governmental officers, urging them to take into account the situation from the perspectives of resettled people. This of course confronted me with the harsh realities of a state in political crisis: hidden agendas, corruption, threats. At this stage I found it difficult not to get antagonized against policy-makers who openly served the interests of the Sinhalese majority. It was clear that if there was any space at all for change-from-below, it had to be found within the non-governmental sector.

I also started sharing information with human rights activists,[5] who could use some of our findings for their reports. Given the political repression, the systematic documentation of the history of atrocities is about the only possible form of resistance against the reigns of terror of both the state and the Liberation Tigers of Tamil Eelam.

During the last month of research, I became involved in *direct action-for-change*. A group of refugees in one of the camps in Colombo had organized themselves to oppose the intended closure of the camp and forced resettlement in the Eastern Province. They were Indian Tamils who originally came from the plantation sector, but had established their lives in Colombo years ago. They were badly affected by the 1983 riots, after which they stayed in camps for two to three years. Transported to the east, they were given pieces of land which were too dry to make a living. Education and healthcare, too, were totally inadequate. The new violence in 1990 made them flee back to Colombo, where they had been staying in camps for the last three years. Their children could now go to school, and most of them earned enough in the informal sector to keep their families going. Thus they refused to be 'resettled' in the east where they did not belong. 'We don't want to be refugees, we don't want charity or relief, we only want a piece of land in Colombo where we can build a little house, live in peace and earn our living. We are from here,' they said.

The army and police came by night to close the camp. A group of 125 people – men, women and children – stayed back on the street. It was the rainy season. From that night onwards until the end of my stay, my research activities became largely determined by the needs of these people, who had been displaced by force even from their refugee camp. Together with my Tamil assistants I visited churches and charitable institutions in search of an alternative place for them to stay, went back to the people on the street to see how one pregnant woman was keeping and to talk with the leaders of the group – who were all males. I participated in meetings of non-governmental organizations discussing the problem, interviewed state officers in charge of the camps, and talked with political activists. By acting as a broker of information I tried to influence the decision-making process and support countervailing power. When I had to leave the country, most of the refugees on the street had found at least a temporary place to stay.[6] These last weeks of research came close to *action-research*, and I am sure that, had I been able to stay longer, the elements of *shared defining power*, *advocacy* and *action* would have prevailed in my approach. However, in the context of civil war and repression, the space for a truly transformative approach which would benefit the interests of any group of internal re-fugees in the long term was severely limited.

Conclusion

This case study shows that feminism provides a perspective on systems of domination which is also relevant in studies not just confined to 'women'. My work with refugees benefited from feminism's appreciation of the het-erogeneity of experience of people in particular categories, yet their shared positioning in systems of domination. What counted as knowledge and the methods to produce it were equally informed by feminism. Through 'con-scious partiality' my aim was to gain knowledge less distorted than that originating from agendas and perspectives of the more powerful. Through a dialogic approach I tried to do this *with* participants rather than *on* research subjects so as to enable them to influence the agenda for advocacy and action. Even if fully transformative research was not possible in those conditions, its components do change the power relations in research in a very practical way. This shows the challenge feminism offers to both sup-posedly neutral positivism and apolitical forms of post modernism.

3. Paradigm shifts and the practice of participatory research and development

ROBERT CHAMBERS

'Participation'

The language of development rhetoric and writing changes fast. The reality of development practice lags behind the language. Sometimes the language lapses into history, as with 'take-off into self-sustaining growth' which took off into self-negating decline. In other cases words persist and prevail, whatever happens to the field reality. 'Participation' is one such word which is experiencing a renaissance in the 1990s. So widespread is its use that some talk of a paradigm shift to participatory development. This chapter examines this view, arguing that reversing power relations is the key, and the weak link, in achieving participation.

There are three main ways in which 'participation' is used. First, it is used as a cosmetic label, to make whatever is proposed appear good. Donor agencies and governments require participatory approaches and consultants and managers say that they will be used, and then later that they have been used, while the reality has often been top-down in a traditional style. Second, it describes a co-opting practice, to mobilize local labour and reduce costs. Communities contribute their time and effort to self-help projects with some outside assistance. Often this means that 'they' (local people) participate in 'our' project. Third, it is used to describe an empowering process which enables local people to do their own analysis, to take command, to gain in confidence, and to make their own decisions. In theory, this means that 'we' participate in 'their' project, not 'they' in 'ours'. It is with this third meaning and use that we are mainly concerned here.

The paradigm shift, from things to people

The new popularity of participation has several origins: recognition that many development failures originate in attempts to impose standard top-down programmes and projects on diverse local realities where they do not fit or meet needs; concern for cost-effectiveness, recognizing that the more local people do the less capital costs are likely to be; preoccupation with sustainability, and the insight that if local people themselves design and construct they are more likely to meet running costs and undertake maintenance; and ideologically for some development professionals, the belief

*Listening and learning in Nainital, Uttar Pradesh, May 1990. In the fore-
ground a senior government official listens in conversation with a local
woman. In the background another learns from a local man about the map
(centre) he has made. Outsider PRA facilitators would now no longer transfer the villagers' map from the ground onto paper (top left): they would ask
the villagers to do this themselves.* Photograph: Robert Chambers.

that it is right that poor people should be empowered and should have more command over their lives.

The new stress on participation can also be understood in terms of a deeper and more pervasive shift in development thinking. In development, paradigm shifts differ from those in the physical sciences. 'Paradigm' is used here to mean a pattern of ideas, values, methods and behaviour which fit together and are mutually reinforcing. In the physical sciences, one new paradigm tends to replace an old one. In development thinking, paradigms tend to coexist, overlap, coalesce and separate. As Norman Uphoff has argued (1992) thinking in development needs to be 'both–and' rather than 'either–or'. However, to illuminate major trends it can still help to set out polarized extremes. Arguably, the big shift of the past two decades has been from a professional paradigm centred on things to one centred on people.

The paradigm of things was dominant in development in the 1950s and 1960s, with emphasis placed on big infrastructure, industrialization and irrigation works. Economists and engineers, and their top-down physical and mathematical paradigm, determined norms, procedures and styles. Economic analysis continues in the 1990s to be the dominant mode of development thinking and practice, but the paradigm of people has come

Table 1: Two paradigms: things and people

Point of departure and reference	Things	People
Mode	Blueprint	Process
Keyword	Planning	Participation
Goals	Pre-set, closed	Evolving, open
Decision-making	Centralized	Decentralized
Analytical assumptions	Reductionist	Systems, holistic
Methods, Rules	Standardized Universal	Diverse Local
Technology	Fixed package (table d'hôte)	Varied basket (à la carte)
Professionals' interactions with clients	Motivating Controlling	Enabling Empowering
Clients seen as	Beneficiaries	Actors, partners
Force flow	Supply-push	Demand-pull
Outputs	Uniform Infrastructure	Diverse Capabilities
Planning and Action	Top-down	Bottom-up

to be increasingly influential. This is shown by the burgeoning literature on people and participation (e.g. Cernea 1985, 1991; Uphoff 1992; Burkey 1993), by the increase in numbers of non-economist social scientists in some aid agencies, notably Overseas Development Administration, and by the development and spread of participatory approaches and methods. Social anthropologists and non-governmental organizations, in particular, have shifted the balance from things to people. The rhetoric of development now widely favours putting people first, and often, putting poor people first of all.

In theory, the shift from the paradigm of things to the paradigm of people entails much change. Top-down becomes more bottom-up. The uniform becomes diverse, the simple complex, the static dynamic, and the controllable uncontrollable. The future becomes less predictable. The transfer of packages of technology is replaced by the presentation of baskets of choice. Most difficult, the paradigm of people implies the third meaning or use of participation, an empowering process, with a shift of power to those who are local and poor.

In practice, the top-down reality has, though, changed rather little. Many reasons can be adduced to explain this. The paradigm of things remains strong, not least because things are still needed: bridges are needed which are strong, safe and durable. Other reasons include, first, 'normal professionalism' – the concepts, values, methods and behaviour dominant in professions – which seeks and values controlled conditions and universal truths (Chambers 1993 chapters 1 and 6). A second reason is 'normal bureaucracy' – the concepts, values, procedures and behaviour dominant in bureaucracies, with their tendencies to centralize, standardize and control. Third, there are 'normal (successful) careers' in which promotion separates power from field realities, and fourth, 'normal teaching' which reproduces normal professionalism, transferring knowledge from the teacher who knows, to the pupil who is ignorant.

Normal professionalism, bureaucracy, careers and teaching combine in top-down standardization and pressures for speedy action. Most importantly there is power. Participation as an empowering process implies loss of central control and proliferation of local diversity. The powerful are threatened with loss of power.

Power relations: uppers and lowers

Human society, in this context, can be thought of as patterned into hierarchical relationships, by analogy described as North and South. Many relationships are vertical, between 'uppers' and 'lowers'. Individuals are multiple uppers or multiple lowers, and a person can be an upper in one context and a lower in another.

North-South, upper-lower, patterns can be thought of as a magnetic

33

Table 2:   North–South, upper–lower relationships

Dimension/context	North Uppers	South Lowers
Spatial	Core (urban, industrial)	Periphery (rural, agricultural)
International and development	The North IMF, World Bank Donors Creditors	The South Poor countries Recipients Debtors
Personal ascriptive	Male White High ethnic or caste group	Female Black Low ethnic or caste group
Life cycle	Old person Parent Mother-in-law	Young person Child Daughter-in-law
Bureaucratic organization	Senior Manager Official Patron Officer Warden, guard	Junior Worker Supplicant Client 'other rank' Inmate, prisoner
Social, spiritual	Patron Priest Guru Doctor, psychiatrist	Client Lay person Disciple Patient
Teaching and learning	Master Lecturer Teacher	Apprentice Student Pupil

field, where the magnets are mutually reinforcing in orientation. In the normal strong North–South field, if lowers participate, it is in activities determined by uppers. If there is a revolutionary flip, lowers become uppers, and a similar situation is reproduced, as in the USSR under Stalin and China under Mao. Participation which empowers requires a weakening of the magnetic field at various levels, with scope for lateral linkages with peers, colleagues, neighbours, and fellow citizens.

The roles of dominant uppers have then to change. From planning, issuing orders, transferring technology, and supervising, they shift to convening, facilitating, searching for what people need, and supporting. From being teachers they become facilitators of learning. They seek out the poorer and weaker, bring them together, and enable them to conduct their own appraisal and analysis, and take their own action. The dominant uppers 'hand over the stick', sit down, listen and themselves learn.

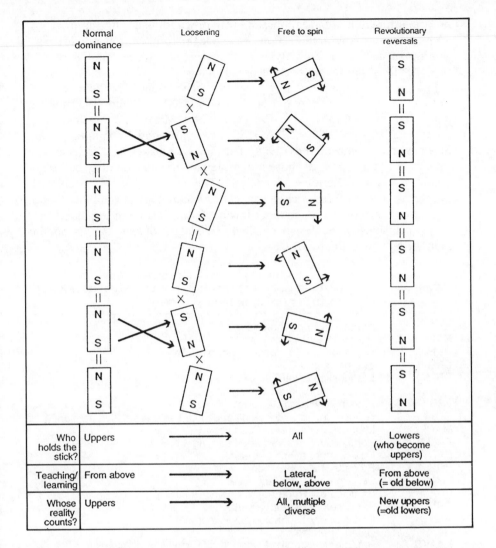

	Normal dominance	Loosening	Free to spin	Revolutionary reversals
Who holds the stick?	Uppers	⟶	All	Lowers (who become uppers)
Teaching/ learning	From above	⟶	Lateral, below, above	From above (= old below)
Whose reality counts?	Uppers	⟶	All, multiple diverse	New uppers (=old lowers)

Figure 1: *Dominance, reversals and freedom*

Change and spread

The extent to which this has already happened is difficult to judge. While the top-down paradigm of things remains dominant, many changes have occurred and together have a momentum towards the paradigm of people. Perhaps the most notable has been a proliferation of schools and methods for participatory approaches. Twenty-nine which have developed since the 1970s have been identified (Table 3) and others could be added.

These new approaches and labels reflect deep and widespread shifts of emphasis and changes in methods and behaviour, especially but not only in non-governmental organizations; and with or without adopting approaches such as these, many organizations have sought to move towards less authoritarian and centralized styles of management. Three families of approaches illustrate the more widespread changes.

First, a huge literature now testifies to the greater participation of farmers in agricultural research and extension (see Amanor 1989 for an annotated bibliography; also Farrington and Martin 1988; Chambers, Pacey and Thrupp 1989; ILEIA 1985; Farrington and Bebbington 1993; Scoones and Thompson (eds) 1994). Farming systems research in its classical style made a huge contribution to professional understanding, based on outsiders' data collection and analysis. The overlapping approaches of farmer participatory research, participatory technology development, and farmer-first approaches in contrast involve farmers more in the identification of priorities, in the design, conduct and analysis of experiments, and in monitoring and evaluation.

Table 3: Some participatory approaches which have developed since the 1970s (in alphabetical order)

AEA	Agroecosystem Analysis
BA	Beneficiary Assessment
DELTA	Development Education Leadership Teams
D&D	Diagnosis and Design
DRP	Diagnostico Rural Participativo
FPR	Farmer Participatory Research
FSR	Farming Systems Research
GRAAP	Groupe de recherche et d'appui pour l'auto-promotion paysanne
MARP	Méthode Accéléré de Recherche Participative
PALM	Participatory Analysis and Learning Methods
PAR	Participatory Action Research
PD	Process Documentation
PRA	Participatory Rural Appraisal
PRAP	Participatory Rural Appraisal and Planning
PRM	Participatory Research Methods
PTD	Participatory Technology Development
RA	Rapid Appraisal
RAAKS	Rapid Assessment of Agricultural Knowledge Systems
RAP	Rapid Assessment Procedures
RAT	Rapid Assessment Techniques
RCA	Rapid Catchment Analysis
REA	Rapid Ethnographic Assessment
RFSA	Rapid Food Security Assessment
RMA	Rapid Multi-perspective Appraisal
ROA	Rapid Organizational Assessment
RRA	Rapid Rural Appraisal
SB	Samuhik Brahman (Joint Trek)
TFD	Theatre for Development
TFT	Training for Transformation

Source: Cornwall, Guijt and Welbourn 1993:14

Second, much work has been done in developing approaches to the participatory management of local natural resources. This includes joint forest management in India (Poffenberger *et al.* 1992 a and b) and elsewhere, where forests are managed jointly by local people and by Government Forest Departments; irrigation management (Bagadion and Korten 1991; Uphoff 1992) where small systems are managed and maintained by communities, and lower parts of larger systems are turned over to groups of irrigators to manage; and watershed management where farmers plan, act, monitor and evaluate measures for soil and water conservation on their fields (Fernandez 1993; Shah 1993).

Third, several streams of approaches and methods – applied social anthropology (e.g. Rhoades 1982), agroecosystem analysis (Conway 1985), farming systems research (Gilbert *et al.* 1980; Shaner *et al.* 1982; FSSP 1987), participatory research (much of it flowing from the work of Paulo Freire) and rapid rural appraisal (Agricultural Administration 1981; Longhurst 1981; KKU 1987) – while continuing as useful practices, have also intermingled in a lively confluence of innovation bearing various labels, including participatory rural appraisal (PRA) (Mascarenhas *et al.* 1991; Chambers 1992b). Rapid rural appraisal leading to participatory rural appraisal is one example of a shift from outsiders' data collection to local empowerment as the dominant mode. The view is strongly held among leading PRA practitioners that processes should only be described as 'PRA' if they are empowering, especially for those who are poor, weak and vulnerable.

These three families of approaches have spread rapidly among nongovernmental organizations, and are now, in the mid-1990s, spreading significantly in some large government organizations. These are little researched and not well documented, so that it is difficult to assess the scale and depth of change. There is a danger of misleading positive feedback (Chambers 1992a; 1994) including special cases. Nevertheless, there are sufficient examples of government organizations concerned with agriculture, forestry, irrigation, and soil and water conservation, especially in Asia and Sub-Saharan Africa, to suggest that despite setbacks slow shifts towards greater participation are occurring on a wide scale.

The paradigm shift in practice

The shift towards empowering participation has been helped by new practices. Four stand out. First, again and again it has been found that activities it was supposed outsiders had to perform can be performed as well or better by insiders – local people, and whether literate or non-literate. This depends on outsiders encouraging them and giving them confidence that 'they can do it'. These activities include appraisal, analysis, planning, experimenting, implementing, and monitoring and evaluation. Beyond this,

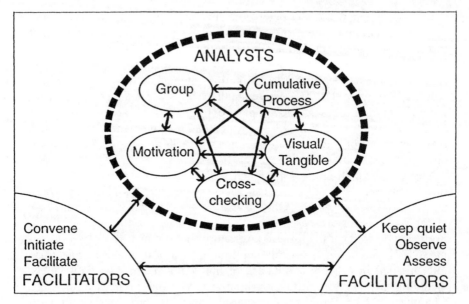

Figure 2:   *Group–visual synergy in PRA*

local people are good extensionists, and facilitators for each others' analysis. (A village volunteer has sent a note to an Aga Khan Rural Support Pro-gramme staff member in Gujarat saying – we are going to conduct a PRA – you do not need to come). Villagers have also presented their analyses in capital cities (with PRA in Colombo, Dhaka and Gaborone). They have also begun to become trainers for non-governmental organization staff.

Second, increasingly, technologies, approaches and methods are spread laterally by peers rather than vertically through transfer of technology. Farmer-to-farmer extension, both within and between countries and ecolo-gical zones, is becoming more prevalent. In PRA, the best trainer/facilitators for other villages and other villagers are local people who have already gained experience. (The best teachers of students are also often other students, a lesson which hierarchically organized universities might do well to note and act on.)

Third, group-visual synergy refers to what often happens when a group of people engage in a visual form of analysis. Examples are mapping, scoring with seeds or counters, and making diagrams of changes, trends and linkages. As groups cumulatively build up a visual representation of their knowledge, judgements and preferences, they tend to increase in commit-ment and enthusiasm, and to generate consensus. The role of the outsider is to convene, initiate and facilitate such a group process. It is the insiders who are the analysts. The outsiders observe, and can see and judge the validity of what is being shown and shared. There are opportunities to encourage and support weaker and shyer members of a community, either to join in with a group, or to form their own. Both the outsiders and the analysts find the process interesting, and often fun.

Fourth, a key element usually missing from earlier participatory efforts is the behaviour and attitudes of uppers. Empowerment of the poor requires reversals and changes of role. In PRA this has come to be recognized as more important than the methods. In consequence, much PRA training stresses how uppers behave with lowers, and handing over the stick, sitting down, listening and learning, facilitating, not wagging the finger or lecturing, and being respectful and considerate. With hindsight, it is astounding that this has not been regarded as fundamental in development work, and that it is only in the 1990s that it is coming to the fore. Some of the new approaches and methods, especially of PRA, make reversals less difficult and improbable than they used to be because they are found to be both effective, interesting and fun.

Traps and problems in participation

PRA and other participatory approaches face many traps and problems. No listing is likely to be complete, but some of the more obvious and important are the following:

Who participates? Missing the poorer

A pervasive problem is upper-to-upper biases, interacting with the local elite and with men, and missing the poorer and women. Finding and involving those who are normally left out, and what has been termed 'the analysis of difference' (Welbourn 1991) will always be challenging. Nor is it enough to identify just one category, such as women. For there are poor and less poor women, and many other differences between groups and categories of people. The poorest, who live far from the centre, who are weak, or overworked, or used to being excluded, are easily left out of empowering participatory processes.

Rushing

Facilitators are often in a hurry. Whether they are foreign visitors, government officials, or non-governmental organization staff, unless they stay in villages their visits are constrained by time, and rushing often means leaving out the peripheral and the poorest, being misled by the less poor, and failing to facilitate an on-going process.

Self-sustaining myth

Power relations can lead to mutual deception by uppers and lowers, by visitors and villagers. Inadvertent ventriloquism occurs when uppers are

Who holds the Stick? Viet Nam, December 1993. A village man surrounded by other villagers explains a cement model they have made of their settlement and watershed to two non-governmental organization workers (seated left). The model is kept permanently in the village and is used for resource planning. Photograph: Robert Chambers.

told what lowers think they want to hear. Myths presented by villagers for reasons of hope of gain, fear of penalty, or self-respect and self-identity, can be accepted and disseminated by outsiders as the reality. Visual diagramming methods often diminish distortions, but even with visualization, the public nature of the event can generate misinformation (Mosse 1993). All power deceives (Chambers 1994). PRA methods well applied reduce but may not eliminate the distorting effects of power relations.

Routine and ruts

Stepwise manuals appeal to teachers and students alike, providing secure rules for right behaviour. Participation which truly empowers implies a process which is unpredictable. So the more that rigid rules and sequences are followed, the lower the level of participation is likely to be. The best PRA manual has one sentence on the first page 'Use Your Own Best Judgement At All Times', and all the remaining pages are blank (KGVK 1991).

Cosmetics: label without substance

The greatest danger with participation is that the words will be used without the reality of changed behaviour, approaches and methods. The key remains behaviour. Unless the behaviour of most outsiders changes, participation will not be more than partial.

Implications

The implications of the paradigm of people are many. For it to be used on any scale in an empowering mode implies widespread changes in bureaucratic procedures and cultures, including participatory management. Upper–lower relationships of authority will always be needed, so the shift required is relative, not absolute. It affects almost all human relationships, between uppers and lowers, and between peers. Any agenda might include first, changing the culture and procedures of development organizations (multilateral and bilateral donors, government departments in headquarters and the field, non-governmental organizations, research institutes, training centres, universities and colleges) towards participatory management, decentralization, and priority to the front-line workers. Second, projects concerned with people should become processes of learning, enabling and empowering, with open-ended time frames allowing for participation and change, while blueprint approaches with rigid time frames and set targets should be confined to things, limited to some physical aspects of infrastructure. Third, there is a need to change to more participatory and open-ended social science research, with more of the agenda, appraisal and analysis carried out by local people, and the outcomes owned and shared by them. This implies also changes in relationships between funding bodies and researchers, and between supervisors and those conducting research for theses. Similarly, fourth, determination of priorities in agricultural, forestry, fisheries and other natural resource research should be much more by and through the analysis and experience of local people, weighted to give voice to women, weak and poor people. Fifth, approaches and methods in teaching and training should change away from the lecture mode to shared learning, peer instruction, problem solving, and social settings in which the shy and retiring feel able to contribute, and in which all teaching and training includes experiential learning concerning upper-lower behaviour and attitudes.

All this means that the new challenges for the twenty-first century face the rich and powerful more than the poor and weak, for they concern reversals, giving things up. For the rich to give up their wealth, without being forced by countervailing power, is difficult and improbable; but for uppers to give up dominance at the personal level, putting respect in place of superiority, becoming a convenor, and provider of occasions, a facilitator and catalyst, a consultant and supporter, is less difficult; for these roles bring with them many satisfactions and non-material rewards. Perhaps one of the biggest opportunities now is to enable more and more uppers to experience those satisfactions personally, and then themselves to spread them, upwards, downwards, and laterally to their peers. For participation, in the full empowering sense of reversals, is not for one place or one set of people, but is itself a paradigm – a pattern of ideas, values, methods and behaviour – which can apply to almost all social activity and spread in all directions.

Acknowledgements

For comments on a draft for this paper I am grateful to Susan Wright and for ideas about uppers and lowers to Jenny Chambers.

4. Participatory research and participant observation: two incompatible approaches

SUSAN WRIGHT and NICI NELSON

Anthropology as a fieldwork-based discipline came of age in the early twentieth century. Despite subsequent radical changes in outlook, analytical approaches and theoretical developments, one thing has remained unchanged: participant observation is still enshrined at the heart of the discipline. In the later part of the twentieth century, the descendants of Malinowski and Boas, in the main, use participant observation to collect their data. The meanings of 'observation' and 'participation' and the relationship between them, however, have changed. From the 1930s onward, the primacy of participant observation as a qualitative data-collection method has been tentatively challenged by the parallel development of participatory research. However, this approach has had little impact on anthropology, and the lone participant observer is still the typical role model for fieldwork. Participant observation can be said to be more 'participatory' than most other social science research methods since it attempts to frame its analysis in terms of local criteria of relevance. In this paper we wish to examine the limits of this 'participatoriness'.

After a brief description of the two methods, participant observation and participatory research, we will ask if a creative synthesis is possible. It is envisaged that there should still be a role for the researcher or intellectual seeking 'world-ordering knowledge' (Hobart 1993: 1). By this we mean a body of theory and information which is shared beyond the local context, comparative in scope, integrated into international intellectual traditions and written in an international language. There would also be greater reciprocity between the holders of world-ordering knowledge and of local knowledge. It is suggested that such a synthesis of the two approaches would produce a more theoretically dynamic, and active social science.

Participant observation

According to the founding myth of British social anthropology (Kuper 1983: 10), it was during confinement on the Trobriand Islands as an enemy alien for the period of World War I that Malinowski 'discovered' that it was a long and intense period of living with the studied group, working in the vernacular, and in isolation from European contacts, which enabled the ethnographer to 'grasp the native's point of view, his relation to life, to realise *his* vision of *his* world' (Malinowski 1922: 25). Simultaneously, a similar methodological development was made in the United States by the ancestor of twentieth century American anthropology, Boas. He emphasised an emic approach to data collecting: 'If it is our serious purpose to understand the thoughts of a people, the whole analysis of experience must be based on their concepts, not ours' (Boas 1943: 314). On both sides of the Atlantic, a long-term, intensive, personalized, qualitative research method evolved – which came to be known as participant observation.

Under Malinowski's method, observation and interrogation played a much greater role than participation. Indeed, it seems that he never actually took part in the key institution, the *kula* expeditions which were the focus of his book: when the Trobrianders set off on their sea voyages to engage in elaborate gift exchanges, because he had once brought bad luck, he was left on the beach (Stocking 1992: 49). For Malinowski, the sole point of participation, of living in his white tent beside village houses, joining in Trobriand fishing trips, and watching people plant yams was to obtain accurate observations. By gradually losing curiosity value, the researcher was thought to have minimal influence on events and to be able to make objective, naturalistic and undisturbed observations. This included documenting differences between what people said they did, what they actually did, and what they thought about what they did. Thus observation was supplemented by questioning on these 'concrete occurrences' to discover what different individuals thought about them, revealing beliefs and apparent contradictions, and pushing them on occasion 'to the metaphysical wall' (quoted in Stocking 1992:45). The aim was to reduce these observable phenomena, interpreted through questioning, to general rules and theories of society and culture.

Both the rigorousness of the data collection methods and the production of general laws were the grounds for claims to 'scientific' status. The method drew heavily on natural science where the treatment of observation as the only source of real facts reflected a positivistic stance. Facts were to be collected 'objectively' without being influenced by the values of the researcher. Malinowski recommended researchers to keep a diary as a safety valve, into which to channel personal cares and emotions and keep them separate from scientific notes. His own diary, containing details of boredom, hypochondria, sexual desires and racist attitudes reveals his attempts to separate what he thought and felt, from his 'work', which he wrote up with a very different dispassionate and authoritative tone (Kuper 1983: 13).

The myth of Malinowski as sole founder of participant observation is now disputed, as many of the characteristics of the method had been established by his predecessors. Haddon introduced the term 'fieldwork' derived from naturalists' ideas of 'intensive study of limited areas' (Stocking 1992: 27) and at least seven men and women from British universities had spent periods of a year or more doing such intensive fieldwork before the first world war (ibid: 30). Also before that war, Rivers had formulated many of the characteristics in his 'concrete method'

in which the worker lives for a year or more among a community of perhaps four or five hundred people and studies every detail of their life and culture; in which he comes to know every member of the community personally; in which he is not content with generalised information, but studies every feature of life and custom in concrete detail and by means of the vernacular language (Rivers, 1913 quoted in Stocking 1992: 39).

Whereas Malinowski cannot be credited with founding participant observation alone, the distinctive advances he did make were: first, to leave the colonial ships and verandahs and to live in a tent in Trobriand villages, and second, to link the collecting of ethnographic data with the production and testing of theory. Despite this more modest role, the myth of Malinowski's founding of participant observation persists. Stocking helps to explain why. The history of a discipline coalesces around 'pattern-making figures' who 'mold the models and write the rules of subsequent inquiry, embodying the discipline's fundamental methodological values in their own heroic efforts' (ibid: 280). In Britain, Malinowski deliberately archetypified the role of 'the Ethnographer' so that in the 1920s his students went into the field confident of doing ethnography 'in a different, more efficient, more reliable, more 'scientific' way than the travellers, missionaries, government officials whom they were pushing to the margins of the discipline' (ibid: 281).

The Ethnographer, equipped with scientific method and theory, was intended to gain professional authority for the discipline. Anthropology's authority derived from the ability to understand cultural difference, that is the ways of life and thought of people constructed as non-Western or 'other'. Malinowski claimed this knowledge was a necessity for all 'practical men' in the colonies (Pels and Nencel 1991: 4). Such men [sic] did not always concur, perhaps because anthropology paradoxically also critiqued the Western civilizing mission it claimed to serve. When Malinowski was 'selling' anthropology, its purpose was to contribute to Western, scientific, technical, managerial, 'world-ordering knowledge' (Hobart 1993: 1). Malinowski referred to 'the feeling of power given by the sense of control of human reality through the establishment of general laws' (quoted in Pels and Nencel 1991: 3). The political nature of anthropology was disguised by its presentation of a politically innocent method and a value-free theory to broker cultural difference. As Pels and Nencel argue, 'Classical anthropology hid its political projects: the responsibility for the creation and legitimation of professional anthropology and for the support of colonialism was covered with the cloak of the neutral and value-free study of cultural difference' (ibid: 8).

Hobart (1993) has revealed the nature of such 'world-ordering knowledge'. It is based on Western rationality and categories, it constructs 'others' as underdeveloped and ignorant, and not only contains a moral judgement about 'them' but is agentive. That is, it depicts a state of affairs requiring action and intervention by the party doing the depicting. 'Others' are constructed as unknowing, inert, passive political subjects or pliant consumers, rendered silent or ineffectually critical. In other words, the growth of world-ordering knowledge is predicated upon the growth of others' ignorance.

Hobart (ibid.) sees this system persisting through 'development'. This is despite a crisis in anthropology in the 1960s and 1970s which Pels and Nencel (1991) attribute to a breakdown in classical anthropology's authority. At the same time as anthropology's colonial niche was lost, a wider critique of the scientific paradigm revealed the discipline's theory and method not to be neutral, but part of Western ideology. At a more abstract level, by the late 1970s the discipline's division of humanity into schemes of contrasting 'cultures' was also seen to be part of the conceptual underpinning of colonialism and continuing Western domination. Said (1978: 1989) implicated anthropology in Orientalism, a process by which the West has repeatedly attributed to 'the Orient' negative collective characteristics, continuously reproducing an oppositional 'other'. Through this discourse, the West has produced a definition of 'itself' as different and superior. Said shows how Orientalism as a discourse is not 'merely academic' but is 'disciplinary': from the eighteenth century onwards, it has become an authoritative and institutionalized way of dealing with the Orient

> dealing with it by making statements about it, authorizing views of it, describing it, by teaching it, settling it, ruling over it: in short Orientalism [can be analysed] as a Western style for dominating, restructuring, and having authority over the Orient (Said 1978: 3).

Anthropology came under attack from anti-imperialists, from people in previously colonized countries, and from ethnic minorities in the metropol. Within the discipline, critiques abounded from feminist, marxist, 'critical' and interpretive perspectives. The critiques led to re-examinations of the way anthropology constructed its object of research; they attempted to reformulate the subject/object divide, and explored the consequences of this for both fieldwork practice and the production of anthropological texts.

The 'colonial critique' (Asad 1973) was a criticism of early ethnographers for not examining their positioning within the colonial system, and for regarding colonialism as inevitable or, worse, benign. Many of the earlier generation of anthropologists felt that they had fed information into the system in a genuine attempt to help 'their people'. Advocacy had been the ethnographer's way of trying to mitigate the worst excesses of the system. Unsatisfied with this, other strands in the discipline called for a critical analysis of the place of anthropology within contemporary imperialism and world systems (Gough 1968). These critiques were connected to a debate about the way anthropology constructed its object of research, and especially the way ethnographies of small-scale 'communities' made them appear timeless, self-sufficient and bounded. The call was to locate both the researcher and the people studied within a historical context, and within nation states and international systems so as to give a much bigger 'field' of research and to focus on the workings of systems of domination (discussed further in Wright forthcoming).

Such approaches argued that the object of anthropological study should no longer be the cultural difference of a homogenized 'other', but categories of people (such as 'class' or 'women') who were subordinated by the working of systems of domination and oppression. These categories of people were however treated as universals. For example, the subordination of women was taken to be worldwide. Feminism in the 1970s was based on the argument that experience of oppression generates consciousness, which in turn defines identity and thence political understanding and action. 'Women' were presumed to be in essence homogenous and to have shared experiences which were the basis of unity and solidarity. It was not until the 1980s that the voices of black women were heard, saying that their experiences of oppression were different and were as much about race and class as about gender. They were pointing out that the experience of white women from the West had been privileged: their way of seeing and defining the world had been claimed as universal, with the accompanying claim to authority to speak for others (Moore 1988: 190; Hooks 1982; Mohanty 1988). This realization has led to a breaking down of universality and the generation of a new meaning for 'difference'. Women are now recognized as having multiple dimensions of difference – gender, class, colour, race, age and culture – none of which can be given primacy. Each of these differences is infused with hierarchies of power and they intersect differently in each specific context, producing ambivalences and contradictions in power relations. Moors summarizes the argument:

> Women are not *a priori* seen as a specific category with innate attributes, but as subjects in a process which are defined and define themselves in relation to others. Taking a perspective in which the subject is not seen as unitary implies a plurality of differences, continuously shifting and sometimes contradictory. Yet, by simultaneously concentrating on the lived experience of concrete women in specific contexts existing patterns of domination can be illuminated (Moors 1991: 121).

Analyses which gave primacy to class and treated it as a universal have followed a similar route. The kind of knowledge that is now sought is not Malinowski's objective general laws, nor the subsequent universal, disembodied knowledge, but 'situated knowledge' (Mani 1990: 25-6). The problem is to find ways of representing similarities and attaining solidarity whilst recognizing the multiplicity of intersecting differences. The central question has become: how are differences constructed and how are they linked to processes of domination?

In a critical or interpretive model, fieldwork came to be recognized as a totalizing experience which draws on all the anthropologist's resources: intellectual, physical, emotional, political and intuitive (Okely 1992: 8). Participation was no longer considered merely a means to collect data based on observation and questioning. Participation came to mean actually joining in everyday activities and acquiring performative competences.

> Anthropologists, immersed for extended periods in another culture or in their own as participant observer, learn not only through the verbal, through the transcript, but through all the senses, through movement, through their bodies and whole being in a total practice (Okely 1992: 16).

Knowledge is not only cerebral but embodied and 'we use this total knowledge to make *sense* literally of recorded material' and we analyse it through 'profound resonances' between the personal, political and theoretical (ibid:16, 18).

'Reflexivity' became a key descriptor of this process of analysis but problems arose over the multiple meanings of this word. Detractors confused reflexivity with narcissistic, self-indulgent, navel gazing. Some of the new genre of accounts of fieldwork came close to presenting experience in the field as a means of learning more about their own personality, giving little insight into the people with whom this self was interacting (Caesara 1982). Instead, reflexivity is a process of continuously moving from the intensely personal experience of one's own social interactions in the field, to the more distanced analysis of that experience for an understanding of how identities are negotiated, and how social categories, boundaries, hierarchies and processes of domination are experienced and maintained. Reflexivity is the means through which the fieldworker's double perspective of insider/outsider, stranger/friend, and participant/observer is kept in tension. At the analysing and writing stage, Scholte (1974) advocated a reflexive critique. This was first in order to situate the researcher and the field in wider hierarchical systems. Second, it was to make an 'anthropology of anthropology' – a critical awareness of the meta-narratives we construct, our representations of culture and difference, how we give them textual authority, and how these connect to or contest projects of domination.

In the resultant published texts, interpretive and critically reflexive anthropologists have tried to represent the research process as a dialogue, especially between the fieldworker and key informants (see the arguments of Dwyer 1977, 1979 and Fabian 1983; and the texts of Dumond 1978 and Crapanzano 1980 as examples). There has been a concern in anthropological publications to give more equal representation to the voices of people involved in field research and to emphasize the process by which an exchange of information and ideas has produced a shared understanding. It is more rare for anthropologists to be concerned that this dialogue should produce results of relevance and use to their interlocutors in the field. Three examples are of note. First, derived from the political critiques of colonialism and world systems, Huizer calls his approach 'emancipatory action research' or 'liberation anthropology'(1979a: 34). He is committed to producing knowledge for local use on how local elites and development policy-makers maintain systems of dominance. His principles and methods resemble participatory research (see below). Second, Schrijvers (1991 and this volume), drawing on both critical anthropology and feminism, proposed a partial and political dialogic approach to research. Using the five steps of her dialogic approach, all participants are involved in the research process with the intention of bringing about change. The dialogue is with the 'poorest women' (on whose side she identifiably stands), local powerholders, and the staff of development organizations which intend to support the women, although they may feel most threatened by the process. The researcher is dealing with and mediating different dialogues which are taking place simultaneously with people in different positions of power. Schrijvers calls this studying down, studying sideways, and studying up.

Finally, Cameron *et al.* (1992) have a more traditional 'field' (consisting of just studying down and not including local elites or policy-makers) but they introduce a more complex picture by arguing that dialogic research is not just with people but is on, for and with them. The empowering aspects of research *with* people, they argue, happen through interaction during the fieldwork process itself, not through claiming to give people a voice, or through representation in texts afterwards. Research *with* people can take several forms. The researcher can allow people to select a focus for joint work, to facilitate work they undertake themselves and also to provide factual information. Most importantly, the researcher can provide an alternative interpretation of their beliefs, attitudes and behaviour and prompt them to look at these in new ways. Research *for* people can arise if the results are presented in an accessible way so that people can initiate their use in advocacy, but the researcher still tends to be in control. Least empowering is research *on* people which Cameron *et al.* argue occurs simultaneously alongside research *with* and *for* people. Researchers have their own agenda: it may be joined by the priorities of the people but will not be superseded by them. At the end of the research process, researchers must also validate their understanding and interpretation with the academic community. However interactive the research process, they argue that at the writing stage identities become more fixed, and representations become controlled by the author, whose voice is privileged. Also seemingly inevitably, the representations and interpretations in such texts become part of 'regimes of truth' (akin to Hobart's world-ordering knowledge) and may be used in policy-making and social control, even if the researcher feels relatively powerless in that sphere.

49

These examples of dialogic research are relatively rare and have had little impact on the discipline. Anthropologists still see themselves as lone researchers. They tend to take their specialized training into the field situation and set the agenda. Even though, through participant observation, they learn people's criteria of relevance, develop performative competence in everyday life, and generate a shared understanding with key informants, they collect the data in cryptic notes, take the data away to analyse it and eventually create an 'authoritative' account of the results which cannot be unravelled. The account is published at a price few can afford except libraries and relatively well-paid academics, or in journals few read, and in a language which may be inaccessible to those whom the account is about. Even when the people studied speak the everyday language of the ethnographer, the technical language of such accounts make them effectively inaccessible to the untrained reader. In this process locally relevant material is transformed into theories, generalizations and insights suitable for disciplinary knowledge and for the concerns of the international, Western-based intellectual, development and management communities.

Anthropologists have often felt that, because their methodology imposes few outside criteria and is the most responsive to the ideas of those studied, their discipline occupies the moral high ground among social sciences. However, there are limits to the participatoriness of participant observation. The move from positivist to interpretive and critical approaches during this century has been accompanied by a shift in the meaning of participant and observer, and the relation between them. Initially, to be participant meant learning the language and living in close enough proximity to observe and ask questions about all the inter-connected aspects of daily life. Now participation means learning experientially as a positioned and interacting subject. It involves moving between invisible social boundaries – all as appropriate to the widest range of gender, age and social identities that can possibily be negotiated – to acquire an embodied understanding of categories, concepts and hierarchies. Simultaneously, as a distanced, observing outsider, the meaning of these experiences and interactions is analyzed in terms of wider systems.

The concern of social theory is no longer to define the cultural difference of an homogenized 'other', but to concentrate on the ways differences are constructed and how people's multiple differences intersect in varying contexts of dominance and subordination. The relations involved may be extensive if the 'field' is no longer taken to be 'a people' but to include, as does Schrijvers, poor women and members of local, national and international organizations whose interests and actions affect them. Dialogic approaches to fieldwork, trying to understand and change systems of dominance, are still rare. Even if, as Cameron *et al.* argue, research *with* will always be accompanied by research *on* people, the tendency is still to concentrate predominantly on the latter. Using advances in ideas about participation, dialogic research and critical 'anthropology of anthropology' are needed to construct people as potential agents, rather than as passive, ignorant subjects of world-ordering knowledge.

Participatory research

The principle of participatory research is that people become agents rather than objects of research and the priorities of this approach are opposite to participant observation. The first aim is for the research to increase participants' understanding of their situation and their ability to use this information, in conjunction with their local knowledge of the viability of different political strategies, to generate change for themselves. A very secondary aim is to contribute to disciplinary knowledge with its double edge of both advancing our understanding of hierarchies and power, and of contributing to world-ordering knowledge.

If people are the agents of research, then they, with the help of a researcher in the role of facilitator, set the agenda and define the issues to be investigated. The researcher then uses her or his knowledge to help devise the most suitable research strategy and methods. The necessary data collection skills are conveyed to the subjects of the study so that they participate in the research. Similarly, the participants and the researcher discuss the data and work out the procedures to be followed in the analysis, so that they are all involved in reaching the results of the study. In the process, there is an exchange: participants are transferring local knowledge to the researcher; and the researcher is conveying not only research skills, but theoretical frameworks and comparative information which help participants analyse the local situation in terms of how wider systems work.

In using the research to generate change, the point is that participants should take the lead in determining the strategy and the researcher's role in it. As Huizer (1979b) says, participants have much greater local political skills than an outsider can ever achieve, and they have to live with the results of their strategy. A second aim is to contribute the research information, theoretical analysis and outcomes to the global body of knowledge from which researchers will continue to draw theoretical and comparative expertise in future participatory projects. 'Writing up' the research for this purpose is usually but not always done by the researcher.

According to the principles of participatory research, the purpose and flow of expert knowledge changes. No longer is the purpose of research to extract information from the poor and subordinated (the usual recipients of our attention) in order to generate disciplinary or world-ordering knowledge. The aim is to use comparative and theoretical knowledge to enable participants to understand their situation and to work out how to act upon it. It has been grandly claimed that the purpose of social investigation

51

changes from creating expert knowledge as professional property, to generating citizens' knowledge.

Participatory research has developed in three strands and, in the main, these have been along a separate and parallel path to participant observation. In one early moment there was dialogue between the two approaches. We are suggesting that now, there is a further opportunity for dialogue between participant observation and participatory research which should be explored.

Mass-Observation

The first moment of dialogue between participatory research and participant observation was in the 1930s. As described above, this was the start of the professionalization of modern anthropology as a discipline, with participant observation at its core. Three men, an anthropologist returned from Malekula, Tom Harrisson; a journalist and poet, who later became a professor of sociology, Charles Madge; and a cultural analyst and film-maker, Humphrey Jennings, set up 'an anthropology of ourselves' for the people by the people in Britain. This was called 'Mass-Observation'.

There were two aspects to its work. First, it trained two to three thousand 'mass observers' all over Britain in systematic ways to collect information from different sources on a given topic. These observers were sent 'directives', which were a combination of questionnaires and research tasks. They focussed on people's attitudes to national events or issues under political discussion, and on the ways people lived their everyday lives. A second group of mass observers gathered in 'Worktown' (Bolton) and systematically observed and recorded the ways people behaved at work, at leisure and at home. They even followed them to Blackpool when the mills shut down, to see how they spent their summer holiday. These two strands of Mass-Observation had quite different relations between the subject and object of study. In 'Worktown', observers (sociology students, photographers, poets) treated the residents as objects, and this roused hostility (not least when they observed and timed people's sexual antics on Blackpool beach). In contrast, the Mass-Observers who received directives, as well as collecting information from others, also used themselves as subjects of study. They considered themselves to be participants in a radical study of the British people by themselves.[1]

At that time, the state was considered a benign, neutral mechanism whose ability to work for the public good depended on the quality of information received. Mass-Observation, by making the experience and ideas of people available to the state, was considered a project of mass empowerment.

One of the criticisms made by university-based 'professional' social scientists was over the process of collecting data by the people for the people. The Mass-Observers were trained in systematic ways of observing and recording

52

information. The critics pointed out that Mass-Observation seemed to consider that rigorous recording obviated the need for selection, as if it created transparently objective social facts. Marshall pointed out that 'observations of ordinary citizens are shot through with selection and interpretation' (1937: 49), and there was nothing in the method to cope with that and make the process scientific. Mass-Observation took an idealist and surrealist approach to revealing truths about society by the careful juxtaposition of 'actual' data, as if it were speaking for itself (whereas, although there was little editorial script, there was a considerable editorial role in the production). This form was used in written productions (e.g. Jennings and Madge's *May 12th*, or Jenning's *Pandaemonium*), as in the montage of documentary film (Jenning's '*Spare Time*' provided a link between the two movements).

This method of collecting data and representing 'everyday life' was possibly not understood and certainly not approved by academic anthropologists. Firth (1939) argued that an inquiry should be informed by a theory of society in order to delineate a particular problem on which facts will be collected (ibid: 177). These facts will be 'built up' to discover 'the formal structure of society' (ibid:166) and 'how this structure actually manifests itself in the lives of individuals' (ibid). Without such a clearly established theory of society informing Mass-Observation's process of data collection and interpretation, far from the facts 'speaking for themselves', they would be 'so much lumber' (ibid).

While Marshall emphasized the need for scientific methods to control bias in the selection of facts, and Firth stressed the need for a theoretical underpinning of the whole process, both agreed that this could not be done by the masses themselves. Harrisson (1937) suggested a model for anthropology drawn from ornithology where there is collaboration between a few experts and hundreds of amateur bird-watchers (1937: 47). The academics argued while there could be observation of the masses, it could not be done by the masses. They held out some hope for the 'Worktown' study, but none for 'the anthropology of ourselves'. This work could only be done by 'carefully selected students' after 'elaborate training' (Marshall 1937: 49). These academics were engaged in drawing up exclusive and professional boundaries as part of the process of institutionalizing their new disciplines. None of the academics addressed Mass-Observation's central problem of dissolving the observer/observed divide (Stanley 1990: 11) in order to make the understanding of society available to and useful for ordinary people instead of being the preserve of the professional few.

Participatory research and development

A second strand in the history of participatory research was its association with radical approaches to development in the 1960s and 1970s (Hall *et al.* 1982, Kassam and Mustafa 1982, Society for Participatory Research in Asia

53

1982; Fals Borda 1988). In post-colonial states, especially India and Tanzania, participatory research was formulated as an alternative to community development policies, which, it was argued, instead of giving people a voice in their own development, incorporated their energy and intiative into the new state and capitalist systems. In South America participatory research was associated with approaches to development informed by dependency theory. This opposed development programmes which promoted oppressed people's participation in unaltered systems and thereby maintained existing relations of dependency and domination. These alternative approaches emphasized the need to develop a critical consciousness through which people would perceive the economic, social and political systems which made them poor, invisible and silent. The aim of research on these systems was to enable people to act individually on themselves and collectively on these relations so as 'to take more control of their lives'. This approach was informed by Freire's (1972) critical approaches to adult education. Participatory research was also being used in adult education in the United States. In the Highlander Centre adult educators worked with poor people in the Appalachian mountains to question and challenge social injustice, especially labour and civil rights. This was based on the premise that in education, so in research:

> By treating people as objects to be counted, surveyed, predicted, and controlled, traditional research mirrors oppressive social conditions which cause ordinary people to relinquish their capacity to make real choices and to be cut out of meaningful decision-making. The collective processes of participatory research help rebuild people's capacity to be creative actors on the world (Maguire 1987: 30).

In one adult education project, participants used local historical archives and land-holding records to understand how their industry had developed (Gaventa 1980). By analysing the industry's social and economic relations, they could see how their powerlessness was constructed, and how their behaviour and responses reproduced that powerlessnesss. There were a few other experiments in using participatory research as a development method in the First World (Gedicks 1979; Maguire 1987; Wright 1992). Mostly these radical approaches were used in the Third World. In 1977 an International Participatory Research network was set up which brought together the Indian, Tanzanian and North American experience, and for a short time there was a branch in Britain.

In this phase, participatory research became part of a development process, and it was heavily influenced by theory. The process of participatory research, as described above, therefore became more elaborate. Often people who were placed in the most oppressive social relations were least likely to be formed into a group, or even to perceive themselves as having shared interests. This became especially clear when the gender dimensions

54

of this approach began to be considered. In this case, the starting point would be for the researcher to act as catalyst to group formation. The second step was to develop a critical consciousness of the systems through which they were subordinated, and thence to define the issues for research. The third step was to use a participatory research method, as described above, to understand how these forces operated and how to influence them. The fourth step was to create a space for alternative development under their own control (Oakley and Marsden 1984) or to gain respect as equal partners with professionals and authorities in a joint process of development (Marsden and Oakley 1990). The long-term development aim was to gain some permanent control over resource allocation and decision-making (Moser 1986).

A number of practical difficulties with this approach can be identified. Not least, there is the number of roles that the researcher has to play. There is also the question of how the poor empower themselves through information alone, when they do not have the ability to accumulate the capital necessary for self-directed and controlled development. The strength of the approach is that it presents the possibility of a partnership between researcher and participants in which both have knowledge to contribute, both can learn from a process of critical reflection and analysis, and both are open to personal transformation and conscientization (Maguire 1987: 37). As in all participatory research, it entails a shift in power – a change from the traditional research relationship between subject-researcher and objects of study, to a more equal partnership between researcher and participants. However, the participatory research and development process takes a long time. Not only do poor people rarely have the time or energy to fit another major task into their day, but it is increasingly unlikely that researchers will receive funding for the complete commitment over the extended period that this method entails. Time requirements was a major weakness in this approach, and it is this issue that the third phase addressed.

Participatory rapid appraisal

Speed is one of the considerations in participatory rapid appraisal (PRA). This approach arose from Chambers' (1983) compelling critique of the practice of agricultural experts in overseas development. He describes the speedy site trip which misses the poorest, least powerful, most invisible and silent people, who are yet the intended beneficiaries of development projects. Where an agricultural expert does encounter one of these beneficiaries, the style of communication may mean that the person does not feel empowered to say what they know and feel. It follows that development projects are likely to be devised without the expert knowledge of the farmer, without an understanding of her or his perceptions of problems, and without their ideas of what would bring them benefits. Sometimes it is not even clear who 'the poorest of the poor' are in any location, and what resources or opportunities they have or need for development.

Chambers (1992), colleagues at the International Institute for Environment and Development (IIED) (who produce *PRA Notes*), and practitioners mainly in the Third World have been developing a number of techniques through which local knowledge can be collected and analysed by the people concerned, with the outside expert acting as facilitator. The initial concerns were agricultural development and resource strategies (see Shah, this volume) but others have applied the techniques to health issues, and a specific gender dimension has been developed. Cresswell (1992) has pioneered the use of the techniques in Britain. Other techniques have used visual aids and drama (although the latter has a further separate tradition in participatory development, Mavrocordatos and Martin this volume).

Cornwall (1992) describes two categories of participatory rapid appraisal techniques. First, diagramming includes making maps and models to denote distribution of resources, watershed systems, landholding, or the composition and wealth-ranking of households. Diagramming also includes making seasonal calendars of rainfall, food availability, workloads of household members, disease, income and expenditure; circle diagrams of relations between institutions; and transects across an area which are walked, combining observation with commentary. The second category of techniques is ranking and scoring exercises. These include matrix ranking to explore local criteria for choices and preferences; proportional piling as a rapid indicator of perceptions of income, expenditure, or time spent on activities; and well-being ranking based on local definitions of stratification.

Diagrams and ranking exercises are done on the ground in a public space using easily available materials such as stones, beans, and coloured sand. For example a matrix grid is drawn on the ground and people are asked to distribute a number of stones or beans between the squares according to criteria that they determine. Participation does not depend on literacy but it does rely on representing ideas or quantities through symbols. It may be questioned whether this does not require skills analogous to literacy, but facilitators report that the exercises are quickly picked up and also easily passed on to others. In order to make decisions about criteria, ranking, or the meaning of concepts such as wealth, the people engage in discussion with each other, from which the researcher can learn mainly by listening. Problems of outsiders understanding the particular cultural mode of representation employed are overcome by 'interviewing the diagram' at the end.

The techniques require the researcher to be aware of who is involved, so as to see which categories of people are absent and whose voices predominate among those present. It is also possible to ask different categories of people, such as young or old, men or women, to draw separate maps, calendars, ranking diagrams and so on. They are asked to present their results to each other, thus exposing differences between the viewpoints of people who are used to setting the agenda for the village and those who are usually silenced or excluded.

Participatory rapid appraisal starts from a consideration of practical issues, rather than being theory-driven. Like other participatory approaches it is based on a paradigm which prioritizes the empowerment of people as subjects of research in a process of change. Unlike participant observation, the positioning of the researcher is not problematized, but tends to be thought of as neutral facilitation of change in the distribution of power. This shift of power is sought, not only in the research relationship, but also in the institutions concerned with agricultural development. If their extension workers are to adopt participatory rapid appraisal, to carry the results through requires an ability to recognize the expertize of local farmers as against that of professional experts; to find more empowering ways of communicating with local experts; and to develop decision-making procedures which respond to ideas from below, rather than imposing policies and projects from above.

Participant observation and participatory research

In the development of their theory and method, participant observation and participatory research have separate histories, with very few moments of interchange. Participatory research uses many methods associated with participant observation (observation, semi-structured interviews, focus group discussions). Participant observation could usefully add certain participatory techniques to its eclectic repertoire of methods, although this is impeded by the disparaging tone often used by anthropologists when referring to participatory rapid appaisal (Cornwall 1992: 12). Their theoretical approaches of participant observation and participatory research may be at greater variance than their methods and it is questioned whether a dynamic synthesis can be produced, or whether they derive from two incompatible paradigms.

The first point of difference is over the meaning of 'participation'. It was suggested above that the meaning of the participant element within participant observation has changed. Initially, participation was a means of gaining close enough access for accurate observation. Now anthropologists consider physical and emotional involvement through full participation in everyday life (not just getting close enough to watch and ask about it) as an essential means of learning about the society studied. However, it is still 'our' research on 'their' life. In contrast, the 'participant' in participatory research refers to their involvement in the research process.

The second point of comparison is over the research relationship. Participant observation traditionally has been based on divides between

57

researcher/researched and subject/object. Although there have been some initiatives to involve people in dialogic research, in the main this divide remains. Participatory research envisages a partnership based on more equal power relations between the researcher and participants in which participants are positioned not as objects of research but as active subjects.

The third point is that in participatory research both the process and the results should be empowering for the participants, whereas in participant observation the processes of collecting and analyzing data are usually not transparent, and the written results not accessible. The participant researcher's questions sometimes prompt key informants to generate a critical distance from their own lived experience and 'treat the familiar as strange'. The 'analytical imagination' (Lederman 1986: 368) which can then develop from daily sharing of an informant's local understanding with the researcher's wider analysis of social systems, is considered as a side-effect of the method as far as informants are concerned. This empowering element of research *with* people could be developed more strongly in participant observation.

The aims of participatory research are to empower more widely and systematically. It has been envisaged as an exchange where 'experts' impart research and analytical skills, while participants contribute local knowledge and as a result, the latter understand and 'own' the research. It is necessary, however, to consider who is empowered by involvement in this process: it will not be all the people all the time. Maguire suggests that leaders and organizations may become involved in participatory projects in order to enhance their own power-base and with no intention of supporting participatory decision-making (Maguire 1987: 44). However participatory rapid appraisal techniques may identify different sectors of the population. Indeed, they can be used to identify the poorest, who otherwise would not come into contact with development researchers, and to make explicit the very different knowledge and views held by different categories of people.

The fourth difference is that the purpose of participatory research is change, whereas this is variously denied or treated as an incidental outcome of participant research. Participatory research is used regularly to inform the design of development projects and is followed up with work on the skills and organizational methods people need to access authorities and participate in the policies arising from the research (Shah this volume). However, it can be argued that participatory rapid appraisal has a limited conceptualization of change. With its emphasis on speed, it has lost the radical theoretical underpinning of earlier participatory development. Participatory rapid appraisal relies on trying to change the behaviour and attitudes of individual experts. Participatory development tried to generate consciousness of how the silence and invisibility of the poor was maintained by the workings of economic and political systems and to analyze how to influence them. True to its time, it relied on an understanding of

58

large-scale systems of dependency and domination. New theoretical approaches to these issues are being developed by anthropologists who are questioning how people's multiple dimensions of difference are constructed, infused with hierarchies of power, and how they variously intersect in different contexts and are linked to processes of domination. This provides a theoretical framework for thinking critically about processes of change from which participatory research could benefit.

The fifth point of contrast is over the kind of knowledge generated. Traditionally, participant observation has studied 'down' and passed the knowledge 'up'. More recently, by widening the 'field' to study 'up', that is, by including those in powerful positions in government and development organizations and by taking a dialogic approach to fieldwork, there is the possibility of some information passing 'down'. However, in Cameron *et al.*'s terms, research *with* people is still rare. They argue that all anthropological research (however many other prepositions it carries) is *on* people, following disciplinary agendas. Disciplinary knowledge both contributes to and critiques world-ordering knowledge. It especially questions the construction of holders of local knowledge as ignorant, passive and ineffectually critical. The contradiction in anthropology is that little has been done to make such people active agents in fieldwork practice. In contrast, participatory research generates local knowledge for local use, while it seems to make little use of theoretical and comparative information to develop an understanding of the local within global systems. Even if participatory research is 'written up' this tends to be through accounts of method. So far few of the insights and experiences gained from participatory projects have contributed to the body of theoretical knowledge on which future projects can draw.

From these points of comparison it is possible to see that the two research approaches contain very different ideas of participation which cannot easily be fused. If the intention is to change the relationship between researcher and researched, so that the latter become participating and acting subjects in their own research, then there is much to learn from participatory research. Paradoxically, participatory research seems to be based on a limited theoretical understanding of processes of domination and change, with potentially much to learn from anthropological theory. At the moment participant observation and participatory research have opposite priorities, yet a synthesis would seem to hold the possibility of combining an approach constructing people as active agents in research with new theoretical understandings of wider processes of domination, in which both researcher and participants are located and which they are in different ways seeking to change.

5. Theatre for development: listening to the community

ALEX MAVROCORDATOS and PATHIKA MARTIN

All these aspects [peasants' knowledge of erosion, reforestation, farming, religion, death, etc.] are contained within a cultural totality. As a structure this cultural totality reacts as a whole. If one of its parts is affected, an automatic reflex occurs on the others (Freire 1976).

In early 1989, a new development project began work with the Bobo people in the Tominian District in the east of Mali. The Bobo are a minority group (constituting about 1 per cent of Mali's population) and relatively disadvantaged. In addition to the shortage of schools, clinics and other modern facilities, they are threatened by declining crop yields in the face of a growing population. Long-term use of new tools and chemical fertilizer has damaged soil fertility and extension of the area under cultivation has aggravated erosion by wind and rain. The Community Environment Project was set up by SOS Sahel to offer technical support to farmers in an area suffering from land degradation and falling yields.

SOS Sahel is a UK based non-governmental organization with particular expertise in the areas of soil and water conservation and agroforestry. It has also experimented with a variety of methods for making its approach in the field as participatory as possible; one of these was the creation of the Drama Unit.

Since at least the 1970s, when development agencies began to experiment with what they then referred to as the 'folk media', theatre has been recognized as a powerful medium of communication for education and community development alike. Dramatic sketches have transmitted messages, particularly around health and family planning, or on the benefits of literacy. The performers were often community workers or actors from outside. Less frequently, but more interestingly, the people themselves may have performed plays which they had created together with the community activists. These plays aimed to portray the problems facing the community, and explore relevant solutions. Sometimes, as in Zimbabwe, 'popular theatre' was used by the liberation struggle as a means of raising awareness among rural and urban people. In Latin America Augusto Boal drew on Freire's pedagogy to design a *Theatre of the Oppressed* in which scenarios of oppression are

61

replayed by members of the audience – repeating the actions of the protagonist – either as a more accurate representation of reality, or as a 'rehearsal for revolution'. Our own aim was to leave behind any didactic pretension, and without any dominant ideology to give a voice to those in the village communities who had not the power, or the habit, of speaking out. The task of the Drama Unit was to 'tune in' to the mood and views expressed by the community. Working from traditional performance forms – dance, drama, story-telling, song – villagers and Drama Unit together would develop a style of improvised theatre. This was intended to improve and develop communications between the project and the villagers with whom it worked, while also supporting existing cultural forms. Linking a theatre programme to the Community Environment Project would provide an ongoing internal evaluation and feedback system: 'a way to listen'.

The first phase of the Community Environment Project (hereafter the project) ran from 1989 to 1992. A field staff of ten men and ten women was recruited, most of whom originated from the Tominian district and were native *Bwa* (Bobo language) speakers. The project was headed by a Malian national from outside the area but three middle level staff were also Bwa speakers. Three expatriates worked in Tominian for the first two years of the project, one of whom had skills in 'theatre for development'. He and his local counterpart formed the Drama Unit. While the project headquarters were in the village of Tominian itself, the field staff lived and worked in outlying villages at distances of between 25 and 80 kilometres from the project base. The number of villages working with the project rose to 40 after four years.

Establishing a base

Our first task was to find out how it would be possible to open a channel for communication using and supporting local traditions of artistic expression. There is very little written research on the Bobo and our understanding was formed through contacts with the communities themselves, or with the field workers and emigrants from the villages now living in Tominian.

The Bobos' older traditions had begun to break down along with the overall social and climatic shifts. In the dry season, masked dancers used formerly to sweep through the villages to the sound of flute and drum, swathed in leaves from head to toe so that those present were no longer aware of the person inside. They were a cleansing force, purging the village of its errors and appeasing the ancestors; they were a preparation and a prayer for rain. The festival could last for days, and was indeed that 'exercise of a dangerous and terrible act' that Antonin Artaud (1965) wanted all theatre to be, for these dances were an integral part of life and (agri)culture. While the ceremonies might have become briefer, there were still days when strangers were unwelcome in the villages. The arts and the villagers' lives in general continued to form a continuum between sacred and profane.

Aside from the necessary animal sacrifices, the festivities of marriage and baptism were at the other end of the continuum. There, as in the weekly drinking parties, the singing and dancing were clearly secular. And to the regret of many, the *ONI-yô*[1] dance had disappeared from the marriage ceremony.

Between the sacred and secular extremes were the worksongs. Many farmers had begun to till their own fields, alone, using donkey ploughs; communal songs had disappeared along with teamwork. While harvesting remained a group activity, only some farmers could still afford to call out the *griots*, who are the village musicians or praise singers. When the *griots* did bring their drums to the harvest, the pace would surge with the rhythm and the songs that praised the labourers. Far from being mere flatteries, the praises the *griots* sang were regarded as a necessary spiritual food which visibly improved the execution of collective work.

It appeared that the Bobo had no traditional form of 'theatre' as such and that the Drama Unit would have to work from music, story and dance. If it was appropriate, theatre would come later.

Among the first villages invited to work with the project was Tana, a village of some 500 people which appeared to be a close-knit community and keen to work with the project. Tana also boasted a particularly strong *griot* presence. We were pleased when the village elders welcomed our cultural initative, and agreed to host the opening experiments in development theatre.

The griot project

By the start of the rainy season in mid-1989, ten Community Environment Project workers were ready to move into their village posts in five host villages. With farming in full swing the villagers had little or no spare time. Meetings were rushed, tired affairs between evening food and bed. We were able to proceed quietly, watching and chatting. Much of our time was taken up with observing the work in the fields, and recording some of the *griots*' harvest songs.

We saw that this musical encouragement during the harvest could be applied to the collective soil and water conservation work that the project planned to initiate and the *griots* looked like promising partners. A caste apart, these families were once supported by the community, but this was no longer the case. Leather craft and weaving, once just a supplementary income, now provided a meagre livelihood. The *griots* had to farm what unused land they could solicit, and they were not farmers by tradition. Many older *griots* advised their sons to seek their fortune elsewhere.

This faltering tradition was an ideal base for us, seeking to nourish the custom just as it was breaking down. The songs praised and exhorted speed and skill, but they carried an implicit understanding of the work in hand. If the *griots* learnt about new techniques such as water-harvesting, their (improvised) songs could expand to include both technical encouragement and talk of a greener future. Their songs would reach farmers who had never attended meetings or trainings.

The *griots* were happy to co-operate the following year. The singer, Ennemo, began by casting his new songs in the traditional mould but week by week, they became more specific. He sang of the flowing rainwater trapped in catchment pits, the soil that would no longer be washed away in the flooding and the vision of trees and millet sprouting in abandoned fields.

Some villages no longer had resident *griots* as the young men had left their villages in search of city money and their old fathers no longer sang. Once Tana had completed its anti-erosion work, Ennemo was available for work elsewhere. The Drama Unit provided him with a bicycle to carry him (and his partner) to Ba'assi to animate the conservation work there. In So'ura we invited the *griot* from a neighbouring hamlet, and he came regularly to sing for the diggers.

Ba'assi and So'ura both reported substantial increases in output when the *griots* were there in March and April. Given time and more training we had hoped that these two *griots*, and others like them, could become the holders of a basic technical knowledge, sought by their own community or even neighbouring villages.

By the end of 1990, the project had contacted a dozen or so new villages and the Drama Unit planned to extend the *griot* project accordingly. But poor rains had driven many young men off in the quest for cash; many of the original singers were travelling from village to village with their balafons (a type of xylophone), playing for tax money. It also became apparent that we had made an important mistake in the first season. Since the *griots* had sung at our invitation, they were seen as our financial responsibility and in 1991 they barely sang in the first villages. Elsewhere we were more circumspect. The villagers of Tierakui themselves arranged for their *griot* to accompany their diggings and he quickly adapted his lyrics. The *griots* of Yabara also turned out but kept to the traditional style. It was planned that the fieldworkers themselves would take part in monitoring and developing the content of the songs. Meanwhile, *griots* from a number of villages were brought together to produce an audio cassette of songs on erosion control which have now been heard many miles from the project site.

Theatre is a language

Theatre for development is often expected to be a mechanism for transmitting a message, but it does not have to be didactic, nor directly polemic. By expressing everyday realities, or even mythical ones, the performers can invite the audience to look into a mirror – perhaps for amusement, perhaps

64

for instruction and perhaps in the attempt to find a way through difficult times. If villagers were to use the language of theatre to express their circumstances and explore their problems they could together decide on a course of action. The role of the project in this was to listen, rather than merely trying to transmit its point of view.

When we sought to introduce the idea of theatre, the Chief of Tana replied with a proverb: 'If someone asks you to make a rope out of sand, you'd better ask to see the old one first.' The villagers were perfectly willing but, having no experience of theatre, they would first need to see for themselves what it was. With the 1989 harvest complete, and many granaries filled, they were free to turn to other activities. There is always plenty of work during the dry season – brickmaking, building and repairs, as well as straw mats and baskets to be sold at market to complete the village tax. One evening a week was set aside to reach for this 'theatre', this rope of sand.

It was mostly young men who volunteered as performers; women were said to be too shy. On their suggestion, early rehearsals with warming up exercises were replaced by the *ONI-yô* dance which led seamlessly into improvized sketches. Simple images of farming, hunting, courtship and marriage soon gave way to more complex scenarios on similar subjects which told us much about village life and customs. Under Tana's harmonious surface, there were many currents of duplicity and distrust which later surfaced in problems with collective working.

Plays depicting the soil and water conservation work also showed us that it had been undertaken more in the hope of other rewards than as a means by which the villagers could themselves improve their situation. While formal meetings (and the field workers' reports) had given a different picture of the villagers' collaboration with the project, the plays made it clear that they were far from feeling that they 'owned' these works.

The following year, attendance at the collective works dropped off significantly and we asked the theatre group to show us the problem. After two wooden performances which lectured the audience on the benefits of soil and water conservation, they finally produced a complete history of their involvement with the project – from their perspective.

From the first visits of project representatives, the scene shifts to volunteers labouring over the catchment-pits. In spite of subsequent visits from the management, we see their numbers soon diminish. There are those who mock the volunteers, proclaiming that only beasts go round scratching holes in that fruitless ground. Some of these prefer to weave grass mats for sale in the markets and they gloat later when the volunteers, still penniless, are arrested and beaten by the militia for non-payment of taxes and impossible fines.[2] They say the fieldworkers should have protected them and warn that work with the project could eventually peter out.

65

Dancing the ONI-yô. This dancer, although blind, performs a solo during an evening theatre performance in Tana Village, Mali. Photograph: Alex Mavrocordatos, SOS Sahel.

Even old men got up from the audience and joined in the play, which was received with boisterous attention. Inspired by their own emotion, the actors had surpassed the bounds that a prepared play would have allowed. This was the strength of improvised work. Afterwards, they wondered if they had taken frankness too far but once reassured their plays became bolder. There may have been other underlying causes of the apathy, but these plays opened a dialogue. Subsequent meetings with the project staff and the village authorities yielded a plan of action which was seen to improve attendance at the water catchment site.

In the meantime work had begun in the village of Embere'ui, a community quite different in character, its readiness to embrace change and new ideas was in strong contrast with Tana's conservatism. The village was largely converted from traditional religions to Christianity and it may be that the work with the Church had helped to provoke reflection. Before too long, these performers also turned their attention to the Forestry Department in a play that signalled their (real) fear about a (hypothetical) danger.

> Some village women are in the forest gathering wood when they catch sight of a pair of forestry agents coming their way. They hide behind a baobab tree, and watch as the agents deliberately set fire to the dry grasses. Later the agents turn up in the village, feigning anger, to fine the protesting villagers for the fire damage. Since there are witnesses, the unusually courageous villagers refuse to pay and are taken before the Forestry Chief. The agents are fired and the Chief exhorts the villagers to report any such cases.

Since the project's official partner was the Malian forestry service, the manager decided to discuss the issue with the local Chief Forester before rumour beat him to it. Following these two plays, a formal agreement was negotiated with the Forestry Department to leave the 'project villages' out of their circuit, allowing time for the slower approach to conservation to take effect, uncompromised by punitive measures. The Chief Forester made a visit to Embere'ui in support of the new agreement. This in its turn made an impression on the villagers who said that previously they had never had anything but aggressive visits from the Forestry Department.[3]

There were more plays about corruption and we began to see the characters standing firm against extortionate demands, citing their rights, and succeeding. This revealed a new courage, and a refreshing willingness to act way beyond the mendicant attitude of the earlier plays. Now both villages had had a glimpse of the empowering possibilities which the theatre work might open up for them.

Meanwhile, the village women had yet to perform, although they were a regular audience. But when the Embere'ui men put on a play showing how hard it is to find a good wife and how they are jilted by their fiancées for any man with more money, it proved too much for the women. At last, they mounted a play showing us the hardships of their life, especially having to share a husband and drag him home from the beer-yard all the time. The play generated active *public* debate between men and women. This was unheard of in the past, especially since the subject was intimate and personal. This departure from Bobo mores sprang from the women's anger and resentment at the allegations made against them by the men; now women began to attend meetings, and the women's plays continued.

Initially Tana's women could not be persuaded into the arena. Most of the village's young unmarried women (the likeliest actresses) were away in town in the quest for cash, and perhaps adventure. The many plays concerning the exodus decried it as undesirable and unnecessary for women – resulting in degeneracy, misadventure and the spread of venereal diseases back in the village. Offstage, the men performers (mostly married) insisted that married women would not perform in public – out of modesty. Nevertheless when forward thinking Embere'ui showed the way, the women of Tana, married or not, were quick to respond; they portrayed marital problems, making much of the jealousy between co-wives, and we saw plays from both villages about drunken and negligent husbands, the rural exodus, child ill-health and the massive workload that women must support. In Tana first and later in Embere'ui women began to play together with the men; if their scenario depicted a man, they would solicit a man to play the part.

The Tana performers also produced a play which commented critically on the project's relations with them. They did this using allegory.

A child has been born. Everybody is cuddling the baby, and when visitors arrive they too make much of it, taking lots of pictures and showering gifts as they leave. Back for a second visit, the three find the mother sitting alone, with her child now ravaged by diarrhoea and much less cute. Hastily they pass on by to see the neighbours who are celebrating their own newborn with dance and merriment. Later when the first child gets better, the visitors come smiling back and the play ends when they carry the baby home with them.

Initial discussion after the play centred on child health, an important enough issue, but there was more to it than that. Unprompted the players themselves explained that the sick baby represented Tana; that in the first project year they had been healthy, producing 204 ditches and a tree nursery, and received visitors from Bamako and London too. But after a less healthy season, no-one wanted to know about the mere 59 ditches dug. Project delegations sped by *en route* to healthier places, abandoning Tana.

Theatre had been used to express a sentiment, very frankly – with just a hint of recrimination – that the villagers could not have expressed in a meeting or a conversation. However, the topic was delicate, and they were wary of exploring it too actively.

The language of theatre had been assimilated by the two villages, and learned by fieldworkers and project management. So far, it was the communities who used the language and the project which listened. From time to time the audience would get involved in the performances, entering and perhaps replaying the action, or dictating its flow. However dialogue between villagers and fieldworkers largely remained conventional, using after-show discussions and meetings.

Integration of the drama unit within the community environment project

Funded by Comic Relief and the European Commission, the Drama Unit only came into being after the main project proposal had been written. Although its function was to support the technical side of the project's work, the Drama Unit's objective of encouraging free and open expression by the villagers had the potential to cause political embarassment; it seemed prudent that it should be autonomous.

Until 1990, there was frequent consultation between project management and the Drama Unit on policy and practice but as the scale of activities increased, this level of consultation was not sustained.[4] With changes in project management and priorities, and a shift in later years towards a higher rate of practical achievements in the field, the importance attributed to theatre work within the project fluctuated. In this project, as in most others, the slow and intangible benefits of participatory practices had to be weighed against the project's need to justify its presence to local officials and ordinary people, as well as to far-away funders.

Field staff in general appreciated the revival of the *ONI-yô* and the valorization of their own (minority) culture, but continued to prefer the concept of didactic rather than listening theatre. Compared with agroforestry or soil and water conservation activities, the objectives of the Drama Unit were abstract and the search for an evolving, locally appropriate form left some fieldworkers uncertain of the role of the Drama Unit within the main project. To combat this, formal training of all field staff was planned but never took place because of the full schedule of technical training.

Those staff directly concerned displayed mixed reactions towards the Drama Unit's work. In Tana they tended to interpret the theatre's exposure of problems as policing of their own work, rather than as a tool for broadening their understanding. They reciprocated by swift criticism of our mistakes. Conversely, in Embere'ui the Drama Unit was actively solicited and the fieldworkers themselves ran the rehearsals, demonstrating their enthusiasm for this work and awareness of its utility.

69

Some difficulties encountered

The obvious and major brake on my own activity was ignorance of the Bobo language. Working through an interpreter was viable while setting things up and even in early rehearsals but to pick up nuances one needs increasingly to be tuned to the subtleties of speech and metaphor. My Bobo colleague would translate, but we lost the advantage of two minds, and were often slow to pick things up. Customs can vary from village to village, and unfamiliarity led to one or two errors of protocol.

When we gave the *griots* a bicycle to facilitate work outside their own villages, we offended some of the other villagers. The social situation of the *griots* was fraught: still marked as members of a dependent caste, and yet no longer given the economic security which was their right. For the Drama Unit a close association with the traditional custodians of music and story-telling was logical and we aimed to include them in the benefits the project was bringing to the area. But in the villages, where *griots* occasionally return from the cities richer than their former patrons, any hint of favouritism was bitterly resented.

The problem of dependency was a recurring stumbling-block. While the project was committed to fostering autonomous development, the villagers often took another view, as Tana's play on aid graphically depicted:

> The scene opens with a group of project workers meeting in a village. They propose rearing a new breed of pigs, and hand out clothing and a preliminary 5000 FCFA (about £10) towards the fodder. The villagers say this is not enough and the project doubles the sum, but it is agreed that the amount will diminish with each contribution. They are making bricks to build sties, when there is a visit from another prospective project – grain banks this time. Unconditionally, as an 'encouragement', a large advance of money is given, plus stocks of maize, millet and even rice. When the original man comes back, his grant now down to 250 FCFA (about 50p), the villagers tell him to keep his money, as they are with someone who looks after them properly.

Neither drama nor soil and water conservation work was paid, but there were benefits such as subsidized tools and credit schemes and in Tana the actors repeatedly asked for financial support of various kinds.

Tana's material emphasis was symptomatic of their declared powerlessness in the face of failing rains, and the express view that only we, the outsiders, could do anything. It also provided an escape from difficult issues, such as the distribution of land or power in the village, or the sensitive details of community collaboration. Both villages were willing to deal with problems in their relations with the outside, be it government, the project, or other organizations. But apart from the generalities of family or marital life, the actors usually slid away from exploring the internal tensions within their village – which may have been the most significant factors affecting their work with the project. Embere'ui was more courageous in this respect but may have expected too much; after two years, the evaluators found the performers disillusioned by the lack of change in response to their plays.

Lack of response was a perennial problem. Sometimes the players made concrete requests which the project was unable or unwilling to satisfy. The 'aid' scenario just described may have been a request for more lavish assistance, or a warning that the villagers could look elsewhere for collaborators. This is a subtle paradox: the villagers' reluctance to accept responsibility could actually become a tool for negotiating a better deal. In the context of the development industry within which non-governmental organizations sometimes compete to extend their spheres of influence, this suggests that self-declared beggars *can* sometimes be choosers.

Conclusion

The utility of the first two years of the Drama Unit's work in Tana were summed up by one elder with a Bobo proverb: 'The hyena says: Good news makes the night pass quickly in a termite heap'. Our interpreter explained that if something is worthwhile, one agrees to do things that otherwise one would not do. Initially a number of Tana elders came along to support the actors (and probably to keep an ear on the proceedings) but by the end of the second season they were regularly taking part in the action, either by proxy or with direct interventions. Their readiness to perform suggests that they saw some value in this new forum. Similarly, the theatre evenings eventually gave women an opportunity to speak up in public about some of their problems. The type of themes treated overall – as well as their presentation – made the theatre evenings qualitatively different from most village meetings.

The first years showed promise of laying the foundations for a constructive dialogue between project and villagers, and of stimulating discussion as a first stage of praxis within the villages. It would be dangerous to claim that any lasting empowerment could be achieved by this means in the short space of four years. However, the Drama Unit's experience does suggest that theatre allows – even occasionally obliges – people to speak more boldly than they will in more conventional exchanges. For this frankness to have a lasting effect, both goodwill and constructive response are essential. While theatre can strike some sparks, sustained participatory practice is needed to fan them into a flame.

6. A multi-method approach to the study of homelessness

FATIMA AKILU

During the course of this century ways of studying homeless people in Britain have changed. In the 1930s most of the writing on homelessness was carried out by novelists. For example, George Orwell in *Down and Out in Paris and London* (1949) provides an insight into the day to day life of the homeless man of the time as he saw it, but offered little in the way of explanation as to the causes of homelessness, or of the ambitions of homeless people. Attempts at more objective accounts followed, but an approach towards empirical collection of data did not arise until the 1960s (Wallace 1968; Bahr 1973; Bogue 1963) where data were obtained from social survey interviews.

The sociological approach was to continue as researchers became predominantly interested in observing trends in homelessness. Most of the studies were carried out by agencies conducting their own independent research (Commission for Racial Equality 1984; The London Housing Inquiry 1988; SHIL 1988; Housing Working Group of Reading and District Council of Churches 1990; Randall 1989). Panoramic surveys were common, with most of the reports recording anecdotal material which tended to reflect the political biases and views of homelessness held by particular agencies. Much of the statistical information gathered on homelessness was from survey agency or local authority records (Thomas and Niner 1989). These reports saw homelessness as first and foremost a housing problem and published papers which were geared toward housing policy and provision. They were sometimes instrumental in acquiring housing, but ignored the support needs vital to a large number of homeless people.

The first authors to question methodology in studies on homelessness were Greve, Page and Greve (1971). In their study they made use of information gained from local authorities and voluntary agencies. In addition they utilized questionnaires and recording schedules, to enumerate the housing needs of the homeless. Their work led them to conclude that there was considerable scope in the field of homelessness for combining action and research. The call for a combination of methods to be used in homelessness research, was reflected in ensuing research. *Single and Homeless* by Drake, O'Brien, and Biebuych (1982) was more comprehensive in its use of varying methods than previous work done in this field. Three quantitative and two qualitative measures were used which consisted of:

○ *Referral agency survey* in which a national referral agency in London was used. Ten per cent of the case records kept from January 1967 to 1976 were examined.

○ *Survey interview* which consisted of a structured questionnaire administered by interviewers recruited locally and trained in London.

○ *Night shelter survey*. This was a study of six months' intake at an East End night shelter.

○ *Participant observation*. The purpose of this was to provide information on how it feels to be single and homeless.

○ *Group discussions*. Six group discussions were held in various hostels and day centres.

New approaches based on the use of a combination of methods were to dominate the early 1990s. They included the approach taken by the Department of Psychology at Surrey University in 1989. Their contribution has broadened the perspective on homelessness to one with a psychological basis. In their attempt to build up a picture of different types of people in different homeless facilities, including the streets, they used three different measures: a telephone survey using a structured questionnaire; a follow up of the telephone survey using face to face interviews; and observations by interviewers of the physical conditions and atmosphere of hostels they visited.

Other homelessness researchers have combined survey interviews with participant observation methods (Henslin 1990). These go a step further in contributing to an increased understanding of homelessness and bear some similarity to participatory research methods. The distinct advantage of participant observation in homelessness research is that it is less structured and more open than the survey interview, enabling the researcher to collect information on non-verbal behaviour as well as providing access to processes and dynamics of social situations as they unfold. The researcher can reformulate the research problem and analyse the data as he or she progresses (Dean 1967; Finch and Mason 1990). Thus the fieldworker is less committed to perspectives which may have been misconceptualized at the onset of the project. The researcher has closer contact with the field situation and is therefore better able to avoid misleading or meaningless questions. Yet this method is not problem free. A considerable amount of time is required to carry it out and this is often not within the scope of many research projects. The way entry is gained and, once established in the group, the degree to which the researcher identifies with the group and the ways people adjust their behaviour in her or his presence all affect the quality of the research (Crano and Brewer 1973; Webb *et al.* 1966; Bailey 1987).

In order to provide a more comprehensive picture of homelessness, and of the very heterogeneous people who become homeless and their experi-

73

ence of it, these later studies have recognized the need to use more than one method. Studies are still, however, over-reliant on survey methods, which are not without problems. One major disadvantage is that the researcher or body commissioning the project decides on the questions of interest and determines the path of the investigation. The power therefore rests with them and the respondent is little more than a passive agent who has very little information regarding the aims of the survey and the role he or she plays in it. Although these methods have provided a wealth of information on the facts and figures and experience of homelessness, they have not devised a way that allows homeless people to speak for themselves. What is required is a research strategy which combines qualitative and quantitative methods, is participation- and action- oriented, and in which homeless people are able to speak for themselves and can determine the issues concerning their homelessness which are of most importance to them.

The use of participatory research methods

This realization that homeless people had not been allowed adequate autonomy in detailing their own experience derived from a problem encountered during the early phase of a survey on homelessness undertaken for my Ph.D. thesis. I realized that the experience of homelessness that I was witnessing while working as a volunteer in shelters and hostels for the homeless was not reflected in the interviews I was undertaking for the main part of my survey research. Moreover, the survey method limited homeless people's involvement in generating information about their situation.

An example of a discrepancy between my work at the shelter and my research interviews was demonstrated in an interview I carried out with a young homeless woman.

> I first met Sally at the Girls' Friendly Shelter in April last year. I carried out a two-hour long interview with her. She was twenty-five years old and had first left home at the age of twenty-one. She left home due to an inability to get along with her mother. Sally says she was an unwanted child and that she was blamed for her mother's strokes. Since leaving home she has been in trouble with the police several times, and was on probation at the time of the interview. She got married three years ago to a man who was violent towards her and subsequently she left him. Sally stated that she saw herself as: '. . . a bit of a waster I suppose. I could be doing something about it but I am not. I could get a job, but I'm just dossing about' (Fieldnotes: interview with Sally).

At the time of the interview Sally said that she had made friends since she had been homeless, and that she had met them at the shelter. I knew Sally for 17 months in my work both at the Girls' Friendly Society, and latterly at the YMCA. During that time I have learnt that Sally is a lesbian, and that this was the major conflict she had with her mum. Her family found it hard to accept this part of her life and it led her to leave home at the age of twenty-one. According to Sally, she tried to conform to her family's wishes but it did not work out and she became homeless. I also discovered that, contrary to what she stated during the interview, Sally was extremely isolated at the Girls' Friendly Society. The other girls were aware of her sexuality and shunned her. When I came to interview her she had been in her room for about two weeks without talking to anyone. When she later started living and working at the YMCA, she seemed happier. The residents and staff knew that she was a lesbian and accepted her.

The information I began to acquire in my capacity as a shelter worker led me to question some of the methods I was using and to conclude that in order to acquire a broader understanding of the people I was interested in, I would have to devise a research design that would require a greater level of involvement from the homeless. This new-found research awareness led to a desire for experimentation with a more participatory approach. Time spent in hostels indicated that a large number of young homeless people experienced considerable amounts of boredom. Out of a desire to alleviate this arose two projects (a mural painting and a film documentary) which homeless people designed and implemented. This strived to encompass a more participatory-based research design. These projects are described below.

The mural project

As a result of my work with homeless young people residing in a variety of temporary hostels and shelters in Reading, I realized that most of them spent their day, when not at the DSS or council offices, sitting around in hostels, walking the streets or watching TV. The idea for this project came about as first a means of reducing the boredom experienced by the young people, and second a means of closely keeping in touch with a small group of homeless young people in order to get a better understanding of what they perceived their situation to be, not only in terms of homelessness, but its associated difficulties.

It was essential for the project to attract a small number of homeless people who had easy access to one another and who would be able to work closely for a period of at least two months with the aim of producing something tangible at the end. The group members were four men under the age of 25 who were living at the YMCA. I had, at an earlier date, interviewed each man on a range of issues related to their homelessness. I approached all four men in the first week of December 1990, and proposed the idea of working together. The central theme of any work we were to undertake was to focus on homelessness.

Planning for the project took place over a period of a month. The central aim was to get them to talk about how they wanted to portray their own personal experience of homelessness on a mural. The variety of things that they expressed were, first, the physical aspects of the experience of homelessness. This included the inability to sleep at night due to fear of being attacked, and sleeping in cardboard boxes, in train or bus stations or the night shelter in Reading, which they felt was grim and dark. Second, they emphasized the emotional aspects of feeling bleak and isolated. They felt their principles had dropped; they had no self respect. Homelessness was felt to be soul-destroying and feelings of paranoia were expressed as well as self-pity. Third, they identified social aspects – notably the fact that homelessness prevented them from socializing, because it robbed them of their self confidence. There was not much for them to do during the day and they experienced intense boredom. Also discussed was their perception of themselves, which they saw as being different from the older homeless. They were in the YMCA, they had hopes and aspirations, and saw themselves as eventually getting out of their present predicament. However they felt they did share some similarities with the older homeless including the fact that they saw themselves as failures, that they lacked independence in the hostel, and felt unable to save or plan for the future. A lot of homelessness was believed to be self-induced: '. . . it happens to people who can't cope, people unable to face the world'.

We concluded that the mural should have a side that would be indicative of the experience of homelessness and a side that would represent the things they desired. We felt that it was important that the two sides were visibly different, not only in the images they portrayed, but in the varying moods depicted. We talked at length before deciding that colour would be the distinguisher. One side would be done in black and white, it would represent the bleakness of the different stages of homelessness and colour would be gradually blended in, highlighting the affluence shown on the opposing side.

Materials consisting of paint, cardboard and an overhead projector were donated to the project by Reading University Students Union. On January 15, 1991, we met for the first time at Silver Street where the mural was actually to be painted. We used the overhead projector to project the images that we wanted onto a large board which we had sand-papered and painted white. These sessions were relaxed and cordial. Throughout the painting period attendance was high. We met everyday at two o'clock and worked for five hours and the painting was completed in two weeks.

The project was seen as a success, and we were able to complete it in the time we had allotted. There were no drop-outs and the attendance rate was extremely good. We felt our greatest achievement was that we were able to develop good working relationships, and we were able to maintain this long after the project was over. Other positive things that evolved from this

Homelessness Mural, Reading 1991. The left side, representing the bleakness of different stages of homelessness is in black and white. Colour is gradually blended in until affluence is highlighted on the right.

Photograph: Fatima Akilu.

project can be seen in the changes that occurred in the young men. Kevin has become involved with a local magazine based at Silver Street where the mural was painted. Rodney, though still suicidal, has agreed to see a psychiatrist on a regular basis. He discovered he enjoys painting and would like to go to art college. Not long after the project ended Brian began to look for a job, which he obtained, in Swindon. Steven is the only member of the group whose situation remains unchanged.

This project dispels the myth that homeless people are not like everyone else. There are difficulties in homeless people working as a group on any long-term project because of their unsettled lifestyle – not only their lack of mobility, but appointments with DSS, probation officers and other agencies make it difficult to meet. We overcame these and began supporting each other. The men I worked with were ordinary people with very realistic hopes and aspirations. They all had plans for their futures. They showed little self-pity and saw themselves as eventually getting out of their present predicament. They clearly saw themselves as temporarily homeless and felt unable to identify with those older homeless using night shelters, whose situation seemed more permanent. Homeless people are not an impossible group to work with as this study clearly demonstrates. They have definite views of their situation, and what they feel would alleviate it, though we were unable to depict all of these clearly in the mural.

The documentary film project

The second project was a film documentary of homelessness in Reading. I was approached by four young people residing at the YMCA who had heard about the work on the mural. They asked if I would organize another project on homelessness, using a video. They wanted to make a documentary that could be used in schools to inform young people about homelessness. Two members of the group dropped out in the first two weeks, due to personal problems. The responsibility for the project was taken by the two people who remained. They were encouraged to keep their own record of all our meetings as well as notes of progress and attendance. In addition to record keeping, the young people between them wrote a letter asking for financial assistance for the project. The first version is shown below:

C/O Y.M.C.A
PARKSIDE RD
READING.

Dear Sir/Madame,
Well let me introduce myself as the secretary of a young but amateur group of people from the Reading YMCA. We are hoping to film a documentary on homeless people in Reading. We are depending on people like yourselves and your company to offer us any help and advice that you might have on filming and also how if any which firms to approach or trusts to get financial backing from, as your help and co-operation will be gratefully received.

Yours Sincerely

This letter went through many drafts before they came up with the version which we all deemed satisfactory (see opposite page).
On the basis of this letter we received two grants which enabled us to hire the equipment we required. All our finances were handled by James, who kept a detailed account of our expenditure. During the two months we worked together James, Rachael and I had long discussions with groups of homeless people living at the Girls' Friendly Society and Church Housing hostels in Reading, on their experience of homelessness. The discussions were all taped and transcribed. Based on the information obtained from these discussions they came up with a picture they believed to represent

their homelessness. The discussions also provided us with enough information to enable us to formulate a script for the documentary interviews, and come up with a list of questions to be used in the interviews.

Our list of questions for interviews to be filmed included the following:

1) Have you ever experienced living on your own?
2) What was the reason you left home?
3) What did you do when you left home?
4) Have you ever slept rough?
5) What kind of experiences have you had while being homeless?
6) Have you looked for work and accommodation?
7) What type of work did you have before becoming homeless/ have you ever lost a job through being homeless?
8) How do you see yourself?
9) Have you thought of counselling to help you cope with being homeless?
10) Are you on any medication? What is it for?

The next step of the project involved approaching young homeless people from two hostels, and requesting their consent to take part in the documentary. The actual filming of the interviews took place over the course of a weekend. Each interview lasted half an hour or more. Seven people were interviewed and all of the interviews, with the exception of two, were carried out by James and Rachael.

The documentary was edited in two phases. The first version contained three minutes of each interview, chosen by James and Rachael. It covered a wide variety of areas, which included the reasons for homelessness, the experience of homelessness, use of drugs, mental health problems and the level of support available to homeless people. In July 1992 we received a day's training on editing. This led us to discard the format we had used for our initial edit. The technique we decided to use for the second version consisted of shorter segments of interviews, which were interspersed with shots of homeless people and the town centre. This approach meant that we had to leave out large areas of the interviews and concentrate on two questions. To decide on this it was necessary to consult all our participants. A meeting was organized with all the people interviewed, James, Rachael and myself. They were shown the first version of the tape. Initially three people wanted to maintain this version. After a lot of discussion we reached an agreement to shorten the tape and concentrate on just two questions. The questions we decided to include were, the reasons for homelessness, and what people did when they became homeless.

Responsibility for the project was divided between James and Rachael. James was responsible for secretarial duties, such as record keeping and monitoring meetings, while Rachael was in charge of field organization, which entailed contacting homeless people for the interviews. It was important that all the members of the group had an equal say in all the stages of the documentary. The form that decisions were arrived at consisted of four stages. First, there was an initial general discussion on all the issues we wished to cover, and second, a further discussion where each member stated their final point of view on the subject. Third, the group talked about how each person's perspective fitted in with the general objective of the documentary. Finally, a series of continuing discussions were held until unanimous agreement was reached on which views failed to meet our objective. These were excluded.

The project enabled a group of homeless people to form and to develop an open and participative method of making decisions. They proved to themselves that their lifestyle does not prevent them from working together. For the two people mainly involved, the project caused them to use a vast array of communicative and organizational skills. The result was a piece of research on reasons for and experiences of homelessness which the people defined and carried out for themselves. The video documents their experiences of homelessness in the setting of Reading, and gives them a voice, as it has been shown in schools and clubs in the area. The aim of the documentary was to highlight the experience of homelessness, setting it in a background that was of direct relevance to Reading. The logical process for the documentary was to begin with interviews of the homeless and progress to detailing information on temporary accommodation.

Conclusion

The success achieved with both projects, depended on the housing stability of the people involved. For both projects the core members of the group were residing at a stable hostel, where they were under no impending threat of losing their immediate shelter. Once that was established, of crucial importance was the role of the researcher in creating a strong trusting relationship with the project participants, as well as creating an atmosphere that encouraged active participation of all the members equally. There were certain factors that threatened this at certain times, such as the dominance of some members, in direct opposition to the reticence of others. All members were made to believe that it was their project and each member was of equal importance. At the inception of both projects it was made clear that the emphasis would lie in our understanding and interpretation of the group process in which we would engage. It was the learning process that was to be of utmost importance, rather than the actual finished product.

Participants were given complete autonomy in deciding how they wanted their situation portrayed. The goal we strove for was one in which the distinction between researcher and subject was removed. Group members were equally responsible for the creative thinking that went into the formulation of the different projects as well as their implementation. It is important to note that, the homeless people were not necessarily presenting their own personal view of how they felt, but of how they viewed homelessness.

While both groups were situationally very similar (living in medium-stay hostels), there was a distinct difference in how they wished to be portrayed. The first group, who worked on the mural, clearly sought to distance themselves from their situation. They argued that the hostel represented a home, while homelessness was indicative of failure. They stressed that they differed from the older, more long-term, homeless, and expressed a strong belief in the impermanence of their situation. In the mural, the side in black and white representing homelessness was only tolerated because of the knowledge that soon they would form a part of the scene depicted in colour that they so envied. This contrasted greatly with the group who worked on the documentary. They saw themselves as victims, there was a general desire to show 'how awful homelessness can be, so that other people would not have to suffer the same fate'. Their aim clearly was to raise the public's awareness of the unpleasantness of being homeless, while at the same time highlighting the different facilities available, should one become homeless. It was evident that the homeless people who took part in both these projects had a clear idea of how they wanted to be portrayed, and which issues raised were of the most concern to them. The differences obtained in portrayals of homelessness in the two groups was partly a reflection of the medium used. Television represents a more vulnerable medium, as it is more conducive to self disclosure than a mural.

In addition to the benefits mentioned above, the two projects provided homeless people with an opportunity to organize themselves, while learning skills such as record keeping, book-keeping and writing funding proposals. From a research point of view, the use of participatory methods provided a qualitative understanding of homelessness, proving that it was possible for the most unsettled and disenfranchised population to contribute to their own definition of their situation. Given the opportunity, many young homeless people are well able and willing to take responsibility for their lives. These projects not only demonstrate this but suggest that future work with the homeless should be designed in such a way that the homeless are allowed a far greater chance to make a contribution than they have been able to in the past.

7. Farmers as analysts, facilitators and decision-makers

PARMESH SHAH

In most development programmes farmers are informants or at best data collectors. They do not participate in analysing data and taking decisions based on the analysis, nor is their inherent analytical capacity used. Although the resultant development process may lead to tangible development results in the short run, it does not encourage sustained innovation by the local villagers or institution building at the village level.

In contrast, the Aga Khan Rural Support Programme (AKRSP) in its work with village communities, has tried to involve villagers in collection, analysis, and use of data, and as facilitators of a participatory appraisal and planning process.

The Aga Khan Rural Support Programme is a non-governmental organization established in 1985 to promote and create an enabling environment for the village communities to manage their local natural resources in a productive, equitable and sustainable manner through their own village institutions. It works with about 200 village communities in three Districts in Gujarat State of western India. The process involves participatory appraisal and planning for the development of natural resources in the village and the formation of village institutions for implementing village natural resource management plans prepared by the villagers. The villagers are encouraged to develop a local cadre of village extension volunteers who develop expertise in appraisal, planning, implementation, management and monitoring and also build functional linkages with other state, non-governmental, co-operative and financial organizations in the area. These volunteers and office bearers from the community are accountable to the village institutions and are paid performance-related incentives by the village institution. The village institutions are federating into a regional organization which will become a support organization for the village institutions working in the area. It will spearhead development of new village institutions and development of functional and management expertise at village level.

Aga Khan Rural Support Programme mainly functions as a support organization. Initially it facilitates development of appraisal and planning skills among the village extension volunteers selected by the community. It also provides training inputs for development of these skills. It then facilitates the formation of village institutions and enables the community to assess the support it will require for strengthening them. It tries to provide training support in technical, financial, management and monitoring areas. The emphasis is not on creating a large support organization which has expertise in all functional areas but on encouraging villagers to volunteer to become village para-professionals in different areas depending on their interest and aptitude. Participatory Rural Appraisal (PRA) is used as a major training and planning methodology to enable village volunteers to become village analysts, managers and institutional change agents.

Participatory Rural Appraisal enables village volunteers to develop as analysts and increases their capacity to interact with all sections of the village community and develop a common perspective on village natural resource development. This facilitates the development of functional leaders in the community who are able to do more objective planning as compared to traditional leaders who mostly develop plans according to the needs of government departments and external institutions.

Participatory mapping–types and applications

In the process of using Participatory Rural Appraisal, participatory mapping by the village community has emerged as a key method to enable village communities to engage in problem-solving, analysis, appraisal, planning and decision-making. Maps are prepared on the ground using a number of local materials such as stones, seeds, twigs, and local colours. Use of these symbols enables a number of illiterate and inarticulate people in the community such as women and landless people to participate. Women generally like to make maps at separate locations where they can be more relaxed. Indeed, when different sectors of the population make their own separate maps, they reveal very different perceptions of a problem or situation. If each group presents their map to an assembly, voice can be given to those more marginalized sectors of the population who are usually silent in the development process.

There are five types of participatory mapping methods and these will be discussed in turn.

Resource maps

These maps indicate the majority of the natural resources in the village including land and water, local land-use classifications and the catchment and command area of each resource. It also shows the quality or status of each resource and its likely users. People also indicate quantitative data regarding use of these resources. The following types of resource maps are being prepared by the villagers:

(i)   An inventory of the village's natural resources in terms of local land-use classification systems. These are important for further discussions on the priorities for development of natural resources by various

84

groups in the village and for deciding the transect groups for further exploration.

(ii) A map of the existing status of resources. For example, a tank which gets breached during a rainy season, heavily-eroded areas in the village, degraded forest areas, a dried-up community well, a water-logged area, an area affected by salinity. These are shown through colours, sticks, leaves and other symbols on the ground and on paper. This helps in identifying the problem resources, encouraging further discussion and focussing discussions on a particular problem.

(iii) Maps showing the utilization of various resources in the village. For example, an aquifer map showing the extent of dried-up and active wells and a canal command area map showing the extent of utilization of the irrigation system.

(iv) Maps showing the uplands, midlands and lowlands in the village and the characteristics of these land types.

(v) Maps showing the quantum and extent of resources. For example, area of degraded land, command area of a small irrigation project, catchment area of a percolation tank and number of trees on the common land.

(vi) Maps showing the users of various resources e.g. a community well, common forest land, rivulet or a *nalla* (small stream carrying seasonal flows of rainwater), lowlands and drinking water village pond.

In the initial stages of the development process these maps help in identifying and making an inventory of the various types and characteristics of village resources. This process of mapping ensures that all diversity is taken into account during further discussions with the villagers. Maps focus discussion and lead to a sound basis for trying out other analytical methods like transect walks and focus group discussions. This ensures that more people participate effectively in the discussions and have a common framework for further discussions. The maps also provide a check-list to ensure that issues identified at the start of the project are not missed out in later stages.

Watershed maps and models

A watershed is a delineated area in which all precipitation is drained into a single drainage outlet. For effective conservation of soil, moisture and nutrients in an area for optimum productivity and income, a watershed needs to be treated through biological and physical conservation measures.

Watershed maps and models are prepared by extension volunteers from the village who are given the responsibility by the village institution for providing support services to the members for the watershed management programme. The maps prepared by the volunteers include the following aspects:

(i)   All major runoff flows in the village's land.
(ii)   Delineation of the watershed (showing the delineated boundaries).
(iii) Drainage outlets in the village.
(iv)   Main *nallas* and the watercourses.
(v)   All land resources in the village (private lands with names of farmers and local land-use classifications; common lands with local names).
(vi)   Delineation of the drainage outlet groups in the village.
(vii) All locally tried out soil and water conservation techniques and physical soil and water conservation structures and methods.

This mapping is done through the following steps. First, extension volunteers go to all the high points in the village and mark out the entire micro watershed including landmarks like major *nallas* and rivulets, the highest tree in the village, the highest hillock and the roads which act as watershed boundaries in a number of cases. Second, extension volunteers choose different watercourses to walk along. They meet the farmers on the way and discuss with them these resources in relation to the watercourse and runoff flows. This enables qualitative and quantitative information to be collected on these watercourses and on the drainage outlets. Third, drainage outlet groups (groups which have lands on a common drainage channel and need to co-operate for effective conservation and utilization of rainwater) are also identified and mapping is done jointly with them. Fourth, the watercourse maps and the information collected from each outlet is aggregated to develop an aggregate watershed map (on paper).

These maps are used for decision-making among the drainage outlet group members and in the village meetings. The preparation of maps and discussions around them enable the group members to develop a common watershed identity. They gain ready access to a discussion and decision-making framework which could be used at all stages: problem identification, generating alternatives/options, prioritization of the alternatives identified, appraisal, technology generation and adaptation, financial analysis, implementation, monitoring and impact study and evaluation.

This process is followed by making an inventory of all existing soil and water conservation practices and treatments carried out by the farmers; finding out which of these treatments have worked and in which conditions. Based on these maps, discussions are held with each farmer and a treatment plan for the watershed is evolved. This incorporates traditional technologies which have already worked and have been tested in the village and new treatments evolved as a result of discussion with the villagers. The map shows treatments for each type of land with the type and specifications of the conservation and harvesting structure required, and identifies common property structures requiring community action. Symbols and legends are used for each type of structure. A watershed status and treatment map prepared by extension volunteers is illustrated in Figure 1.

Location of Nullah plugs for reclamation and erosion control

Figure 1: *Watershed status and treatment map for Pangham village, Bharuch District. Prepared by extension volunteers and aggregated from outlet maps*

These documents become the framework and base line maps for further discussion and group meetings. They help in monitoring progress during the implementation of the watershed programme and are used in assessing its impact. Subsequently they are used for conflict resolution between outlet groups and for resolving conflicts related to common property structures. Such maps have also been used to introduce accountability systems where payments made to members are depicted in the map and are read out aloud to make the system more open and transparent to the members. It helps in raising difficult issues and makes possible the discussion of issues requiring community and peer pressure on people who are not co-operating with the group.

87

Thematic maps

These relate to a particular aspect of a problem or illustrate the diversities in a village in relation to a particular issue. The topics depicted can include crops, weed or pest incidence, input usage, soil moisture, credit sources, the command area, aquifers and livelihoods. These maps are frequently used to focus the efforts of village extension volunteers and to enable the development of specific and adaptive solutions within the village. An aquifer map prepared by the villagers is illustrated in Figure 2. These maps and the analysis based on them help to ensure that the range of solutions offered to the villagers takes into account the diversity in the ownership and nature of resources, and in the access to inputs and technical solutions. Such maps have been used to evolve specific technical guidelines for agricultural extension and to discuss innovations and experimentation. They are also useful for deciding the nature, size and the number of experimentations required for a dryland-farming extension programme.

Social maps

In heterogeneous societies with a number of caste, social and economic groups, it is important to know the stratification of the communities both in terms of resources and their access and distribution. These have implications for the solutions and their likely applicability. These maps show the distribution of households in terms of different caste and social groups in the village. The social map is then extrapolated with other resource and thematic maps and the problem identified can be correlated with the social aspects. This is linked with ownership of assets and wealth groupings for the village. Making such a map helps to analyse how each solution identified by the community affects different social groups and particularly the poor. After more experience with this kind of analysis people can cross-reference social maps with other maps to understand the social implications of their existing endowments and the solutions identified by the community. These maps are an important mechanism by which social or equity analysis becomes an integral part of the appraisal process by the community.

Monitoring/impact maps

These maps are prepared by villagers at various stages of the project – appraisal, implementation, management, monitoring and evaluation. Baseline maps are prepared by the community before the project starts and show the existing productivity of resources and utilization of natural resources. The variables included are access of the poor to these resources, availability of fuelwood and fodder to women and poor people and existing

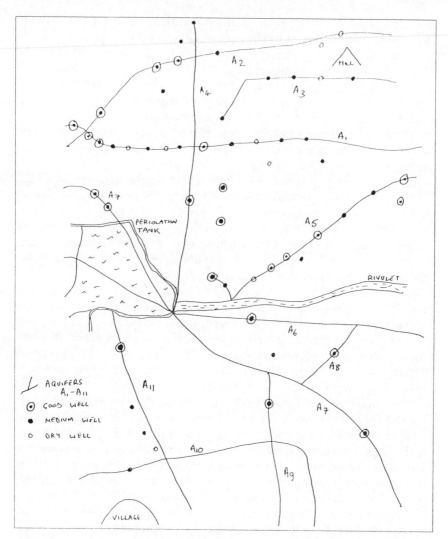

Figure 2: *Aquifer map showing impact area of percolation tank. Kansala village, Surendranagar District. November 1990. A_1–A_{11} are aquifers identified by farmers. Original map shows names of all well owners*

productivity of the marginal lands belonging to the poor farmers. These are shown with symbols representing the degree of access and the productivity. Grains of a particular crop are used for 100 kilogram units of production and stuck onto the map to show production and the productivity figures. Net incomes are also shown in multiples of 100 rupees. Access to a common property resource is also discussed in a small group when each

89

individual indicates the type of products and the extent of its availability from the resource. The information from all the groups is put together on the map which acts as a common framework for discussions village-wide. Those who are unable to attend the initial meetings are contacted individually so that they can record their observations when they have time.

In this manner the responses of most participants of the programme can be collected over a period of time. This information is aggregated onto one map and then presented by those farmers who have been involved in data collection to other farmers in a meeting. The information is cross-checked and verified before finalization.

After some time, when development activities are well advanced, the same process is used to make an impact map. It is possible to do impact studies and to aggregate, process and analyse data rapidly in the village itself with the people and to use it for a subsequent appraisal and planning process by the community. One can have a very high sample size and still be able to do the exercise in less time and with more reliable results than other conventional methods of measuring impact.

To measure the impact of finer aspects like erosion control, moisture retention, and any corresponding increase in productivity, analysis through the diagraming of the field is encouraged. These maps also help in technology generation, adaptation and evaluation for watershed and dryland-farming extension programmes. An impact study through mapping is being tried out in credit, biogas, forestry and water-resource development programmes. Participation of the local people in designing the impact studies can be considerably enhanced by making people draw an impact diagram. This impact diagram helps people to map various possible benefits and to establish which have occurred from an intervention. A diagram for assessing the impact of an irrigation tank prepared by the villagers is illustrated in Figure 3. Different social and economic sections of the village community are encouraged to take part. After discussion in a village meeting the variables are finalized and included in an impact study.

The base-line and impact maps are available to the village community for analysis and reference. The main findings are presented in village meetings. This has enabled people to understand the linkages between investments and benefits. This process also helps the farmers and the community to do economic analysis both jointly as well as individually – a process which is extremely helpful for illiterate people to understand the concept of economic viability. Each group in the community is able to do its own analysis separately and they can be aggregated for the whole village. Advantages of undertaking action on a community basis become clearer and no longer remain abstract through this process. For example it is possible to identify the reduced cost of fertilizer (through group collaboration), increased prices of output (through pooled marketing) and decreased cost of plant protection (through community action). All these linkages

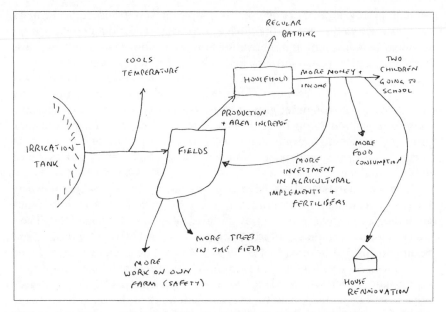

Figure 3: *Impact diagram of irrigation tank in Gadechi village, made by Savsi Bhura (farmer) in Surendranagar District. Redrawn from original*

between community action and their economic implications become more clear through this process of preparing maps, their analysis and presentation. It becomes a simple way to make an economic analysis which could be adopted by any inhabitant of the village irrespective of whether he or she is illiterate or inarticulate.

Participatory mapping has been effective in breaking communication barriers. Use of visual communication methods has enabled inarticulate and illiterate sections of the community including women and other marginalized groups to participate in the development process. It has helped local people to make a resource inventory, use indigenous knowledge and undertake problem identification and analysis. The process of mapping has also proved to be a useful mechanism for conflict resolution and participatory decision-making. The process has proved to be useful for better targeting and effective implementation and management of development programmes.

Enhancement of the farmers' organizational, analytical and communication capacities

In the Watershed Management Programme, the processes of participatory mapping were shown to enhance farmers' organizational, analytical and communication capacities so that they were able to participate much more actively in development processes. In preparing watershed maps, farmers did 'transect walks' across the village resources. Their data collection on resource management and innovations involved observation, detailed discussions with individual farmers, and debate with outlet group members as the map was made on the ground and as a watershed treatment plan was gradually devised. Subsequently the map was made on paper so as to be able to discuss it with other groups in the village and with external officials. This exercise was done by the farmers themselves and not by outsider professionals from governmental or non-governmental organizations (as is normally the case) and people became more confident in analysis and decision-making.

Farmers' analytical skills have been enhanced in a number of ways. Extension volunteers encouraged farmers to make line diagrams about technologies they were trying out in different zones of village land. They concerned, for example, different ways of building earthen *bunds*, or experiments with different depths of ploughing. These were presented to other farmers, resulting in an inventory of local technical innovations or, where inadequacies were identified, the incorporation of further suggestions from outsiders. A plan to test out the impact of these innovations on problems associated with particular land or soil types was set out in a line diagram which was used to discuss the ideas with men and women farmers in the field. Extension volunteers followed farmers' experiments in the field, producing technical guidelines from the results. At the end of the agricultural season, diagrams representing the performance of, for example, many small *bunds* in comparison to a single large contour *bund* were presented by extension volunteers in feedback sessions to farmers. Farmers were involved in evaluation of the experiments and in planning further refinement of the technologies. The advantages of this approach are that the extension volunteers and the farmers both become more observant and are dynamically engaged in developing and adapting technologies and experimenting with them. They do not stick to a blue-print technology. They are able to discern the benefits and problems of various technologies suggested by outsiders and learn to experiment with them. It becomes a learning process in which innovations are constantly encouraged.

Farmers also carry out monitoring and impact studies using a range of participatory methods. As a first step, they are able to decide upon, and represent diagramatically, the impact study variables for the watershed management programme. Such impact variables include moisture retention, soil depth, extent and the type of erosion, land reclaimed due to silt deposition and the number of intensive rainstorms required for good growth of biomass and the crop. Impact diagrams prepared by the different groups affected by the intervention show all the impact points and the linkages which could result from the intervention. These include economic, social and other factors (both positive and negative).

Further analytical skills developed by farmers concern cost-benefit analysis and equity mapping. Using standard symbols, each community member shows the productivity and income of their land to monitor the social impact of interventions. Others are able to point out any discrepancies. The data is collected, aggregated and analysed on the spot in a cost-benefit analysis by the people themselves. Further questions are asked: what is happening to the poor as a result of this intervention? Is the impact positive or negative? What are the impact points? The poor sections of the community are encouraged to indicate answers to these questions. It has been our experience that it is difficult to get responses by direct questioning on a number of complex issues. For example, how are certain castes trying to corner all the benefits of the programme? However, people do not feel threatened to respond on these issues while diagramming. It is easier to show on a diagram whether a particular intervention in the village has led to increased employment or income, has improved access to common property resources or has improved the social standing of those who are a part of the village institution. Similar questions also relate to the negative consequences of an intervention. This helps to focus discussions on the equity aspects of any choice or decision the community takes.

This information is shared with all village community members. The form of presentation enables villagers to understand viability aspects which are difficult to discuss. Maps and diagrams promote discussion on issues like 'Can we undertake a soil and water conservation programme on credit next year as the programme has proved to be a viable activity in the current year'. Other people point out how much they have lost and why. Discussions on issues like why certain people gained more and certain people gained less involve seeking differences between various households in the community and analysing the reasons for different performance. This enables the village institution to provide appropriate support to different groups in the village. A continuous framework for analysis emerges through this process.

A further skill acquired by farmers was as facilitators for the participatory planning process. Many village extension volunteers have taken part in a number of participatory appraisal exercises together and with the Aga Khan Rural Support Programme(AKRSP) team. They have been formally exposed to Participatory Rural Appraisal and Planning methods during this process. They were then asked to conduct certain participatory planning exercises in groups independently of outsiders in a new village (not their own) which had shown interest in the approach and had asked AKRSP for collaboration. The all-villager group conducted these exercises, further innovated on certain methods and developed a village team in the process which was confident of undertaking these exercise independently of AKRSP. These teams are doing planning exercises in a number of villages involving mapping, transect diagraming, interviewing, group

93

discussions, prioritization and preparation of a village natural resources management plan. It is observed that they enjoy the process and are able to carry out most of the exercises with the community. During the process they further innovate, strengthening the argument that Participatory Rural Appraisal and Planning is a creative process for the villagers. They also retain the equity orientation when they are on their own.

Farmers made a presentation of a plan for the long-term management of their natural resources to a team of district officials in Surendranagar district in Gujarat. They used the maps prepared by them earlier and made a number of on the spot and extempore maps and diagrams to reinforce their point of view. The officials and villagers then split into transect teams and the villagers showed them a number of problems and solutions proposed by them in the plan. Finally there was a discussion about certain doubts raised by the government officials. The villagers answered most of the points raised and the village plan was approved by the government team in principle. There are a number of such instances where the villagers have been able to present their plan to outsiders in an effective manner.

Conclusion

Participatory methods using visual and verbal modes of communication have been effectively used for appraisal, planning, monitoring and evaluation in development programmes. However it has been observed that the use of participatory methods by itself is not sufficient for sustaining the participation of people in the development process. The other aspects which need to be strengthened are the development of local institutions and processes leading to delegation and decentralization of decision-making and resource allocation. A number of programmes which initiate participatory methods in the initial phase are not able to sustain participation as outsider professionals are not prepared to make major reversals in the decision-making and resource-allocation mechanisms. This involves changes in power relationships. Use of participatory methods to enable development of local institutions is an important first step towards changing power relationships.

8. Who speaks for whom? Outsiders re-present women pioneers of the forests of Mexico

JANET TOWNSEND

I tell you, nobody knows it better than the one who is living through it, the one who is living this whole thing. Anyone can say, 'This woman is very stupid'. (Lucía 1990, Mexico).

The question is, how dare I represent, re-present, Lucía in this article?

Advocacy

For academics, it is a very attractive project for the subjects of research to set the agenda and for academics to represent them, re-present them, act as advocates for them under their instructions. Many researchers feel unhappy about the extractive approach to research (Cresswell 1992) when we go to communities, learn from people, leave and re-present our subjects to the academic world (Ong 1988; Mohanty *et al.* 1991). This benefits our careers but rarely our subjects. Advocacy beckons as more ethical, but is still problematic. Joke Schrijvers (1991) has described her struggles to work with the powerless while authority remains with her.

Working with poor, isolated rural women in Mexico as I shall describe, we sought to know what solutions they proposed to problems which they identified. In drawing up recommendations, we found conflicts of opinion between 'Us' and 'Them': who decides? A majority of the women perhaps wished us to focus all our efforts on bringing them to the attention of companies wishing to exploit them as homeworkers. We did not do that: should we have done? Aihwa Ong has warned us, 'when feminists look overseas, they frequently seek to establish *their* authority on the backs of non-Western women, determining for them the meanings and goals of their lives' (1988: 88). At worst, the operation may be merely voyeuristic (Hawkesworth 1989). We would wish to think of building coalitions (Goetz 1991), but what real coalition was there between women pioneers and visiting academics? Was there a way in which we could usefully represent, re-present, what we think we heard?

In this case, our subjects had great faith in the power of the written word, the power of experts. They set a great value on our level of education; they saw knowledge as power; they believed in the value of truth. They believed that if they could persuade us to tell their stories, it could make a difference to their lives. They were therefore very vulnerable to exploitation by social scientists – by us.

95

How could we live up to their wishes? We are publishing two books. *Voces femeninas de las Selvas* (Townsend *et al.* forthcoming [a]) was our first priority and has been in press in Mexico since 1992. It seeks to tell of the lives of pioneer women, in Spanish, in non-academic language directed primarily at Mexican non-government organizations. Selected life histories are set in the context of their communities, with a summary of our overall recommendations, which I shall present below. *Women's Voices From the Rainforest* (Townsend *et al.* forthcoming [b]) compares findings and life histories from Mexico and Colombia with an international literature review, for a more academic readership. Can either book avoid being a classic colonial discourse, written with the authority of power about others who have no direct voice? We select, we edit and we re-present even the life histories.

The research

For thirty years, I worked when I could with families seeking to make farms out of the rainforest, particularly in Colombia. These people are pioneers, civilizing the wilderness, although to outsiders they may be destroyers of the great wealth and joy of the forests and even of the forest people. In 1984 and 1987, I worked with women pioneers in Colombian rainforests, seeking to explore the gender divisions of labour. Women's accounts of their problems and needs drove me to an extensive literature survey of women's experiences in settling 'new' lands (locally called pioneering/land settlement/colonization/ transmigration) (Townsend 1991; Townsend *et al.* forthcoming [b]). I found that, in moving to 'new' lands, women widely suffer losses of five kinds: rights to land, access to income, leisure, public services and, above all, the social networks which are the main guarantee of their rights and one of their main life satisfactions. I attribute the frequency of this pattern in very different societies to the international culture of 'development planning', in which 'land settlement' is such a popular if often disastrous intervention (Hulme 1987).

But this was the outside, academic view, already identified by Robert Chambers (1969) without achieving change in the processes. I wanted to work with women pioneers, to learn about the problems which they identified and the solutions which they proposed. I did this in Mexico, first on a pilot study with Jennie Bain in 1990 (Townsend with Bain 1993) and then with four Mexican women colleagues: two sociologists, Ursula Arrevillaga and Socorro Cancino, and two agronomists, Silvana Pacheco and Elia Pérez (Townsend *et al.* in press [a] and [b]). [1]

From June to August 1991, the five of us worked together in ten remote settlements scattered across the poor, tropical south-east of Mexico. Each had been carved out of the tropical forest in living memory and all were Spanish-speaking. Nine settlements were *ejidos*, where land is owned communally and plots of equal size are held by *ejidatarios* but there are also landless labourers. Each *ejido* had been encouraged to set aside one plot of land for landless women, for an Agricultural and Industrial Women's Unit (Arizpe and Botey 1987).[2] To be a Unit, at least 15 'landless' women, who could range from the wives of *ejidatarios* to the near-destitute, had to form a group and, if they wanted credit, had to work the land collectively. The Unit would have one family-sized plot of land between them. They had no experience of collective work or group organization and usually no training, but the women greatly welcomed the chance to meet and generate a little income.

In eight settlements, we used a random sample and questionnaire survey of households for background information about each community. In all the settlements we depended on focus groups and life histories to learn about women's lives and priorities. We sought women's evaluations of the potential for action, individually and through focus groups. We recorded 27 brief life histories. These villagers were remote and saw few outsiders, but their access to collective consumption (roads, water, electricity, health care) depended mainly on successful negotiation with the distant and powerful. That perhaps explained their enthusiasm for our project and their willing contributions to it. To them, it was of the first importance to be represented to the outside world, and educated outsiders were potential allies. They warmly welcomed the concept of advocacy research.

Successful research for advocacy demands an awareness on the part of the researchers of the personal and and theoretical views which are informing the work. Although I doubt that we can jettison our conceptual baggage as Aihwa Ong requires (1988: 88), this awareness admits the possibility of adjustment if women emphasize features of their lives which do not fit personal or academic preconceptions. In my case, I arrived as a socialist feminist and therefore placed emphasis on the household rather than the individual or society as the unit of study, and on production for income rather than control of reproduction as the immediate issue. My Mexican colleagues all came from a socialist intellectual and political tradition but had less formal background in feminism. As I shall show, our methods enabled us to shift our ideas in the light of the women pioneers' analyses and priorities, but left us uncomfortable with the differences of opinion which remained between Us and Them. Our methods were also designed in the light of current practice around 'development' for women in Mexico.

There was much 'development' work with rural women in Mexico at the time, mainly by government agencies, most of it strongly oriented to income-generation or to educating women to perform their current roles 'better', through, for instance, courses on nutrition and hygiene. Any financial assistance was directed to women's immediate practical needs in their current roles, not to any possibility of strategic change. In Caroline Moser's terms (1989) this was an 'efficiency' approach which greatly increased demands on women by developing their efficiency as producers, reproducers and managers. Such efficiency was in the interest of the welfare of their children and menfolk rather than their own welfare, let alone their empowerment. Projects sought to meet women's 'practical' needs (Moser 1989; 1993), not to change women's position.

We were critical of existing work with women, but most of the women who talked to us would have welcomed 'development' work of any kind and expected to be able to turn it to their advantage, which raises the question: whose agenda is all this? Of the six of us who have worked on these projects in 1990 and 1991, five are Mexican, but only one of us had actually grown up in a village in a house with a mud floor, thatched roof and a total lack of services. She has qualified as an agronomist since then, changing her understanding and preferences. None of us were from the regions in question or had kin or even friends to approach.

I certainly went with a male agenda, for I excluded the personal from my initial enquiries. My concern was with sustainable livelihoods, the differentiation of the peasantry, sources of income, education and services. I habitually talked at the household level, having a socialist feminist preoccupation with production. I was fascinated with the possibilities of home gardens for sustainable agriculture, for instance. Individually, in unstructured interviews, pioneer women also talked a great deal at the household level. It was in focus groups and life histories that the content changed, that women's concern was for themselves as individuals as well as for their families, and that they changed our understanding. But would they have approved our final conclusions? We did supply each focus group with a report of the meeting and we sent typed overall evaluations to each community and to such officials as they requested. We did not, however, return to the eight communities, which are scattered across a vast area, with the final list of 'our main proposals' for women to evaluate. This paper, alas, was not agreed with them. Our account here is necessarily a brief representation, our re-presentation, seen through our eyes, of women's problems and solutions.

The communities

All the communities were new or recent, and at some stage of a transition from forest through crop production to ranching: a transition from the heavy demand for labour when the forest is first felled to the low demand for labour of extensive cattle ranching. Although women did little agricultural work, this transition radically altered women's lives. They were the reproducers, bearing the children, cooking and laundering for children and men, bringing up the children and providing constant emotional support. When the forest was first felled, families needed all the labour women could reproduce, with skills learned within the family, and most women were experts in reproducing such labour. Under cattle ranching, it was only people with formal education and specialized skills who could comfortably meet their basic needs. Most women did not know how to qualify their children in this way and large families lost their previous advantage, since demand for unskilled labour was much reduced and wages were low. Many young couples – or rather, young men – had decided on small families, while many older couples were painfully divided, the women wanting sterilization and the men seeing it as a threat to their masculinity.

Women's priorities

In focus groups, we asked women in small groups to answer

○ Do I like being a woman? Why? (or why not?)
○ What are our problems as women in this community?
○ How shall we solve them?

Most 'liked to be women', because of 'the children', 'the work that women do' and/or 'the house and home', and there were few dissidents (Townsend *et al.* in press [a] and [b]). To our surprise, the problems which many women identified as most immediate and most intractable were those of (male) alcoholism and violence and of women's control over their own reproduction – conventional Western feminist issues raised by them, not by us. These evils were often expressed as bad for the children rather than for the battered mothers, for children went hungry when men spent their wages on drink, and children in small huts were exposed to the 'bad example' of domestic violence.

Women's expressed wants proved often to be for their families, whether for income or services. Employment was a priority in all the communities because of the transition to ranching: most women would have welcomed almost any form of exploitation (of their men or of themselves) which offered additional income to the household. They spoke positively of new forms of employment elsewhere in Mexico which privileged geographers might see as highly exploitative, such as packing plants in the strawberry industry (Rosaldo 1990) or homeworking and subcontracting (Benería and Roldán 1987; Wilson 1991). They sought training in handicrafts, or the chance to devote long hours to embroidery to sell for a pittance, for the family. All eight communities lacked some or all public services, and women were intensely conscious of their and their families' needs in this area. Again, they sought training as well as investment.

There was a remarkable enthusiasm for women's group action, considering that many women were extremely isolated ('I have to ask my husband's permission to visit my mother down the road') and that our subjects ranged from the near-destitute to women who had themselves built economic

99

success. Yet for all their isolation and conflicts of interest, most women wanted more collective action and were eager for training not only to enhance their individual productive and reproductive skills but to co-operate more with other women. They felt invisible to the outside world and our requests for life histories were welcomed while they also responded very positively and constructively to focus groups. Despite all the real diversity and difference among these women, this was a moment when most were eager to act and to organize and when the men, conscious of the desperate need for more employment and more public services, supported them.

Women's proposals for immediate action

In each focus group the question 'how shall we solve women's problems in our community?' produced very fruitful charts. At the end of our fieldwork but still in the field, we sat down with all the charts and our interim reports on each community and sought to group our final proposals by the levels of possible action, above that of the individual and household. We focussed on collective action women could take themselves as well as actions requiring the co-operation of state or non-governmental organizations.

Action at community level

Piecing together our subjects' opinions, we felt that the elected community leaders could do much more for women if women co-operated to bring pressure as they sometimes, but rarely did. First, Mexican women depended on the ability of community leaders (men or women) to secure public services from the municipality and the state and to canalize to them the demands of women. Varied success accounted for much local variation in the level of public services. Second, community priorities were often strongly male-oriented, and gender interests could conflict. For instance, in one community women carried all water almost a mile, but men's prime concern was the poor access to market. In such cases, women could make more direct collective approaches to the municipality and the state and the women of two villages did take advantage of our presence to use us as secretaries for such action. Third, each community had a health committee and could mobilize community labour for projects, from street cleaning to water supply. Fourth, the community could exert pressure on the municipality to close some or all bars (Greenberg 1989). Women in one community had achieved this and found that drunkenness was reduced although not eliminated. In theory, community authorities could act much more often and more strongly over male violence against women. Certainly, there were many actions available to community leaders that would improve women's lives, but women would need to bring pressure to bear.

100

Action by women's groups in the community

Above all, most women told us that women should find ways to act against alcoholism and domestic violence. We had not expected this, and had little to contribute. A minority saw these as individual problems, to be solved by the sufferers: each had either to reason successfully with her partner, or to take the children and leave him, knowing that she would receive no support. These were the common practices, but in focus groups women always identified the problem and usually proposed collective action, such as arranging for a woman to go with her children to another house when her husband came home drunk, or for many women to go to her house and restrain him. The difficulty was that women rarely met as women, unless there was a Women's Unit.

In the Women's Units (above), internal divisions and fraud were common, for there were no local traditions for such groups and training in group practice was sorely needed. Women's Units had a great deal to gain from internal unity and, if they could get it, from training. Their potential was still limited by their access to resources but this was the one forum where women co-operated to achieve a collective end. As outsiders, we felt that the Women's Units were a control device, giving women a little land on restrictive terms, and channelling their energies with little hope of profit. Even so, each Unit became a focus for women's concerns in the community. Women relished the scope it gave them and we had to recognize that the enthusiasm of the members of Units was one indicator of the current potential for women's groups.

Action by facilitators

Our main conclusion was that large numbers of high-grade facilitators, whether provided by the state or by non-government organizations, were sorely needed to enable women, with or without Women's Units, to achieve their objectives. There were two reasons for this. First, women were traditionally isolated and lacked experience in co-operation and indeed in production. Second, the employment and income crisis for men occasioned by the shift to ranching had made women very eager to co-operate.

Focus groups with women generated requests for help in identifying their problems as women, and in developing local solutions to domestic violence and alcoholism, as well as help with reproductive skills and income generation. Training was constantly at the centre. Emma Zapata (1990) has developed training methods which seemed to us to meet these requirements, greatly increasing motivation and shifting the emphasis from efficiency to empowerment (Moser 1989) and we felt that her students could meet the women's requests.

Action by non-governmental organizations

In 1994, many such organizations in Mexico are extremely effective, but they tend understandably to concentrate on urban poverty and accessible rural areas. In pioneer areas and other remote rural areas, there is great eagerness for what they can offer, in particular in training facilitators and in supporting women's groups. Many women also longed for access to specialist groups such as Alcoholics Anonymous.

Action by commercial interests

In some areas, such as the region of Los Tuxtlas, Veracruz, pioneers had developed skills in growing imitation forests in their home gardens. These produced an immense range of products with very low inputs, for biodiversity reduces the need for fertilizer and pesticide. Tropical fruits, medicinal plants, timber, fodder for animals, glue, firewood – all were grown in sustained abundance. The whole family participated, but the mother usually organized the work. This skill was being lost as ranching took over the land, using less labour for less production, because the forest gardens produced for subsistence and there was almost no market (Alvarez-Buylla *et al.* 1989; Lazos Chavero and Alvarez-Buylla 1988).

All over the tropics there is extensive research seeking sustainable forms of agriculture. These home gardens were the only sustainable agriculture in these regions, and could have produced fruit and other products for national and international markets. What was lacking was the immediate market. In Europe, consumers pay high prices for sustainable/'organic' products, but here there is little demand.

Private capital may also turn its attention to the women's enthusiasm for homeworking. Unfortunately, we felt that their comparative advantage for this lay in the extremely low levels of pay they would accept. They had apparently no relevant skills to sell, and it could be impossible for any woman to turn homeworking to her advantage. Here, then, we parted company with our subjects, who wanted the chance to try.

Action by the state: a view from below

It was for the municipality and the regional and national state to respond to requests from communities but the massive cuts in support to rural areas during the 1980s had rendered this very difficult. Nevertheless, there were specific needs which could be met. The municipality, for instance, could act over violence and alcoholism and in many areas of Mexico there were local bans on the sale of alcohol. None of our focus groups or depth interviews had produced any proposals for action by the authorities against domestic violence, for community and municipal authorities and police were all seen

102

as too male-biased for the issue to be considered other than as a bad joke. Again, we were aware of other experiences elsewhere.

Education was highly regarded by the pioneers yet children attended school for years without learning to read. We echoed their constant plea that the Secretariat of Public Education should require teachers to fulfil their contracts and that teachers should be called away less from their communities. These communities were remote and living conditions poor, so that it was understandable that teachers used the excuse of meetings to spend little time in them – perhaps a few days a month. Nevertheless, there were areas of Mexico where teachers were required to fulfil their contract to teach and sanctions could have been more widely imposed. The National Institute for Adult Education had a great deal to offer as members of these communities would work hard and long for a pittance to teach others.

The Ministry of Health could have acted to enforce the law among its own workers. It could, for instance, have made contraceptives available to women without requiring the husband's consent. In law, women were entitled to them, so that we were told that when clinics required a husband's consent to supply contraceptives or to sterilize a woman – as they often did – this is out of fear of male retaliation. In law, women were entitled not to be sterilized without their own consent – but it still happened. Remote communities also suffered from very inadequate provision of health care: there was a shortage of trained paramedics and an even greater shortage of drugs.

Agrarian Reform and the Secretariat of Agriculture were supposed to provide support for Women's Units, but this was often minimal and they could have provided far more training in organization and in real skills for income-generation. Often, the support they offered was token and ineffective, being almost entirely office-bound: Units were lucky if they saw their official helpers for a few hours a year. The creation of a viable Unit was too demanding for that, as the members had to learn not only skills but whole new ways of working and relating to others. Yet these were the institutions which then offered most to women in these communities.

Not all our proposals need have entailed additional resources. These forgotten, invisible communities could have benefited greatly from many actions that were immediately possible. The 'trainers' for whom women called would represent a real cost but would be an efficient investment in human capital and in the future of Mexico.

Empowerment and advocacy

Pioneer women in Mexico feel a strong need for advocacy and welcomed our project warmly, but we have seen that when we came to write our recommendations differences of opinion remained between 'Us' and

'Them'. We fear the homeworking after which they yearn and we have hopes of the law and the police which they do not share, but we had no time to develop these issues. Nor did we have the resources to return with our list of proposals to communities hundreds of kilometres apart, so the recommendations are ours and the authorship remains with us. Above all, our project did not include funding for continuing advocacy but was merely academic fieldwork. The book in Spanish is designed to influence Mexican non-governmental organizations and state departments and we shall send complimentary copies to them. However, we have no resources to negotiate with them for policies and resources, over the months and years. I am too distant, and my Mexican colleagues too involved in their new jobs.

It is important to identify the limitations of specific forms of research. I do believe that the academic 'field visit' can contribute to participatory research, but it is limited by the space and time restrictions of 'fieldwork', particularly when there is no action underway to which it can contribute. Empowerment, for instance, is likely to be limited. We cannot empower others, for individuals can only empower themselves (Rowlands 1994), although opportunities can perhaps be created for them to do so. Many women seemed to find the tape-recorders and focus groups such an opportunity as they took hold of the situation, but this was fleeting. I think that our project did little to enable our subjects to empower themselves over the longer term, for it was too short and too little action-oriented, like most academic 'fieldwork'.

We hope and believe that our research still has a value. But we do not believe that empowerment or advocacy are easy and we fear that academics are too prone to a belief that the mere publication of participatory research is in itself a solution.

9. Participatory research on non-European immigration to Italy

VANESSA MAHER

Background of the study: immigration into Italy

Between the 1970s and the 1990s, Italy received immigrants from more than a hundred different countries in Asia, Africa and Latin America. During the 1970s the immigrants were predominantly students or women, who quickly found an economic niche as domestic servants. But in the early 1980s, a number of factors created an upsurge in immigration generally, particularly that of men. The factors encouraging immigration included the effects of war and of indebtedness on a vast range of countries from Morocco to Latin America, political repression in Iran and Iraq, civil war in the Horn of Africa. By this time most European countries, but not Italy, had responded with restrictive legislation to the increase in immigration. As a result, many immigrants found themselves in Italy against their original intentions because its borders offered least resistance.

During the 1970s Italians had more or less ignored the newcomers, in the hope that they would eventually go away, and in the belief that Italy was a country from which people emigrated not one to which they immigrated. In the 1980s, Italy experienced immigration on a large scale. By the early 1990s between 600,000 to one million non-European immigrants had entered the country. Before 1986, Italy had not updated its immigrant legislation since the Fascist laws of 1931, so the new immigrants had no legal rights and were the responsibility of the police (Reginato 1990). They crowded into the dilapidated city centres, sleeping in parks, railway carriages and even cars. The Catholic Charities' hostels and canteens for the homeless were overwhelmed by immigrants. The government left things in the hands of the well-organized charities; eventually angering the immigrants with this view of them as needing help rather than having rights and useful capacities. The newspapers cited wildly varying statistics and became vehicles of racist stereotypes and confusion. Although many immigrants were employed as workers in small factories, restaurants and building sites and as domestic servants, the newspapers insisted that all immigrants were pedlars, drug dealers or sex workers. Pedlars themselves became the target of small shopkeepers and, in 1989 and 1990, of racist attacks in several Italian cities.

105

The setting up of a research group

The setting up, in 1988, of a mixed research group, composed of four Italians, ten immigrants and myself, to carry out a qualitative enquiry of an anthropological kind into recent immigration to Italy, was a creative response to the situation. It was a departure from established procedures in Italian social research; it also represented a more positive approach to the issue than that prevailing in politics or the media.

The impetus for setting up a research group came from a series of informal meetings held in June 1988 at the tiny research centre of a leftist trade union. The meetings included people of varied interests and political alignments (henceforth referred to as The Promotional Network or Network). The purpose of these meetings was to learn more about recent non-European immigration and to disseminate more accurate information to the public. The Network included officials from local authority departments, the Director of the Municipal Foreigners and Nomads Office (a priest), members of Catholic charities, trade union officials of various political tendencies, lawyers, teachers of Italian courses for immigrants, members of civil rights groups, sociologists who had worked on Italian emigration, a demographer working on current immigration and a Rwandan, known as the 'professor' for his authoritative role among immigrants in Turin. I was invited to the meetings of the Network because I had been working on a research proposal to do an anthropological study of employment of recent immigrants. Since employment issues were a major focus of anxiety for the Italian press, I proposed to examine the formal and informal qualifications of the new immigrants, the areas of competition and complementarity with young Italians, and the cultural obstacles to the employment of immigrants. A key feature of my proposal was that the research should be participatory, for methodological and ethical reasons.

The Network eventually agreed to promote three research projects. The first was a statistical study, to be carried out by a local authority department with the university demographer. The second was a questionnaire survey on the attitudes of Piemontese to the new immigrants. The third was a modified version of my participatory proposal to be carried out by immigrants. The sources of finance were at that point undefined. The three groups were in frequent contact, met at conferences and sent observers to one another's meetings. From the planning stage to the publication of the results the anthropological project lasted three and a half years, from June 1988 to December 1991. Roughly half of this time the research was financed and encouraged by a research institution, the Institute for Economic and Social Research on Piemonte.[1]

The group which carried out the research was sustained by more than funding during the research period. Firstly there was the stimulus, support and interest provided by the Promotional Network. Secondly the members came to recognize the advantages which the research group offered as a source of intellectual support, pooled information, friendship, respect and affection. Lastly, the group felt that it was contributing something of use. In the later stages of the research, for example, it was able to meet the demand for clarification on immigration issues which came from schools, cultural associations and local authorities.

The research group

The Promotional Network requested me and the Rwandan 'professor' to recruit the research group for the participatory project. He was the only immigrant member of the Network and had at first opposed the participatory nature of my proposal. His reaction was the first manifestation of immigrants' awareness of relative social power and fear of being 'used'. This ultimately became a primary issue for the research group. During this period it became clear that prospective participants do not necessarily leap at the chance to do participatory research. The 'professor's' decision to support the research was critical for its success because of his initial caution, his experience and his prestige amongst both immigrant community and concerned Italians. I recruited an Iraqi Kurd with an Italian degree in Political Sciences, an Iranian student of Political Science, a Moroccan graduate in Business Studies, and two Italian graduates in Cultural Anthropology. The Rwandan 'professor' invited an Eritrean engineering student, two Somali women, one with a degree in law, the other a political science student, and the same Moroccan I had approached. This coincidence helped lessen his initial distrust of me. However, this method of recruiting, at first, produced divided loyalties in the group. Later we were joined by a Moroccan husband and wife (invited by the first Moroccan), an Ethiopian–Italian woman working in a local authority and two women and a man (Turin University students) from the Ivory coast. Half the research group were women, reflecting the importance of women in the immigrant population.

There were various other participants. F, the researcher from the trade union which had been the catalyst for the Network, gradually became the key figure in the group, for his wide knowledge, personal warmth, political acumen, wide acquaintance among 'concerned' Italians and central position in our information network. He was among the warmest supporters of my proposal. At his behest, a university sociologist organized invaluable lectures for us by researchers on immigration and civil rights workers. This sociologist wrote up some of the results. We also had an observer from the Foreigners' Office, preparing a degree thesis in comparative immigration law. For about a year, a postgraduate anthropology student from Chicago carried out research under my supervision on the

107

Senegalese in Turin, and although he did not collaborate closely with the group we learnt much about the Senegalese through him and his wife. His work was also a useful illustration for the non-anthropologists of what was meant by participant observation and reinforced the anti-questionnaire lobby.

The group varied in size and composition over time. Eight of the research group followed through the work from beginning to end, modifying the analytical categories, carrying out interviews and participant observation, and writing the research report. The rest took part only for a limited period.

Several factors contributed to the instability of the group. The main one was that the researchers, like other immigrants, were engaged in unskilled, irregular work, while having housing and healthcare difficulties. The finance we received was not enough to pay researchers a living wage, so they could only do research part-time. This is probably common in participatory research and makes progress slow. Further, some of our researchers were engaged in helping newly arrived or less educated immigrants cope with various bureaucratic procedures or to find work, accommodation and language courses. Others gave talks in schools, set up a radio programme for immigrants, or provided information for political refugees. Those from the Horn of Africa assisted refugees from the civil wars there and raised humanitarian aid. The Gulf War caused feelings of despondency and insecurity in other researchers. At this time many north Africans were leaving Italy because they felt themselves, with justification, to be the object of suspicion and hostility. (Some employers did actually fire north African and Middle Eastern workers.)

We were unable to involve leaders from the Chinese, Philippino and Egyptian communities in the group and consequently it proved difficult to interview their members after this initial setback. We decided, given the heterogeneity of Italy's immigrant population and the initial structure of the research group, to restrict our research to Africa and the Middle East, working through personal networks of research workers.

No one person dominated the group throughout the course of the research. This was one of its achievements. The meetings were a curious mixture of formal discussions in the whole group and informal ones involving two or three people. Some centred round a theme such as 'Islam and commerce', 'prostitution' or 'new churches in west Africa'. Others were commentaries on interviews, conferences, books, newspaper articles and current events. At the beginning members invited interested parties to our weekly meetings, but later we had one 'open meeting' a month. I think this attempt at maintaining an open channel of communication between the group and the outside world was important in securing public approval, in particular that of immigrant interviewees and associations who felt that our group was not exclusive.

108

The most insidious danger for the group lay in the stereotypes which members of the group held about one another. Each person held stereotypes about members of linguistic groups other than their own, which were matched by reciprocal prejudices. If the premise for good anthropological fieldwork lies in a temporary suspension of value judgements and a critical awareness of one's own cultural conditioning, some members of the group were already well-equipped but others only achieved a degree of critical awareness during the research. Although many of the researchers did not know one another and, as it emerged, held certain prejudices towards one another, they established a common ground during the first few meetings. As a group they forged a broad ideological stance, seeing themselves collectively as the 'South' pitted against the 'North', the objects of Western stereotypes of 'under-development', the ex-colonized against the new imperialists, Blacks against Whites, immigrants dealing with European injustice and racism.

Since I was the only anthropologist in the group (apart from one Italian graduate), and had drawn up the proposal, I had to explain the aims and methods for the first few months and I became the focal point for this forging of a common 'southern identity'. According to the stereotype, I incarnated their common enemy. I was British, therefore identified with many colonial wrongs.[2] I was an anthropologist, so suspected of dealing with 'primitives'. In addition, I was female and trespassing across gender barriers; born and brought up in east Africa, therefore probably racist, a university professor and so probably arrogant. Finally it was assumed I was doing research on immigrants to make money or to further my career. Even the fact that I had written a book on women in Morocco turned out to be a handicap. For the first few weeks I produced credentials. For example, I provided copies of my books together with a flattering review by Fatima Mernissi, a Moroccan sociologist admired by members of the group. I made it clear that I had no political patrons and was not earning a penny by the research.[3] But I also insisted that it was not enough to be born in a society to have an analytical knowledge of it. I maintained that immigrants were not free of racist stereotypes, nor, I argued, was it illegitimate or racist for people of one country to write in their own language about another. I also made it clear that I always tried to make my analyses in a hypothetical form. Gradually, our mutual perception became more complex and less ideological. However, the immigrant researchers' refusal to recognize 'outside' competence on their countries of origin persisted, acting as a levelling mechanism as between the researchers and the 'scientific advisers'. Their ultimate acceptance of me and their recognition that I was less ignorant than many people about their countries seemed based on my having been born in Africa.[4] This seemed to be another way of affirming experience over analysis as a source of understanding.

Methods

Our main frame of reference was the Manchester school – and related approaches to social networks.[5] We emphasized the interrelations of social networks in Italy and in the place of origin. We also worked through the social networks of the researchers to ensure relationships of trust with interviewees. The focuses of our analysis were: social perception, the situational definition of social identity, normative ambiguity, new forms of ethnicity among immigrants, the role of personal mediation (both positive and negative) in Italian society and its effect on the relationships of immigrants.

The research was conducted through interviews and participant observation in all the social situations frequented by immigrants and the research group. Ninety life-histories were compiled, based on multiple interviews and visits. While the members of our group were well-educated and experienced immigrants, we made an effort to contact people of different backgrounds, including recent arrivals. We included so-called clandestine immigrants and those in trouble, as two of our members acted as interpreters in the courts of law and the prisons. As quantitative data became available we adjusted our sample to include people of particular geographical or social origins.

Interviews were negotiated through trust relationships between the interviewee and members of the group, on the condition of guaranteed confidentiality. For this reason we did not use a tape-recorder. The interviews were conducted using participatory methods, which allowed the interviewee to set the direction of the communication, although the researchers also gathered basic socio-economic and demographic data on the individual's history and experience in Italy. As the material accumulated, new hypotheses could be formulated. It was soon clear, for example, that work was not the central concern of most immigrants, but rather a means of survival. The research began to branch out in directions which were not those provided for in the original proposal.

Each interview was conducted by at least two people, one culturally 'near' to the interviewee, the other 'distant', not necessarily Italian. The 'near' researcher guaranteed the unambiguous comprehension of what was said, sometimes translating from the mother-tongue of the interviewee. The 'distant' researcher asked for explanations of matters that might have been taken for granted by those culturally near the interviewee, but which could be most interesting. Of course the 'near' researcher was often, but not always, the one that had contacted the interviewee. Interviewees were always invited to attend as many of our meetings as they wished, especially before being interviewed, and were given the completed life-history to correct or censor.

The form of the life-history was easily recognized by those of the group who had no prior knowledge of anthropology and sometimes was familiar to the interviewees. (Biographies and autobiographies are a conventional literary form in north Africa, for example.) It was the unit accepted for payment on a sort of piece-work basis by IRES-Piemonte, and this led to a methodological prominence which was not part of the original proposal. Its importance in this context led to an underemphasis of participant observation carried out by members of the group, and a relative lack of analysis of the social relationships in which immigrants were currently involved in Italy.

Political analysis: the taboo of participatory research?

There was a conscious effort in the beginning to avoid including political or religious leaders in the research group, in order to avoid creation of an hierarchy between the researchers and other immigrants. However, it soon became clear that most of the group were keenly political and active in voluntary associations. It was felt that their high motivation was essential to the group. Their involvement with such activities made their research commitment erratic but it also gave the research group credibility in the eyes of the immigrant community. The initial resistance to participatory methods gave way gradually to acceptance by the group. It is important to note that when the proposal was discussed the equal status of all the participants was one of their primary considerations. The following statements were to this effect:

'The starting point of the work is that I don't begin as a loser. Everyone has the same rights as I have.'
'You Europeans see us from the point of view of technology. We start out from our point of view. For Italians, if a person is poor materially, he is poor culturally.'
'Each of us must say what he thinks, this is the starting point.'

After the first few months, when outsiders asked who ran the research or where the questionnaire was, I was not the one who explained its aims and methods.

Practical applications of the research

The research was intended to convey to the general public and to administrators, teachers, social workers, and health personnel an idea of who the immigrants were, in cultural and personal terms, and why they were in Italy. We were often pressured to propose solutions rather than provide an informed analysis. Until the end, we avoided communications with the media. Nevertheless, we discussed our provisional research results with countless cultural associations.

Towards the end of the research, members of the group stimulated a number of initiatives which in 1992 appear to be assuming institutional

111

form. There were two publications, one to inform immigrants of their rights after the 1989 'Martelli Law' on immigration, another provided a general forum for political discussion. We also had a series of talks with representatives of Health Authorities, Family Planning Clinics and Psychiatric Clinics. Members of the group gave talks on our research within a series on racism organized for sixty secondary schools. The association Produrre e Riprodurre of the feminist 'Women's House' in Turin formed an association with immigrant women to get municipal support and finance for a co-operative and an Intercultural Centre for immigrant women to socialize, explore employment alternatives to domestic work, and on the weekends to meet their children, who spent the week in Catholic hostels. The same group obtained EC funds to train fifteen immigrant women as 'cultural mediators'; health personnel from several districts offered in-training facilities. This is the only course, so far, to have found jobs for its trainees.

Among the most important and practical results of the research is the substance it has given to the concept of 'cultural mediator', who may be defined as someone, ideally an immigrant, who promotes communication between people who have different cultural understandings. This means defending the immigrants' right to self-determination and dignity, helping them to exercise their rights and use social services, providing 'cultural information' both to immigrants in difficulty and to relevant Italians. The mediator also helps immigrants to deal with cumbersome bureaucratic procedures. Since 1992, local authorities together with Harambe: a Multicultural Association founded by immigrants (some of whom were from our group) and the feminist association Produrre e Riprodurre have obtained funding for four training courses for highly educated 'cultural mediators' in the health and social services. Although there is no guarantee of employment, some immigrants are becoming visible in roles which carry higher status and are closer to their real capacities than that of unskilled labourer or domestic servant.

Conclusions

There were many power issues at stake during this research, some of which were negotiated within the research group while others were not. Among those which were not negotiable was the relationship with the financing body, which finally published the results in its own name. Its mode of payment both presumed an hierarchical structure within the group and favoured certain research methods (life-histories) at the expense of others (participant observation). However, the financing body never interfered with the conduct of the research. The Promotional Network sent observers and guaranteed our work to the financing body, but did not attempt to control our activities. This reassured members who often felt pressured by religious or political groups to exhibit themselves as their clients, and were afraid of being 'used'.

Within the group, considerable efforts were made to ensure democratic procedures and effective participation by all members. All members introduced themselves to newcomers and observers, and 'rounds of opinion' were asked for on controversial points. For the purposes of the research, the world was divided up into the Horn of Africa, the Maghreb, West and Central Africa and the Middle East. The researchers allocated themselves to one or more areas by affinity or interest. The members of the group interviewed each other 'to see what it felt like to be interviewed' and discover the role of stereotypes and ethnocentricism in their approach. This made them more willing to allow the interviewee to direct the interview. All members were invited to take part in drafting the final report, and considerable effort was invested in making sure their pieces were integrated satisfactorily.

But the other side of participation was social control. Those who participated less often in the activities of the group tended not to respect the agreed division of labour. The group exercised a form of ideological control (over those scientific advisers who did participate fully) by emphasizing the primacy of experience over analysis as a source of understanding. In their turn the scientific advisers as such exercised some control, but also redirected social and economic benefits to the researchers through training in research methods and in the analysis of Italian society, as well as through the distribution of research funds, and the promotion of the researchers as representatives of the group and as public speakers.

Many of the members of our group received recognition within it for the fact that for years they had been unacknowledged mediators between immigrants and Italian institutions. Our research reinforced a growing demand in the immigrant community and the Italian social services for a professionalized 'cultural mediator', a practical attempt to correct the imbalance of power between immigrants and Italians in key situations.

The research group provided, in the terms of organizational sociology, a 'transitional situation' in which the members tried out shifts in power, which did not take place in the structure of the larger society, but which represented a hypothesis for social change. Perhaps many 'participatory' development projects have this character. In anthropological terms, the group was a 'liminal space', which divested the participants of their habitual social roles, annulled the barriers of rank and ethnicity, and subjected the members of the group to socializing experiences unavailable in the 'outside world'.[6]

10. Power to the people: rethinking community development

DONALD CURTIS

If there is any evidence that power in contemporary developing countries is moving to the people it is not because of any thought-out policy or government programme, but rather because of the widespread failure of the state. People are seeking to do for themselves something of what politicians and developers of all kinds have been promising and sometimes delivering but which, in times of recession and adjustment, suffer increasingly from shortfalls and frustrations. The problem now is for policy to catch up.

In many Nigerian villages today for instance, one may find a number of public services being organized on an entirely local basis, while others are managed in partnership with national, state or local governments. In the first category one may find roads, drains and culverts, security services (called vigilantes), revolving funds to keep clinics supplied with medicines, as well as a structure of decision-making bodies to serve the public interest. In the second category, in which state and locality combine, are school and clinic building, wells and other infrastructure projects. Village development case histories show that the larger part of local infrastructure is the product of past or present 'self-help' of the pure or assisted kind.[1]

The poverty of development thinking

How has it come about that both development theory and constitutional theory have been so slow to recognize local initiative and responsibility as a basic reality? The answer to this question lies in the pervasiveness of modernization notions in development work, leading to an emphasis upon macro strategies and bureaucratic management, with consequent association of village institutions with backwardness and traditional values. These modernization ideas are combined powerfully with the vested interests of élites, for whom a disintegration of local institutions may offer opportunities for personal gains. For instance, élites often benefit when arrangements for common land management break down and privatization of land becomes a possibility.

One small niche within development thinking has nevertheless persisted over the years, offering some sort of grounding to the idea that communities (however defined) can have a role within the development process. This is community development. Community development enthusiasts like to think of themselves as a part of a movement, with journals (the Community Development Journal and others), conferences, leading figures and common beliefs. The community development movement, like its French counterpart, Animation Rurale, had its origins in the late colonial period in Africa. At that time contemporary thinking was captured and sustained by the reports and writings of practitioners such as T.R. Batten (1962) and Peter du Sautoy (1958), who wrote out of Ghanaian experience, and a Handbook (HSMO 1957) produced from a conference which sought to summarize the findings and principles of the movement as a whole.

It is easy to look back at some of this literature now and see in it the cultural condescension of an urban, schooled, (and in its leadership, Western) élite, pronouncing upon the need to help a rural, unschooled, mass. This is apparent in the persistent contradiction between the idea that community development enables people to do something about their 'felt needs' and the equally prominent notion that people have to be educated to determine those needs. This contradiction is still apparent today in the debate about conscientization. Paulo Freire's concept is widely used in non-governmental organization circles. It is interpreted by some as a necessary educational prelude to people being able to look after their own destiny; while others argue that people are able perfectly well to express needs and do something about them, if given the opportunity.

All this is about power, however coyly put. Colonial governments were not about giving people power in a big way, but may have seen that a little bit of power over the allocation of resources for village wells, road access, and the like, would be a way of satisfying pressures for change without undermining central authority. Post-colonial governments seem to have concluded that even a little power was too much to lose. They have used control over development strategy as a means of asserting control over politics, leading to what Kasfir (1976) referred to as a process of departicipation. In its positive expression this entailed service delivery by the state or its local agents, with politicians and bureaucrats emphasizing the entitlement of the electorate to services 'free at the point of delivery'. In its negative aspect this philosophy has led in many cases to severe disappointment as service delivery mechanisms achieved only modest success. In the late 1980s and early 1990s under the influence of World Bank's 'structural adjustment policies', the level of frustration increased in many African countries as service delivery became static or declined. A widespread realization has taken place that services alone do not produce development.

116

The survival of community development

The usual claim is that community development is a total approach to development. Its ambitions are still grand, as is evident in a United Nations' definition which I found posted up on an office wall in Kachia Local Government:

> community development is the process by which the efforts of the people themselves are united with those of governmental authorities to improve the economic, social and cultural conditions of communities, to integrate these communities into the life of a Nation and to enable them to contribute fully to national progress.

But, while community development has had its moments, as when India's post independence rural development was captured by Albert Mayer's pioneering experiments (Dube 1958), the more normal position of community development has been as a line department, in parallel with others such as Agricultural Extension or Health Care. As such it has been a clearly marginal programme, often with a limited budget, poor transport and few resources. In practice community development activity is often confined to a support programme for those communities that have been persuaded that they will get a new classroom, a clinic or whatever, if they make the bricks and carry the sand. In other words, 'assisted self-help' has become the essential formula around which the rhetoric of community development is aired.

Community development has survived in spite of four major kinds of criticism. The first concerns administrative effectiveness. As Schaffer (1969) indicated, there can be no quarrel with the principle that felt needs should be satisfied or that self-help is a good thing, but this statement has no interpretive value; it contains no explanation of the successes or failures of practice. Schaffer's own critique focused upon the incompatibility of the activities that take place in the name of self-help with the need for rational planning of public expenditure and resource commitment. Self-help is inadministrable he claimed: a theme subsequently illustrated with a detailed Kenyan case study by Holmquist (1970) and taken up again with some practical suggestions in an evaluation of a village water supply scheme in Lesotho by Feachem et al. (1978).

A second major critique concerned social equality and was raised by Chambers (1974). Self-help is often socially unjust. Chambers argued that when it comes to contributing to village development activities, the poor do the work while the rich reap many of the benefits, particularly from activities such as road building. If villages impose flat-rate charges upon themselves such charges fall more heavily upon the poor who have less of a voice. This, of course, is not necessarily how the participants see it. For some less well-off people a commitment to paying the same as everybody

117

else may be a statement of political equality, as I heard someone claim in a village in Botswana in 1971 (Curtis 1991b).

The third line of criticism concerns politics directly. Practitioners are often aware that community development activity is very prone to 'political influence'. This is generally taken by the complainants – who are not the politicians – to be a bad thing. Self-help groups are ideal organizations for political capture. A group of people wanting something may be seen as a cluster of votes that can be recruited in exchange for a small favour. Public funds for support of self-help are often managed by politicians directly, without the intervention of the civil service and become ready-made patronage. Community leaders and groups face real dilemmas in deciding how to respond to this patronage.

The fourth criticism concerns power and is of a different order. It is argued that community development ignores the facts of power and will make no lasting impact until the people are empowered to act on their own behalf. Two different approaches have been adopted in reaching this critique. Most popular with non-governmental organizations is the idea of conscientization, seen as a process through which outsiders can interact with villagers to raise the consciousness of the people about their condition, leading to various kinds of action. In so far as this action solves problems the people might be said to have been empowered. Sometimes this process leads people into direct confrontation with previous powerholders such as landlords or political leaders. Often the gain of power is limited to that which flows from the discovery of individual benefits in common action, in which case conscientization is not much advance upon the old community development idea of informal education.

My own studies led me to a more limited but specific notion of empowerment (Curtis 1991a). This is where people seek to provide a service that is truly a common or public good from which everyone will benefit and no-one can be denied access (as in successful protection from flood). To be successful they need to take or be given specific powers of enforcement. Otherwise free riders will take advantage and those people who get together to provide the public good will end up frustrated. Many of the things mentioned in the opening paragraphs of this paper, such as village security, village cleanliness, and protection from flood are of this kind. Others, such as a locally available supply of medicines or school facilities, are non-excludable for reasons of political choice. It has been decided that in principle they should be free at the point of delivery. How these common goods are handled in practice will be considered below.

Looking back upon these criticisms of community development one can see that the first three reflect the dominant development values and aspirations of their time. The 1960s and 1970s were decades in which high hopes were placed by developers on the rational allocation of resources through planning. Allocation by the state was seen as a necessary condition for the

118

advancement of social equality. In the 1980s and 1990s such ambitions have been labelled 'welfarist' and largely replaced by scepticism as to the efficacy of the state and by the notion that any kind of development is better than none.

Let us take the criticisms of community development and set them against contemporary Nigerian field experience.

Criticism 1: Village initiative is the tail that wags the dog

This problem arises when village people start upon projects that require assistance from government, and yet are able to manipulate public authorities into unsustainable commitments to capital expenditure, maintenance outlays or personnel deployment. This administrability problem boils down to two issues, one to do with the capital account, so to speak, and the other with the recurrent expenditure.

How does the Nigerian administration in central or local government prevent community development-inspired initiatives in the villages from becoming pre-emptive of public capital budgets? Amongst local government politicians and community development staff in the three states visited there did not seem to be any general awareness of this as a problem, however hard I belaboured the logic. Subsequently discussions in a workshop with Community Development Inspectors revealed that the problem has at least partially gone away.

This is what seems to have happened. First and foremost is the widespread realization on the village side that there is little money in the public purse and what little there is, is not destined for them. Therefore, village residents do not readily embark on projects that require government support unless they know of specific funds that have been earmarked for the purpose. When they start a project they may put in some requests to test their politician's powers of patronage or the local government purse but they are more ready to be entirely self-reliant than their discourse with the authorities would suggest.

From the authorities' side there is the additional constraint that local governments are the operative agencies in the field but have minimal capital budgets. Where they do engage in capital undertakings local governments usually rely upon funds from the state government, parastatals or foreign funded projects, and such funds are designated for particular sectors. So assisted self-help is constrained in practice to particular sectors. In Kaduna State, at the time of the study, Junior Day Secondary Schools (providing the first two years of secondary schooling) were the focus; in Kano it was TV Viewing Centres, and so on. It is easy for community development officers to establish clear and limited expectations in the villages as to what assistance may be expected from external

119

sources, and to blame higher authorities for any remaining elements of frustration.

Recurrent account problems have long been recognized as a more severe constraint upon all forms of development activity (Feachem *et al.* 1978; Cairncross *et al.* 1980). It is in respect of maintenance of buildings and facilities that the implicit deal between state and village that is embodied in assisted self-help is most inadequate. Self-help village water supply programmes have been based upon the supposition that villagers, having contributed money or labour to the construction phase will be willing to look after the project because they will feel that it is theirs. This is an argument that can be reversed with equal logic by villagers, who having done their bit, will happily leave maintenance to government. The question of who has legal responsibility is lost in such wishful thinking.

With this background it was interesting to find in one Nigerian village an example of a revolving fund, set up to provide a secure source of medicines in the village clinic. In spite of the fact that local government has a theoretical responsibility for such supplies, the village people had taken their experience of shortages seriously and made their own provision. A capital fund was raised, supplies were purchased and the capital replenished by charging patients for medicines at cost. In this way the problem of recurrent funding, which, like all taxation, they find difficult is moved to the raising of a capital fund which they find easier, and the common good of a local source of medicines is achieved. How well this procedure was working I was not able to establish, but we see in this kind of arrangement the beginnings of local institutional solutions to problems which hitherto have been seen as the responsibility of the state.

The problem of villages starting upon projects with the intention of committing public authorities to expenditure in their direction may not have disappeared, but it is discouraged by low expectations of what the state can deliver. Much more dynamic is the experimentation that is apparent in some villages to find ways, not only of constructing buildings, but also supporting vigilantes and other ongoing commitments.

Criticism 2: Community development fosters inequalities

Whether community development procedures are perceived as being equitable or not will depend upon what they are being compared with. One comparison is with provision through the state which raises taxes and charges and distributes services. If we just look at the delivery side of public service provision, often the aim has been to provide services free at the point of delivery. This is done in order to promote equality of access. If, however, there is any shortfall in provision then such a system redistributes resources towards those who receive and away from those who do not receive. Many countries in Africa today have falling school rolls and decreasing access to free medical services, leading to a situation of increasing inequality in public sector provision.

Many observers are blaming this decrease in access to cost recovery measures; that is the official or unofficial reintroduction of charges for publicly supplied services. The poor, they say, cannot afford to pay. Whether or not that is the case, it is interesting to note that, in many Nigerian villages there is a willingness to make contributions in cash or in kind to village-level funds, which is not there when it comes to paying local government or other taxes.

One reason for the willingness to pay local charges in the villages may be that people feel that they have a chance of a direct say in decisions. A second may be that a contribution is a demonstration of equality of status. A third may be that there are specific attempts in these villages to recognize and allow for inequalities in economic ability to pay. Since these allowances for inequality are indirect, a description of such procedures is necessary.

Typically, contributions to a fund for a school building, a rotating fund for a medical supply or whatever, will be at a flat rate. For instance, in one village in Kachia Local Government area, it had been decided that men should contribute 10 Naira and women 5 Naira. On this basis the basic fund would be raised. Villagers were aware however that some of their number would be unable to pay because of poverty and might make allowances simply and unobtrusively by not pressing for payments (even when they have the powers to do so).

On the other hand they also knew that there are some among them, and some absentees who still have an interest in the village, who were able to pay more than the flat rate. To attract some of this extra funding village projects are often rounded off with a 'launching' ceremony at which the wealthy are invited to a round of conspicuous giving. When Mr X makes a contribution at a public gathering he will be aware that Mr Y has already contributed so much and may be inclined to exceed this. Mr Y, on seeing and hearing Mr X making his donation may be inclined to revise his own contribution upwards. Competitive giving enables them to convert wealth to status. The ingenuity of the system as a whole lies in its ability to demonstrate both status equality through the flat-rate charge and status inequality through competitive giving. This kind of contradiction seems to be readily accommodated. These kinds of village-level contributory systems – no doubt there are others – do not have major redistributive goals. They are about increasing project funds. But they are perceived as socially just, they do make allowance for income differences and they do work well enough to keep a certain amount of action in the common interest going in the villages.

The full complexity of Nigerian politics at any level cannot be unravelled on a series of brief visits. Nevertheless one or two remarks can be made about the relationship of political support to community development activity in the villages.

It was clear from discussions that several of the Executive Chairmen of local governments were anxious to keep community development activity under their own direct responsibility. Several were explicit about the links which community development provides to organized groups of people in the villages and the political gains that this can provide. However Chairmen were also well aware of the dangers of the excessive promises that village exposure can lead them into. They no doubt want to be associated with any public resource allocation that takes place but are aware that a promise unfulfilled can cost as many votes as a promise fulfilled will gain.

These points were summarized in an open and frank discussion amongst Local Government Chairmen and Supervisory Councillors that took place in Kaduna in March 1992 at which the option of a more 'enabling' approach to community development was raised (O'Donovan 1992). Participants were open to ideas about political leadership roles that support self-reliance rather than dependency upon public support. This was in recognition, no doubt, that the public sector is often unable to deliver even the patronage funds that can match local initiative.

Community development, the local power mosaic, and development strategy

Only the surface of what is taking place in Nigeria's villages will have been discovered during these encounters. No doubt there is also turmoil and dispute, but the emergence of new institutional forms from trial and error is an indication of the willingness of local people to take on difficult tasks and seek solutions to them.

Community development classically has been concerned with the catalytic facilitation of self-help, what we would now call 'enabling change'. Whatever the interpretive weaknesses of community development, this basic conceptualization fits much better with new ideas about development strategies than it did with the statist or welfarist approaches of the 1960s and 1970s. There is the new scepticism as to the role of the state, shared in part by critics of the left as well as the right, but clearly driven at the present time by the latter. The prophets of the New Right, with their emphasis upon markets as a means of expression of free choice and of relative value, provide the main thrust behind present attempts to liberalize economies and debureaucratize the state, but several other intellectual stimuli pull in a similar direction. Toffler (1990) for instance, sees similarities in the structures of pre- and post-industrial societies and has ideas of 'mosaic' power structures that could challenge the bureaucratic norms that have pervaded development thinking in both Second and Third Worlds. Writers such as David Korten (1990) and myself (Curtis 1991a), take the line that the dominant development paradigms of the 1960s and 1970s have suppressed or hidden non-statist structures and that these must now be allowed more prominence.

There is a long way to go before this kind of critique is widely accepted at practitioner level but the new thinking shares some basic perceptions. The first is that the state is not all-knowing. No longer is it assumed that the agents of the state, whether community development officers or agricultural extensionists, foresters or anyone else, are founts of an invaluable wisdom that need only to be disseminated for development to occur. The second perception is that the state is not all-powerful. Indeed the bluff has been called on the state and progress can only be made if a plurality of sources of power are recognized and encouraged into dialogue. Third, it is accepted that the state is not very wealthy in itself. It does well if it avoids bankruptcy in many cases and can best promote the well-being of the nation if it encourages the holding of personal or shared wealth at many levels and in many institutions in society. These perceptions bring into sharp focus questions about the expression of choice in development, about the growth of non-state institutions, and about new means of generating wealth and well-being. Community development, always at the interface of state and locality, needs to be in on the act.

A new dynamic is emerging at the grassroots in Nigeria, and no doubt elsewhere, which reflects the prevailing conditions of our times. This new dynamic is potentially far more self-reliant in spirit, more institutionally sophisticated, more economically attuned to the local resource base, and possibly less inegalitarian than what has gone before when the modernizing state set the pace and the conditions of participation. Community development workers remain one set of officials who have, or should have, the most day-to-day contact with this changing reality. They should perceive this new dynamic and be able to respond to it.

However community development philosophy has not kept up with these changes. There is still no clear conceptualization of the 'process' that may be expected to take place through community development. There is still the tendency to regress into a paternalist notion of the need to enlighten the villagers. There is still the inclination to use state resources for political patronage. Community development philosophy can catch up with best practice and experience if thought is given to four questions.

The first question is how to facilitate choice, without leading? To a large extent the Participatory Rural Appraisal approach does precisely this and our experimentation with mapping, ranking and so on, during the community development training in Kaduna State proved exciting and enjoyable for officers, villagers and facilitators from academic institutions. Most importantly, it revealed its potential to show up needs and potential opportunities for common or joint action in the villages. The second question is, how to see and understand local institutional development? The emergence of appropriate local institutional structures for management of water supply, common land, forests, and flood protection may occur through trial and error and be disseminated through imitation of best practice, but intelligent facilitation of this process by observant and sympathetic outsiders can no doubt speed the process. Third, how can local government grant powers without facilitating local tyrannies? Kaduna State may have got it right. Proper procedures having been followed, the power to coerce fellow citizens so that they do not free ride upon a service created for common benefit has been granted to village-level bodies, but is specific and limited and sparingly used. The fourth question is how to handle a plurality of levels of decision-making, of interest groups and of formal and informal structures? To get used to dealing with people who are exercising power on whatever scale is something which good community development workers learn without being taught, but there is clearly potential for more conscious approaches to mediating and power-broking. These lines of questioning would move community development away from the role of facilitator of state intervention to facilitator of community responsibility, something that is increasingly being thrust upon communities by the weaknesses of the state.

11. Shifting power, sharing power: issues from user-group forestry in Nepal

C. J. V. GRONOW

In the hills of Nepal there is generally no alternative to community forestry – and its essence is a real transfer of responsibility for forest protection and management from the central government to the users (Banko Janakari 1987: i).

The issues

Nepal's user-group forestry programme has an ambitious objective. In the words of His Majesty's Government, it is to bring about 'the phased handing over of all the accessible hill forests to the local communities' (HMG 1990: 4). Implementation of the policy would clearly involve a massive transfer of power from the state to the villages. This paper examines a government-sponsored attempt to shift power away from the state. What happened when the policy was put into practice? What conflicts ensued? Did the state relinquish its power? It will become clear that even when a policy commitment is in place, effecting it is far from straightforward and the outcomes are not always as expected.[1]

In order to do this two assumptions must be examined. The first is that the power to manipulate forest resources in Nepal lies with the state; the second assumption is that shifting power to the community level (a central feature of participatory development) will invariably be unproblematic. This case study will illustrate the need for caution, careful background investigation and vigilance in using these two assumptions. Before attempting to shift power it is imperative that the basis of both the existing and future institutional arrangements are understood and assessed. Too often the shifts in power are attempted almost blindly.

Vigilance is particularly important in resource management. In law, Nepal's scattered hill forests make up part of the government's vast estate. However, in practice, many a professional forester will explain that the forests are only nominally under his jurisdiction. It is often to prominent local landlords or community groups that farmers have to turn for access to the wealth of the forest. In some cases the District Forest Officer may indeed have the power to restrict access to the forest (reducing locals to pilfering after dark) but not to administer it according to the principles of his profession.[2] Both the state and the users are in effect 'alienated from forest management and regeneration' (Nadkarni et al. 1989: 13).

125

The second assumption concerns the destination of a power shift. Most forests can be managed to achieve a number of product objectives (timber revenues, charcoal, small firewood, fodder) but some of these objectives are mutually exclusive. Along with the range of use options there will be a corresponding range of interest groups. Transferring control to the local level has the potential to increase the supply of forest products to members of the village community (through greater access and better management). However, if care is not taken to reconcile the demands of different interest groups, a shift from the state to the local level may considerably worsen the position of the weaker interest groups. In some cases under-managed, degraded, but open-access resources have been converted into tightly controlled, *de-facto,* private forests.

It is also important to be sure of the degree of autonomy to which a community aspires. Midgley *et al.* caution that the idealism, rhetoric and paternalism of authentic participation must be tempered with a realistic assessment of what is possible and what people really want. They remind us that:

> Concepts of participation that appeal to western educated middle-class activists do not always conform to the expectations of ordinary people. For many people, participation means sharing the benefits that others in society already enjoy . . . it is the act of manipulating the mechanisms of the state that should be taught rather than the rejection of state support (Midgley *et al.* 1986: 158).

This is not to denigrate the value of community participation in resource management. The intention here is simply to point out how complex and risky the whole area of shifting power relations can be.

User-group forestry

Nepal's ambitious forest policy is probably unique in the extent to which it aims to transfer authority from a state forest service to local communities. Before proceeding, a description of the development of user-group forestry and its constituent policies and processes is warranted. Essentially it means a government-sponsored programme of local forestry development which is controlled by user groups for their own long-term benefit. 'User group' refers to a specified group of people who share mutually recognized claims to specified use rights of a particular forest (Gilmour and Fisher 1991: 70).

A policy of involving 'the public' in local forest management was first proposed in the National Forestry Plan of 1976. The plan acknowledged that the condition of the hill forests was 'very poor' and that the Forestry Department alone could not significantly improve the situation. A new institutional arrangement was needed that would also mobilize the resources of the villages. In 1978 legislation was enacted to enable the new policy to be carried through. The Government's commitment to developing community-based forestry, Nepal's popularity as an aid destination and the huge international press for the 'other fuel crisis' combined to ensure that a high level of donor support arrived in the wake of the new legislation. By the end of the last decade most of the hill districts were participating in community forestry activities.[3]

It is now recognized that in the early years the programme operated out of a technocratic, classical forestry paradigm, with the creation of village wood-lots as its focus. In this context 'community participation' largely took the form of voluntary labour and patient acquiescence. The villagers watched the hillsides being planted up and wondered wearily who might eventually benefit from the exercise.

In the mid-1980s the whole programme came under intense scrutiny. Progress on handing over forests had been minimal and the use of the epithet 'community' in connection with the programme was increasingly being seen as untenable. The reappraisal culminated in 1987 in a landmark workshop on community forestry management.[4] The outcome was an admission that: 'in very many places, community forestry has got off to a false start' (Banko Janakari 1987: iv).

The workshop led directly to a commitment to starting again, with user groups at the centre of the strategy and an acceptance that this time full management responsibility had to be handed over. By 1990 everything seemed to be in place: policy, legislation, aid, operational guidelines, even the restoration of multi-party democracy. [5]

Shifting power: forest department reorientation

Impressive work by professional foresters and social scientists has led to a better understanding of the nature of institutional change in Nepal. This has involved the reorientation of the role of the Forest Department, the organization of user groups, and new institutions to support power sharing within a forest user group – notably the building of a local consensus on forest management.

In the past two years many field staff (District Forest Officers, Rangers and Assistant Rangers) have abandoned their policing function, favouring a new role as instigators of user-group forestry. The majority however continue as before. Why is this so? Does it indicate that the Forestry Department does not in fact intend to transfer its authority? Experience in Nepal indicates that we should not be too hasty to pass judgement, particularly at the field level.

The way in which development planners have approached the parallel issues of user-group and field staff involvement in the programme has often been inconsistent. The former is gradually being engendered through well thought out participatory approaches. In contrast, field staff involvement is

127

encouraged by the imposition of directives, targets and blueprints, or at best a training course in extension skills. It is not sufficiently recognized that many of the difficulties besetting forest users are also faced by the field staff; ignorance of forest policy, minimal incentives, insecurity and little back-up support.

In some places a more sympathetic approach to reorientation has emerged employing participatory principles to help the field staff take more control of their position in the programme. Three strategies make up this approach to the reorientation of field staff: participatory workshops, field support and institutional change. The workshops 'start up' the process of reorientation, providing the opportunity for the staff of a District Forest Office to spend ten days freely discussing community forestry issues amongst themselves usually with the help of a professional facilitator. It is often the first opportunity the field staff have had to explore and review the programme they have been charged with implementing, in some cases after years of official duties. The opportunity to reflect upon their own work situation and to have access to the relevant literature is invariably seized upon with relish, as is the chance to experience the 'participatory approach' for themselves.[5] The outcome of most workshops is a decision by the field staff to reorient, to commit themselves to supporting community-led forest management.

The second step, follow-up support in the field, is essential if the reorientation process begun in the workshops is to be consolidated. Where adequate and competent support has been provided, particularly in the form of a role model, field staff have often gone on to become dedicated and accomplished facilitators of user-group forestry. Too often it is the projects that have let the field staff down, by failing to provide the short-term practical and moral support and security that is critical to field staff attempting to change.

Discussions and field support can start off a reorientation process, but they cannot sustain it: institutional change is needed to provide the field staff with an environment conducive to their new role.[6] As two assistant rangers explain:

> Rangers can support user forestry but there must be a consistent application of this policy. At present this new role is not part of our job description, thus only those with a personal interest do the work and they get no recognition for it. . .There has to be a firm and clear long-term policy. Just as for user forestry to work in a village everyone has to agree to support it, so it is the same for us in the Forest Department (Yadav and Deo, personal communication, quoted in Gronow 1990: 23).

While some progress has been made in this area it is generally proving to be inadequate, as evidenced by the increasingly perfunctory nature of the work undertaken in some districts and the level of support services provided to user groups. The signs are not encouraging. For instance, the Forestry Bill which was drawn up in 1991 to replace the interim legislation and confirm the position of user groups had not yet been passed.

It can be concluded that at different levels within the Forest Department quite different positions are being taken regarding community control over the forests. Midgley *et al.* (1986: 147) have identified four modes to describe possible positions of the state vis-à-vis community participation: participatory, incremental, manipulative and anti-participatory stances. All four seem to be present in Nepal's Forest Department. Midgley's analysis serves to remind us that the Department should not be regarded as a monolith with only one fundamental position on power shifts. In addition, the position taken by the state often depends on the specific activity concerned; so while there may be little resistance among forestry officials to the transfer of *de jure* control over a remote hill forest, there is great reluctance to hand development budgets over to local groups. It seems likely that the transfer of forests to user groups will continue but often with minimal operational support for the advancement of user-led forestry.

Sharing power: user-group organization

The process by which forest authority can be successfully transferred to user groups is one which depends on reaching a local consensus on resource use. It is an approach that endorses the viewpoint of many villagers, that if community control is to succeed then: '. . . everyone must agree on how to protect the forest.' The Forest Department's role in this process is to facilitate the reaching of an agreement within the group. Field staff who attended the start-up workshops described earlier usually have a good grasp of the concept of facilitation, having experienced a 'facilitator-participant' relationship during the workshop. This reiterates the point made earlier about the need for a consistent application of participatory principles. If the field staff's introduction to community development is a series of lectures on the subject they can hardly be blamed for setting up a similar 'teacher-pupil' relationship with the users; the medium is still the message.

Once the Forest Department receives an application from a user group, the first stage of the hand-over process is 'investigation'.[7] The boundaries of the forest are mapped by the Forest Department, the social boundaries of the user group are determined, interest groups identified and existing institutional arrangements appraised. In many parts of central Nepal, the state forests are virtually open access lands, all forms of institutional control having long since collapsed. In the case of newly established plantations, the Forest Department will probably still be regulating access to the resource. Increasingly, however, it is the case that some form of indigenous forest management system is already in place.

Many indigenous systems are excellent; they have succeeded in halting the degradation of an open access resource and have distributed forest products regularly and fairly. However existing institutional arrangements are often 'rubber stamped' without further investigation.[8] To do so may involve making an assumption about the system that is difficult to justify. It should not be assumed that an indigenous arrangement is equitable. Indigenous systems are invariably effective arrangements for protecting a resource, but that protection is often achieved at the expense of the least powerful of the interest groups.

The following case study illustrates this fact. When questioned about the distribution of local forest products, a member of a weaker section of a community explained that:

> The Karkis and the Brahmins closed the forest, they are the big people. If we try to take something from the forest we get told not to or else we get hit (I.B.Pariyar 1991, personal communication).

In this case the weaker section of the community, the Pariyars are low-caste tailors, while the Brahmins and Karkis are high-caste farmers, teachers and merchants. The Pariyars' interest in the forest is as a source of low-grade fuelwood (dry twigs and sticks). Unlike the Pariyars, the Brahmins and Karkis have extensive private tree resources. They view the forest as a potential source of additional income, if the growing stock can be protected long enough for its value to increase. The Pariyars need daily access to the forest for minor products; the Brahmins and Karkis require only occasional access to high-value products. In a highly stratified society like Nepal it cannot be assumed that the persistence of an indigenous forest management system signifies that it has the full support of the community; all too often the system is perpetuated by coercion, not consent.[9] Indeed control over the forest resource can be the very foundation on which the social structure of the village has been constructed, often an essentially feudal edifice.

After the 'investigation stage', 'negotiation' is the second phase of the process. Each interest group is encouraged to discuss in detail its objectives and ideas for the future management of the forest. Differences between interest groups are then reconciled through negotiation. If one group refuses to acknowledge the needs of another, negotiation can become extremely tense. In such cases a District Forest Officer has often played a critical role, using his authority to insist that each party's position is respected. In one village an officer successfully intervened on behalf of a minority group which was unable to pay a proposed levy of one rupee on fuelwood. The officer refused to sanction the transfer of the forest if the needs of this group were going to be ignored by the majority, even if the revenue collected was to be used to develop the forest. A compromise was worked out whereby the low income group could receive free firewood in return for providing labour to protect the forest, to the value of one rupee.

In some cases the intervention of the Forest Department has led to remarkable local power shifts vis-à-vis the forest resource:

I had not even imagined that I could step into Bhakimle Forest. But I have got firewood equal to what the other big people have got. They say that I have equal rights over the forest (C.B. Tamang 1990, personal communication).

If a consensus can be reached, a user-group assembly is called to approve a written form of the agreement. This document is known to the professional foresters as the Operational Plan and to the local foresters as 'our rules'. The District Forest Officer will also be called to the assembly to approve the plan, at which point legal control passes to the user group.

The Operational Plan sanctions the activities that individual members of the group can undertake, such as fuelwood collection. It also specifies sanctions that can be taken against individuals who choose to disregard the rules, fines and penalties for example. Sanctions therefore play a dual, and critical role in user-group forestry.

An executive committee is usually elected to oversee the day-to-day implementation of the rules. In earlier years it was believed that the heart of the institutional arrangement should be an organizational structure such as a committee. This strategy rarely worked; committees were either hi-jacked by local élites or were moribund through lack of a mandate from the wider group. Unfortunately planners are still setting programme targets on the basis of 'groups formed' rather than 'agreements reached'.

Initially it was assumed that once a group had gained control of a forest it would cut all ties with the state, aiming for self-reliance, in the mode of 'authentic participation'. The converse is usually true, most groups have clearly stated that they want the Forest Department to work with them to develop their resource. In its rules the group will often define the role of the Forest Department; to provide technical advice, financial support and to help resolve disputes.[10]

Experience in Nepal also reinforces the statement made by Midgley *et al.* (1986: 158) cited above. Donor agencies can (inadvertently) impose on the groups methods and forms of development which they believe to be 'more participatory' but which often only frustrate the group and leave it feeling manipulated. In one such case a request for an increased technical input from professional foresters was denied, on the grounds that the group would be 'empowered' by coming to value its own indigenous knowledge over that of the professionals. The converse was true; the group began increasingly to feel that it was not after all in charge of the development process.

Conclusion

In virtually all cases the physical condition of hill forests has improved under user-group control. Most groups have managed to implement their plans successfully, instituting product distribution regimes, regeneration schemes and protection systems. Where power has been shared within the group the new institutions have also been reasonably equitable. Applications for forests to be handed over are being made at a faster rate than can be processed.

However, many groups are having to shelve their more ambitious plans because of insufficient material and technical support from the Forest Department. It appears that transferring control of the forests from the state to the groups may not be the biggest challenge after all. Ensuring that the state can be and will be responsive to the needs of the groups will probably be the final and most challenging shift.

Acknowledgements

I would like to thank Verity Smith, Heather Payne and Margeret Keen of the AERDD for their help in the preparation of this paper.

12. Empowerment and community care for older people

Kevin F. MEETHAN

The policy background

The introduction of market values to British social policy offers a radical change to the design and delivery of services for a variety of user groups, such as the disabled and frail older people. The new legislation governing the delivery of care for these people, which came into full effect in April 1993, was foreshadowed by the publication of the Griffiths Report (1988), the White Paper on community care (Department of Health 1989) and subsequent implementation guidance (Social Services Inspectorate/Social Work Service Group 1991a, 1991b, 1991c). The new framework was to be characterized by responsiveness to users, a flexible use of resources, and a devolution of responsibility to front-line agency staff. In turn, this involved substantial changes in the pattern of power relations between service providers and service users. First, the users were no longer to be considered as passive recipients of services, but as active participants in the assessment of their needs, which were to be met by the creation of individual care packages focusing on their specific needs. Secondly, the providers' role would be adjusted to that of 'enablers' acting to co-ordinate services between the informal care provided by family and friends and the formal care provided by statutory, voluntary and private agencies. Such co-operation required a shift in the established hierarchies of power that existed between statutory organizations in relation to the voluntary sector and the non-professional informal carers. It was argued that major shifts of this kind would not only reduce the level of residential home and long stay hospital provision, thus enabling people to remain at home – or in the community, but would also be able to provide services that are more responsive to individual needs (or if you prefer, consumer choice) as well as giving better value for money. In terms of the legislation they were to move from being service-led to being needs-led.

Central to the realization of these aims is the introduction of a system of care management and care planning, with local social services departments taking the lead role. Care management is seen as the process through which services are tailored to individual needs. Once an individual has requested help, or has been referred for help, an assessment of need is undertaken which leads in turn to the production of a care plan specifying agreed levels of service. The person who draws up the plan is accountable

133

to the user for ensuring that services are delivered as specified. It is through such a system of devolved accountability to practitioner level that quality of services will, it is thought, be ensured. The production of care plans therefore involves a series of negotiations between the care manager, users, informal carers and service providers in order to reach the objectives of the agreed care package. Once the package has been agreed and implemented, it has to be monitored and reviewed so that changes in circumstances can be accommodated.

Care management is seen as the means by which both the users of services and their carers would be empowered. As the guidance documentation states, they will be

> enabled to exercise the same power as consumers of other services. This redressing of the balance of power is the best guarantee of continuing improvement in the quality of service (Social Services Inspectorate/ Social Work Service Group 1991b: 9).

This is a clear and unambiguous appeal to the values of the market, as if care can be purchased with the ease that other goods and services may be, and that this in itself will be sufficient guarantee of improved quality and standards. Although this may be open to criticism on political or ideological grounds, the legislation nevertheless requires a substantial shift in power away from professional service providers to service users. In turn, this attempt to shift the balance of power towards a needs-led service begs the question of how needs are to be defined.

For the purposes of this paper, it is sufficient to note that needs are one of those 'elastic' categories that have no fixed or essential meaning, but rather are constructed from contingent circumstances, as the implementation guidance acknowledges:

> Care management seeks to recognize the individuality of need by challenging practitioners to identify the unique characteristics of each individual's needs and to develop individualized, rather than stereotyped, responses to those needs within the constraints of local policy and resources (Social Services Inspectorate/Social Work Service Group 1991a: 13).

Empowerment in this sense is seen as an individual's right to choose the services that will best suit their particular circumstances, but in some cases, there is more than the service user involved. Current policy guidelines also recognize the importance of informal carers in the caring process, although it has been noted that such involvement is problematic and often involves conflicts of interest between professionals, within kin groups, and between carer and the cared-for person, all of which have important implications for the care management process (Dill 1990; Lewis and Meredith 1988, Parker 1990). This raises questions not only about whose needs are being met, but also whether or not needs are determined by professional standards or organizational requirements rather than by the complexity of relationships within individual cases (Mannion 1991). In order to address these issues, it is necessary to consider the role of power and control in relation to the delivery of care.

Power and professions

Hugman (1991) identifies three aspects of power within the caring professions. The first is hierarchical relations between occupations. The second is hierarchical relations within occupations and the third, between members of occupations and service users. These three points are developed further below, even though they overlap and interact in a variety of ways (1991: 42–3).

Once considered as an optional extra for the statutory services, joint working has now become a statutory requirement (Social Services Inspectorate/Social Work Service Group 1991a). This in turn raises questions concerning accountability not only within the hierarchy of professions and organizations, but also between them. As the Audit Commission (1992) makes clear, a necessary condition of needs-led services will be a shift from the 'vertical' delivery of services through autonomous hierarchies to the development of 'horizontal' integration of service delivery across agencies. While problems of this kind are not new (Hunter *et al.* 1988) there is no reason to assume that the new framework will be any better (Wistow 1988) without a significant change in what has been termed the 'organizational culture' of service provision (Social Services Inspectorate/Social Work Service Group 1991a, 1991b).

Two aspects of formal bureaucratic organizations are of significance here. First, as Freidson (1984) has noted, professional colleagues are not equal, and are demarcated by rank within organizations. In practice, this means that the concerns of those with supervisory roles are more likely to have an organizational perspective in contrast to the front-line workers, who will be more concerned with the day to day problems of their work (Challis 1990; Lipsky 1980; Reed 1992). Second, within organizations, information – or lack of it – is used in different ways between different hierarchical levels (Berman 1989; Nocon 1989). The information that a manager requires and uses is not of the same order as the information needed and used by a front-line practitioner, the former being more concerned with overall performance and service delivery, the latter with particular day-to-day cases on an individual level. In addition to these internal organizational differences, many practitioners are members of national professional organizations, with their own criteria of acceptable practice and standards. Taken together, the internal differentiation of organizations and the external professional criteria may give rise to tensions between professional models of good practice, and the

135

managerial goals of agencies concerned with the delivery of care within specified budgets and locally defined goals.

Control over information is one of the ways in which professions not only define themselves, but also exercise power over service users. The possession of a specialized body of information by a professional puts them in an asymmetrical relationship with their actual or potential client; they may not regard knowledge of the services available and the means of securing them as a resource to be shared. The withholding of knowledge about such services can be an exercise of power (Allen *et al.* 1992) and a legitimation of professional status through the application of professionally defined eligibility criteria.

That the implementation of the new legislation would have profound effects on the delivery of care is not in doubt. This research aimed to discover whether the new legislation would actually enable users and their carers to have a greater involvement in the way that their needs were defined and the services to meet those needs were determined. In the following section, I will present some examples of the problems encountered in a joint working pilot project, established to provide packages of care for older people by focusing on the systems of referral, assessment and care planning.

The Scarcroft project

The Scarcroft project was conceived and planned as an exercise in joint working in order to test out some of the proposals on community care for older people in one area of York. North Yorkshire Social Services provided the funding and acted as lead agency, while York Health Authority, York City Council Housing Department and Age Concern, York were also involved. As North Yorkshire Social Services were the funders and the employers of the staff, the project was to be line managed through the local area team. The project was housed in its own office within the area in order to be accessible to the public. A full-time co-ordinator was to oversee the day to day running of the project and take overall responsibility (Meethan and Thompson 1993a; Meethan *et al.* 1993).

The agreement to develop the project, itself the result of a compromise over local resource allocation and political pressures (Meethan and Thompson 1993b), was made at a senior management level by a well-established joint working committee. All the agencies agreed to ring-fence service provision in the area. The project workers would be able to use these services in the creation of care packages. This was formalized by the signing of a service exchange agreement which acted as a contract between the agencies specifying, among other things, that all referrals to each agency would be passed on to the project so that those with more than one service need could be identified and receive an assessment.

It was decided at an early stage that the project would operate with two models of care planning. One was be undertaken by ten part-time care planners drawn from the front-line staff of the agencies, such as district nurses and social workers.[1] They would devise care packages for users whose needs meant that they required more than one service from each of the agencies. This came to be known as the main project. The other model of care planning, known as the Intensive Home Support Scheme, was for the very frail older people who would otherwise be at risk in their homes, and therefore previously considered suitable for admission to residential care. This part of the project was to have a devolved budget catering for a maximum of twenty cases per year, and would have a full-time care manager – the Intensive Home Support Scheme Officer.[2]

Referrals

The implementation of care management systems required, among other things, that referral systems and assessments for services were comparable and standardized across agencies. The process of becoming a service user was the result of a negotiation between the potential user and professionals, although it might involve others such as kin, carers, neighbours and friends. It was within this nexus of relationships that power was exercised by the professional by defining and categorizing the user from the initial referral to assessment (Hugman 1991).

Despite agreement at a senior management level, at the operational level different methods of gathering and using client information led to confusion about referrals and criteria for eligibility. Although it was intended to provide packages of care to those with more than one service requirement, there was no consensus on what actually constituted a referral, and whether or not the project should act as a clearing house for all referrals to all agencies. Those who were referred and considered unsuitable for care planning were those in need of only one service, and were passed on (or back) to the appropriate agency. This information in turn was logged in order to show the overall pattern of service need in the area.

Poor communication both within and between the agencies meant that more than six months after the start of the project several staff from different agencies reported that they were not sure whether they were passing names onto the project for information purposes or referring for a care planner's assessment. Even people whose work meant that they were more closely involved with project users could not understand the referral process or why some people were accepted and others were not.

Referrals for one service from an individual agency were not seen as sufficient grounds for care planning, and although the project was to act as service co-ordinator between the agencies, there was no adequate system to cross check referrals to one agency with referrals to the others. In practice this meant that it was difficult for the project workers to link different service needs to individual cases in a systematic way. The function of the project – to provide co-ordinated services on a needs-led basis – was not being adequately communicated within and between the agencies. It seems to have been assumed by the senior management of all the agencies that knowledge about the project would somehow 'filter down' to the front-line workers. Knowledge of the project's existence and the services it provided was mediated through the existing networks of professionals and the standard referral routes. Many of those who were referred were already known to the care planners, who were using their inside knowledge of the project to gain access to resources.

The development of a joint referral system between the agencies was constrained by existing working practices. These emphasized the matching of individual referrals to the existing provision of services. As an example, some agency workers had been told by their line manager that they could not refer the users of their service directly to the project – they had to refer them first to their manager for 'vetting' – despite the planned intention that referrals could come from any source. Although there was an apparent consensus between the agencies at a strategic level, attempting to change from service-led to needs-led provision at a practitioner level was compromised by existing procedures which formalized roles both within and between the agencies, and still matched individual need to existing patterns of service provision.

Assessments

It was originally intended that a common assessment form would eliminate multi-agency assessments, as well as being the means by which an individual's needs would be formalized into a care package. In the early stages of the project, criticism was directed by some care planners against the perceived lack of professionalism by others, in particular the care planners from Age Concern, whose status as voluntary sector workers was conflated with 'amateur'. Those care planners in turn criticised the other agencies for being too bureaucratic. Their approach was to visit the client in their home and gain information through informal talks rather than formal assessments, with the information being written up later. This informality was one of the distinctive features of their approach (Thornton 1989). To some, this informality was seen as unprofessional, and the writing down of information after the visit unethical. In this situation the role of the professional in relation to the user was demarcated by the use of bureaucratic methods such as form filling, with its corresponding air of professional detachment and objectivity (Dill 1990).

Those from Age Concern however saw their role as befriending older people rather than simply assessing their needs. This was reflected in their less formal methods and a more immediate response to referrals than other agencies. The differences between these two approaches reflects the competing values of the statutory and voluntary sectors. It also shows that in this case the development of common assessment procedures did not, at least initially, resolve problems concerning different underlying assumptions between different professions and organizations.

The care planners were able to reach a greater understanding of the problems that they faced individually and collectively. By getting to know each other face to face, formal co-operation within the project also gave rise to informal co-operation in cases where the project was not involved. One of the important aspects in the development of joint working at this level was the realization among the care planners that the use of common assessment processes would not detract from their own specialist assessments. In this way professional boundaries between the agencies and some degree of autonomy could still be maintained, while common procedures could be negotiated.

Professionals outside the project often saw it as a threat to their status and some were concerned that they would lose 'their' cases to the project. This highlights the fact that day-to-day working practices and underlying values of agencies and professions can lead to friction at an operational level despite agreements being made at a strategic level, and further that the adoption of a common terminology (care planning, common assessments) is no guarantee that there is a corresponding adoption of common values (Marsh and Fisher 1992).

Care planning: carers' and users' views

Care management is seen as a continuous process of assessing and meeting needs, and adjusting the care package if necessary. Noting that the monitoring function has tended in the past to be regarded as a passive form of surveillance, the official guidance states that care management:

> stresses the proactive role of monitoring in *supporting the achievement of set objectives over time and adapting the care plan to the changing needs of the user* (Social Services Inspectorate/Social Work Service Group1991b: 77, their emphasis).

The assessment of needs is best demonstrated by the Intensive Home Support Scheme, which dealt with users who required the more complex packages of care. This differed from the main project in several respects. Employed specifically as a full-time care manager, the Intensive Home Support Scheme Officer did not have to contend with competing and possibly contradictory demands between her role as a care manager and other work. She did not have the confusion that some of the other care planners felt regarding who should be managing their project work. A further important element was the fact that the Intensive Home Support Scheme Officer had control over a devolved budget, specifically for use within the scheme. In this way services that were required over and above existing resources could be bought as required (although all payments had to be approved by the accounts department of the county council). The Intensive Home Support Scheme Officer was allowed considerable freedom to plan and implement care packages, so that in terms of management issues, access to resources and the maintenance of professional boundaries, she did not have to contend with the same problems of joint agency working that bedevilled the main project.

Each care package was closely monitored and changed as circumstances dictated, in consultation with the users and carers. The officer kept in close touch with all the clients and their carers, making casual visits to the users' homes, usually once a week. A more formal review system for each care package was held at regular intervals, decided by the users, their carers and the project officer. At these meetings the current packages were discussed, and any adjustments would be specified. In addition, those in day-to-day contact with the project officer kept her informed of any developments so that she could make constant re-assessments of people's needs and appropriate readjustments to their care packages, as the following case study demonstrates.

Mrs A lived alone in sheltered accommodation, and had been receiving home help from the social services for some years. The number of visits had, however, been reduced from every two weeks to once a month, due to service cut-backs. Her nearest kin, concerned about her frail condition and poor diet (partly the consequence of Mrs. A having very poor short-term memory) requested additional help from the social services. This was provided in the form of hot meals, delivered twice a week. The warden of the sheltered housing was still concerned about her condition, and referred her to the social services on two subsequent occasions. The Scarcroft Project was informed of these latest referrals.

Shortly after these new referrals had been received, the home help visited the project office and informed the project officer that both she, the housing warden and Mrs A's kin were becoming increasingly concerned about her condition, so a home visit was arranged. Initially, Mrs A informed the project officer that all was well, but when her kin and the housing warden joined the discussion, problems were identified. Her kin, for example, had been handling her financial affairs for some time as a result of her poor memory. Mrs A conceded that she did in fact have difficulties in coping, but initially refused extra help on the grounds of cost. When it was explained to her that the outlay would be very little, and anyway, would be handled by her kin, Mrs A agreed to accept a package of care consisting of a daily visit and a hot meal from Monday to Friday, with her kin providing support at the evenings and weekends.

Several points can be drawn from this particular case. First, the actual package of care itself was relatively straightforward, although requiring a lot of initial co-ordination between the project officer, the social services and Mrs A's kin. Second, it also shows that the definition of needs, especially with vulnerable people suffering from poor short-term memory may in fact reflect the concerns of the carers more that the concerns of the users.

Third, this case also shows that although service providers must have a thorough knowledge of service availability, there is no way of ensuring that users and carers will have the same knowledge. Consequently, their ability to make informed choices might be limited. In this case, knowledge of service availability came from the home help who was aware of the project, and what it could offer. It is therefore clear that ownership and control over information of this kind is a crucial issue for the successful delivery of individual packages of care.

Responsibility for service provision was exercised by the care manager, acting on behalf of the users, through contracts with service providers. When the services were provided from informal sources, such as kin, or volunteers, the lines of accountability were blurred. Although in the case of the Scarcroft Project this did not cause any difficulties, in terms of the general lessons to be drawn, the issue is to what extent could a care manager – on moral, ethical or indeed legal grounds – have control over the input of an unpaid carer? How can they be held accountable for the actions of someone over whom they have no actual control? There is perhaps a danger here that kin might be pushed into a caring role through the exercise of some putative moral authority by a care manager, perhaps in cases where there is conflict between the needs of the user and their carer (Twigg and Atkin 1994). What is important here is the degree to which carers or users can exercise control over the care package itself.

It was intended that the planning and implementation of the care plan should take the users and their carers as the starting point and encourage them to play as active a role as possible. There is no doubt that this form of assessment and planning was very popular with the project users. However, the context in which these negotiations took place was not value free. Those involved brought with them expectations of each other's role, determined in this case by the context of assessment and review procedures.

The project users tended to defer to what they perceived as expert opinion, not only from the care manager but also from other professionals, most notably general practitioners, whose opinions were rarely challenged. (Meethan and Thompson 1993a). This was not only an acknowledgement of the power of professionals, but was also a devaluation of the views of the users. The deferential attitude towards professionals by the project users shows that within the project, although greater care was taken to listen to the views of the carers and the users, the processes of developing and maintaining a care package were being driven by professional criteria. What was offered was greater transparency of decision-making about choices within a limited range of options, rather than choices between possible options. However, it must be acknowledged that some of the users were happy to let the project officer take decisions on their behalf, in effect, empowering her to act for them.

Conclusion

It is clear that although the new system of care provision emphasized the central role of the user, and indeed their carer or carers, there are still formidable problems to be overcome if the aim of a needs-led service is to be realized. In the introduction I pointed out that the shift to a needs-led system requires the empowerment of users and their carers through involvement in the process of care planning and care management, and that in turn, this would require a substantial shift in power away from the professionals involved in the delivery of services to the service users. I also pointed out that in terms of the caring professions, three aspects of power were involved: hierarchical relations between occupations, hierarchical relations within occupations and relations between professionals and service users.

Relations between the organizations and the occupations involved were compromised in a number of ways, one of which was the issue of management. As the care planners were not, strictly speaking, project workers, the project co-ordinator could not exercise effective management of their work. Therefore there were always competing interests to be reconciled between the agencies involved and the demands of the project work.

The decision to develop the project as a joint concern between the different agencies required each agency to ring-fence existing service provision. The problem here was that the resource bases of the agencies were not equal, so that the agreement simply confirmed an already existing hierarchy of agency relationships, with the social services department as the lead agency, and Age Concern as the poor relation. The initial suspicion of the Age Concern care planners and the suggestion that their methods were 'amateur', confirmed the relative position of the agencies. Although the care planners in the main project were able, after a while, to negotiate working agreements between themselves, this was only possible because they were acting outside the then standard provision of services. Those involved were able to make exceptions to their practices in order to accommodate the new system of working without compromising their professional standing.

Hierarchies and professional boundaries within the organizations also caused problems. As mentioned in the introduction, one of the conditions of a needs-led service is a shift to a horizontally organized system of care delivery that cuts across the current hierarchies. This in turn, will require what the implementation documents terms changes in the 'organizational culture' of all agencies involved. The use of this term could be taken to imply that agencies have common ways of conceptualizing and acting on situations, and that such cultures are unitary in their outlook and effects. Scarcroft however shows that divisions within organizations, such as professional status and control over information, are as much a barrier to joint working as differences between organizations. As noted above, whereas joint agreements are possible at a strategic level, changing the day-to-day work practices of agency workers is another matter. Front-line agency workers may have very different perceptions from their managers as to what joint working means, as well as exercising some degree of autonomy and power.

Relations between the providers were also problematic. As we have seen, the design and delivery of a care plan involved a series of negotiations between the user, carer and the project officer. The project officer, acting outside the mainstream provision of services, did not have to contend with the existing pattern of professional boundary maintenance, and therefore exercised considerable control. This finding has considerable implications for the wider application of care management systems, for unless there is a substantial shift away from organizational and professional constraints, it will be the assessors' definition of needs and requirements that ultimately determines the care package.

This required shift is not all one way. The deference of the users and their carers towards expert opinion raises the possibility that instead of displacing or at least modifying the role of professional opinion, the care managers' judgements will themselves become another form of expert opinion. On the other hand it must also be acknowledged that in the case of this particular group of users, handing control to someone else may also be a form of empowerment.

The incorporation of the users' and carers' needs into packages of care will, therefore, face formidable obstacles unless the current structures of service delivery change at a variety of levels both within and between agencies. The rhetoric of user choice and empowerment is one thing; in practice it needs to be matched by a corresponding unlearning of existing organizational and professional practices and hierarchies at all levels.

13. Local institutions and power: The history and practice of community management of tank irrigation systems in south India[1]

DAVID MOSSE

The development of local institutions is a central strategy in participatory rural development. Forming new institutions involves complex, local and historically specific processes of social re-organization. Yet much participatory development literature uses terms such as 'local institution', 'community' or even 'management' in normative or prescriptive ways, divorcing 'global' development strategies from local social and historical contexts. What is often omitted is an analysis of the interplay of power through which global development concepts mould and are moulded by existing social and political relationships. Practitioners sometimes assume they are creating new local institutions when they are, in fact, recombining existing roles, relationships of power and social status. There is another equally problematic idea, namely that community-based systems return to an ideal old community order, cleansed of the state or the market. In reality participatory institutions are neither as new as they appear, nor a reproduction of the idealized past. They are constituted, negotiated and challenged in the context of existing structures of power which may simultaneously be supported and challenged by powerful project mediators pursuing their own 'participatory development' agendas. The recognition of this social reality is likely to improve understanding of the way such institutions operate.

This paper focuses on south Indian tank irrigation as an example of community management of natural resources. I will examine today's 'participatory' policy and practice in the light of, first, the historical experience of 'community management' in tank irrigation systems,[2] and second a village case of participatory tank development in Tamil Nadu. What light does the historical analysis throw on contemporary local institution building? Can an ethnohistorical perspective help in critical appraisal of the use of concepts such as 'community', 'management' and 'participation' when applied in specific situations? Undoubtedly these concepts are often used uncritically to gloss complex and changing sets of rights and social relationships. Finally, what is the relationship between 'traditional' and modern institutions in irrigation management, and specifically, how effective is the conjunction of contemporary participatory development goals with established village institutions?

144

Tank systems and environmental change

A tank is a man-made reservoir created by a simple earthen embankment that captures surface runoff. Tank *systems* are an important indigenous, decentralized form of irrigation in the semi-dry zones of southern India. As well as collecting and impounding water for irrigation, they enable percolation and recharge of groundwater and provide mechanisms for coping with water scarcity and for flood control. In addition, tanks provide a water resource for pisciculture, silt for fertilizing and clay for brickmaking. The succession of tanks in a chain often links micro-watersheds into a wider system covering a large area. The tank irrigation systems of south India are both a *technology* and a *resource* (Reddy 1989a), and 'need to be thought of in terms of a wide complex of natural resources, physical facilities, land-use patterns, and managerial institutions' (Ambler 1992: 1). Equally they imply a particular system of social relations which defines sets of rights, entitlements and obligations which make co-operation, dispute resolution and collective action for maintenance and repair possible, both within villages and – because of the nature of drainage – between villages. Moreover, this chapter argues that as a *social system* tank irrigation is rooted in and defined by shifting relations of power both within villages (e.g. expressed in idioms of inter-caste conflict) and between villages and the wider political structures of the state.

Tamil Nadu has between 36 000 and 39 000 tanks of various sizes. From colonial times a majority of tanks have formally been the property of the state, administratively controlled by the Public Works Department or the institutions of local government (the Panchayats). Yet, for almost two centuries small-scale tank irrigation systems have suffered low levels of attention and public investment (Ludden 1979). While in the early 1970s tanks were the single largest mode of irrigation in Tamil Nadu, between 1960 and 1980 there has been a secular decline in the area under tank irrigation. Many tanks are now physically in serious disrepair (e.g. silted, encroached upon), and the social institutions which manage the tank systems have in many cases collapsed. Factors which have impinged on the functioning of tank systems and contributed to disrepair at different historical times include changes in village social structures, in the state's involvement in community irrigation systems, and (recently) the privatization of access to water resources through well and pumpset irrigation (MIDS 1988).

Constraints on the sustainable expansion of other forms of irrigation (canals and wells), and the environmental and human costs of neglecting this 'minor' but crucial irrigation system in highly vulnerable agroclimatic zones in south India, have begun to give tanks a higher profile in recent years. State and central governments see the necessity for a comprehensive policy for tank-irrigation development. This is likely to require substantial state investment (e.g. in desilting and repairs) as well as the establishment of participatory arrangements for maintenance and local-level regulation.

Handing tanks over to farmers and giving them clear rights and responsibilities over the resources is seen as an economical way of managing such widely scattered and small-scale systems, likely to lead to better maintenance and higher productivity (Abeyratne 1990: 2; Ambler 1992: 1). Indeed there is a growing consensus that the key to tank rehabilitation is the establishment of formal or informal water-users' associations, assisted with funds, technical support and training, and given legal authority to manage tank systems. Ultimately ownership of tanks would be transferred to these groups (Singh 1991: 21). These institutions would then implement larger-scale capital intensive government programmes of tank rehabilitation and modernization.

This strategy is often justified with reference to 'traditional' community-based mechanisms for water distribution and maintenance, whose erosion is assumed to underlie the decline of tank irrigation. Here, a model of past institutions provides a legitimizing charter for present-day community action. Moreover, in environmentalist discourse the tank is a trope in arguments for more appropriate irrigation technologies; a statement of an alternative set of social relations, and the (Gandhian) ideal of decentralized community-based action, ideologically opposed to large-scale bureaucratically controlled modernizing development (large dams and canals, borewells etc.) (e.g. Shankari and Shah 1993; Agarwal and Narain 1989). An idea of the past thus embodies distinctly modern principles of participation, democracy, and class and gender equality. But, as the case below shows, new institutions based on notions of participation (including women and other excluded groups), free association, equity, and democracy are often 'built' or negotiated in the context of existing organizations based on very different axioms.

Historical change in the institutions of tank management

Tank irrigation in Tamil Nadu has a long and complex history throughout which systems of 'community management' have expressed and been underwritten by local and regional relations of power and patronage. Inscriptions on tank *bunds* (crescent-shaped earthen dams) and in temples which go back to the centuries BC, although found mostly during the expansion of tank construction between AD 750 and 1300 (Von Oppen and Subba Rao 1980; Ludden 1979), only demonstrate the political importance of the construction and maintenance of these *public* resources. Water has always been a *political* as well as a natural resource, and the operation of tank systems regulating its flow have been influenced by changing configurations of power at both village and state level.

146

Pre-colonial systems of tank management, especially those established in the semi-dry zones of southern Tamil Nadu depart significantly in four ways from the popular characterization of 'traditional water management systems' as functionally specific, socially equitable, locally autonomous, and ecologically stable. First, cultivator rights to irrigation water were inseparable from rights to shares in other community resources and services, such as rights to temple worship or to the labour of service castes. These rights and shares were held in virtue of membership of caste and kin groups, and defined not only material entitlements but also social status (cf. Ludden 1985). The system of shares defined 'the community' as 'the unity of a group of kinsmen who together constituted the (locally) 'dominant caste" (Harriss 1982: 130) with privileged access to both the best placed land and to tank water at times of shortage, while other caste groups held only service-related rights and obligations. Second, therefore, tank systems institutionalized *unequal* access to resources within sophisticated systems of water distribution (both within and between villages). These concerned the timing and frequency of water release, amounts of irrigable land (e.g. per cultivator) and the type of crop grown (Reddy 1989b). Third, at all levels (village, region and state) the rights and rules constituting this 'traditional' management system rested on political authority, determined by vertical relations extending from village headmen, through regional chiefs to the king, while tank maintenance itself clearly linked investment and dispute arbitration to revenue flows and political overlordship. The authority and rights in tank systems of village headmen were held by virtue of a relationship with a superior political and military authority, in principle, as royally gifted privileges (cf. Dirks 1987). Finally, the organization of traditional tank systems did not preclude mismanagement or ecological instability. At every historical time for which there are records, tanks are reportedly in disrepair. The political gains from tank building (i.e. the acquisition of new constituencies) often were not matched by local capacity to maintain and repair the systems. By the end of the 18th century many tanks were already in urgent need of repair, only partly due to the extended period of military conflict immediately preceding British rule (Harriss 1982: 73; Lardinois 1989: 24–5, 38–43).

Under British rule, institutions of kingship, caste and property underwent profound changes affecting the operation of tank systems.[3] The consolidation of individual private property isolated rights in land from rights in 'public' resources necessary for its productivity: rights to irrigation water, to forest resources, and to the labour of dependent caste groups (cf. Ludden 1985: 85). The separation of the private from the public domain (economic from political relations) under colonial rule was based on the dismantling of indigenous political systems which had formerly resourced tank systems, and involved assertion of the colonial state's own proprietory right over 'public' resources (e.g. tanks). While incentives for local management were undermined, the colonial government provided minimal compensatory investment (Ludden 1979). Indeed, government spending was largely directed to large, revenue-generating irrigation works in the fertile tracts, while in the more marginal areas, tax systems often discouraged the expansion of wet land cultivation (Ludden 1979; Reddy 1990). In the old regime, as Dirks puts it, 'property only existed in the context of social and political relations' (1987: 125). Under colonialism this system of relationships was replaced by a single emphasis on revenue and the collection of grains.

The dismantling of earlier state forms and the colonial administrative concern with civil order and revenue extraction isolated Tamil villages from previous political linkages. Village functionaries (local headmen turned government officers) initially increased their power. But power was *localized* at the village level in ways which resulted in private accumulation, commercial investment or expenditure on prestige and status (e.g. through temple festivals systems cf. Curtis 1991: 108), rather than public investment in productive resources. Ironically, colonial rule undermined 'traditional water management systems', while inventing them as autonomous village institutions separate from wider political relations.[4]

The centralization of control over minor irrigation, begun under colonialism, continued after Independence. The government retains ownership and responsibility for tank maintenance while the informal rights which operate tank irrigation are not legally recognized. Today, local systems of water distribution and tank maintenance vary. In many villages informal rights, responsibilities and offices (e.g. water guides) are recognized, and sometimes more formal tank 'panchayats' exist (e.g. Meinzen-Dick 1984), but they seldom preclude disputes at times of shortage. Often, the locally powerful ignore existing rights or protect their access to tank water by force.

Where they exist, institutions of 'community management' often continue to protect the interests of a dominant caste group. Indeed in many villages it is the weakening of local authority structures (and the caste institutions expressing these) which has undermined tank management institutions. In addition, the old system of resource sharing and service obligations is losing ground to the market. Reciprocal caste-based relationships between landed patrons and labouring clients through which minimum subsistence (plus house sites, rights to crop residues etc.) is exchanged for labour and services are being replaced by market relations. While high caste patrons disengage from unprofitable obligations, low caste clients often see status gains in withdrawing from traditional service-bound roles (Mosse 1994b). The new institutions of local government – the Panchayats – while being the channel for government funds for minor tank repairs have generally not taken on tank management and, being themselves the product of village factionalism, would be unable to resolve conflicts over water rights. Leaders would probably be unwilling to risk loss of support from locally influential individuals by attempting to curtail their privileged control of water resources.

State policy has had an important influence on tank irrigation systems. Until recently, state governments have given tank irrigation a low priority. The Public Works Department is under-resourced in this area and rarely able to carry out adequate repairs. A policy favouring the extension of privately controlled exploitation of groundwater has resulted in the neglect of public sources of irrigation, and enabled farmers to opt out of local institutions. Finally, changed and diversified cropping patterns have both increased demands on tank water, reduced inflow from catchments, and, because of more diverse water demands and duration, made the management of distribution far more complex (Reddy 1989b).

To conclude, the unchanging traditional community management of tank irrigation is largely fictional. Local tank systems have always been embedded in, and influenced by changing sets of social relations and by wider political transformations. There have been changes in first, the nature of rights in village tanks, from politically defined 'shares' to rights which are tied to private landholding title; second, in the nature of the 'community' of water users, from a caste-based structure of shares and obligations to a set of competing interests loosely tied to caste identity; and third, in the underlying power and authority and the determinants of social status. Such changes continue to influence recent attempts to reconstitute community management in participatory development terms.

Experiments in participatory institutions for tank rehabilitation: case study of Nallaneri village

New participatory institutions of tank management are being promoted in circumstances, and based upon principles radically different from those pertaining to functionally similar forms of organization in the past. Agencies developing these programmes have the difficult task of promoting participatory structures in the context of strongly hierarchical social forms, and of interdependence and informal co-operation presently under threat from contractual norms and market forces. In this final section, I examine the uneasy conjunction of contemporary participatory goals and 'traditional' co-operative institutions.

In 1988 the Centre for Water Resources (CWR) of Anna University (Madras) started an experiment in participatory institution building for tank management in two sets of tanks in Tamil Nadu (with funding from the Ford Foundation). Four tanks were selected as a focus for participatory initiatives from among 150 being 'modernized' under a state-wide programme implemented by the Public Works Department (PWD) with finance from the European Economic Community (CWR 1990; 1991). The CWR project aims to involve farmers in determining the use of Economic

149

Community/PWD project funds locally for tank development. The project brings together technical and community development expertise into small teams which develop *location-specific* tank development plans with farmers. Tank rehabilitation encompasses not just the problems of tank siltation and *bund* and channel repair, but also protective development of the upper catchment. Most importantly, the programme assumes that tank systems can be restored by vesting their long-term management (planning, rehabilitation, maintenance and administration) in the farmer community itself (CWR 1990: 125).

At the centre of the project strategy, therefore, is the promotion of local water-users' organizations which ultimately will assume ownership and management of the repaired tanks. These should represent all interests (landowners and tenants), be democratic, and draw up by-laws setting out membership criteria, subscriptions, the duties of office bearers, and the registers to be maintained. Apart from tank management, water users' associations link farmers to government departments (for credit and other inputs), connect them to sources of marketing advice and agriculture train-ing, resolve conflicts and appoint guards to protect crops and 'water guides' (*nirgatis*) to distribute water (CWR 1990: 125–32). The strategy for institu-tional development can be illustrated with a village example.

Nallaneri is a small village in Chengalpattu District with a total popu-lation of 582 and a caste structure dominated by two castes – high-caste Mudaliars (40 per cent) and low- or 'untouchable'- caste Harijans (60 per cent). Landholdings are small and the land distribution relatively even. Access to irrigation water is, however, more uneven and very few Harijans have rights to water from the two interlinked tanks which irrigate the village's paddy land (CWR 1990).

When the project was initiated three types of water distribution operated in the village. First, during land preparation and transplantation and at times of abundance, an *open system* operated. Water was carried in the entire distribution network and farmers had free access to use as much as they required (ibid: 23). Second after transplantation, water was dis-tributed through each of the different branch channels in turn. The dis-tribution was regulated by a (Harijan) 'water guide' appointed by the farmers. This system could not guarantee delivery of water to the entire irrigable area, and excessive irrigation by farmers during their turn resulted in conflicts (ibid). Third, the village had the vestige of an older 'shares' (or *pangu*) system in which privileged rights to water were exercised (at times of scarcity) by members of a dominant caste and kin-group, who pay an additional village irrigation tax and whose social rank is marked by obliga-tions and privileges in village festivals.

This water management system ensured *unequal* access to water re-sources during times of shortage.[5] There was no overall authority or body to arbitrate disputes, but then the system was firmly based on an existing

150

social hierarchy which excluded non-dominant and Harijan castes (although since water rights could be bought and sold there was some possibility of mobility). The system was inefficient in terms of water loss during distribution to scattered *pangu* holdings, but minimized social conflict. Finally, the system had failed to mobilize resources for routine tank maintenance and repair.

The aim of the small project team[6] working in Nallaneri was to build a participatory water-users' organization in the village to maintain the tanks and ensure that water distribution was both equitable and efficient. Initially they confronted not only an unequitable tank management set-up which failed to maintain the system, but also deep-rooted caste conflict between Mudaliars and Harijans, based on new status aspirations and the loss of traditional rights reflecting a breakdown of earlier reciprocities. Harijans had begun to withdraw from low-status obligations such as labouring within the village or providing temple and funeral services. In retaliation high castes had refused Harijans their customary rights, such as the usufruct on palmyra trees on the tank embankment, held in recognition of these village services (CWR 1990: 45–6).

The project team's first task, as they saw it, was to 'solve the prevailing caste conflict and establish traditional amity among the villagers' (CWR 1990: 47). In practice, the team's interventions further changed the relationship between the two castes. The team first organized reconciliation meetings between leaders of Mudaliars and Harijans. Second, they increased wage rates in the village to prevailing market rates, to keep Harijan workers in the villages; and third, they appointed a Harijan 'water guide' for water distribution. In this the Harijan community were recognized as equal partners in a development effort which effectively changed the local balance of power in a way that was probably a pre-condition for subsequent moves in establishing the water-users' organization.

The project team, together with a core group of village leaders, then initiated a number of practical tasks and collective actions: repairing tank sluices, cleaning channels, soil and groundwater testing, engineering surveys, assisting in linkage to government departments, and lastly agreeing a site for a new community well. These tasks – progressively more complex in terms of their demands on community co-operation – were preparation for the formation of the formally registered water users' society (hereafter 'the Society') seven months after the project began (CWR 1990: 47–55). The form of this Society was negotiated over 12 farmers' meetings (CWR 1990: 56, Annex VII). Significantly, it was agreed that the indigenous water distribution system – the kin-based *pangu* shares – would provide the core of the new institution's structure. Thus the Society had a twenty-one person Executive Committee based on a modified version of the 'shares' system with elected office bearers and three Task Force Committees (for maintenance, water distribution and management), as well as the General

Body open to all farmers. The important change in the 'shares' system introduced by the project was to increase the original six 'shares' to ten by including *all* irrigated land cultivators – even the previously excluded Harijan farmers. Each *pangu* or water shareholding group had two elected representatives in the Executive (in total eighteen Mudaliar and three Harijan members).

The Society meets many of the criteria for successful common property resource management emerging from the literature: an important and clearly defined resource is at stake on which all members of the community depend; there are established, clearly defined, secure and publicized rights in the resource, which are vested in the *local community* of actual users; the organization builds upon an existing institution, has (in its by-laws) established clear rules for the protection of the resource and distribution of benefits, has the authority to impose these rules and effective sanctions against those who violate them, and has mobilized people's contributions towards costs (e.g. Wade 1987a; 1987b; Chambers, Saxena and Shah 1989; Bagadion & Korten 1991; Ostrom 1992). A number of long-neglected tank maintenance activities were undertaken by the Society which had by mid-1989 begun to increase the tank's storage capacity (CWR 1990: 57).

During its first year, the Society increased its general body membership to 95 per cent of cultivators, and improved the representation of women to 32 per cent (CWR 1991: 10). It also extended its exercise of authority by imposing fines for cattle trespass (CWR 1991: xi). Most importantly, the Society undertook to execute tank rehabilitation works under direct contract from the Public Works Department (rather than through a private contractor), and as a way of establishing the capacity to do this, began to mobilize local resources for tank work from contributions (on credit) from members, loans from a local non-governmental organization and seed money from the state government (CWR 1991: xi). The CWR project team provided support in the form of facilitation of meetings, training programmes (e.g. in book-keeping, labour record-keeping), and organized visits to other tank programmes.[7]

The establishment of the Society as a 'participatory institution' for tank development has involved active negotiation between the agendas of the project team and the different groups and individuals within the village. The project's agenda is the promotion of participation and equity in the management of a scarce but common water resource. To achieve this they are obliged to work inclusively while striving for equity. For the project the 'community' of beneficiaries – the users of tank resources (water, fodder, fuelwood, silt, fish etc.) – includes a cross-section of a socially heterogenous villagers. It is impossible to target only the most marginal farmers and to exclude élites. Therefore the project works to protect and promote the interests of subordinate groups (i.e. Harijans).

Given this context, the project strategy involved establishing an institution for water management based on an existing but inequitable system, while exploiting opportunities made possible by wider changes in inter-caste relations to shift the existing system into a more participative and democratic mode of functioning. In fact, the project entered a relatively fluid system as an external agent with significant resources which enabled it to negotiate between different interest groups. This opened up new possibilities in a situation where alternative alliances were already appearing (another non-governmental organization had begun working in the Harijan 'colony' of the village). In effect, the appearance of outsiders with knowledge, contacts and resources, shifted the local balance of power making institutional innovation possible. Harijans obtained new water rights, a Harijan leader was appointed to one of the Society's Task Forces, meetings were held in the Harijan section of the village and various collective actions for tank repair began. Such effects are sometimes glossed as the 'catalysing role of outsiders'.

The institution which resulted from the field staff's early intervention in village affairs did not only reflect the project's agenda. It represented a negotiated compromise between the participatory values enshrined in the project's objectives, a pre-existing pattern of caste hierarchy, and the aspirations of a subordinate group. As in earlier times, the tank institution was more than a system for efficient water management. Since asserting rights in paddy cultivation concerns not only production but also 'assertions about standing, belonging and community' (Spencer 1990: 101; Leach 1961), the project institution (the Society) became a means for renegotiating the meaning of 'community' locally. In creating new statuses and rights, it was also a vehicle for the importation of new values and provided a context for social conflict and caste mobility. The social implications of building on a traditional institution (the *pangu* system) indicative of Mudaliar caste dominance while promoting Harijan participation (albeit nominal) in it as equal members are complex and long running. They clearly show that the Nallaneri tank society is a *political* institution, providing the context simultaneously for the re-assertion of upper-caste pre-eminence, *and* Harijan social protest. (This is detailed elsewhere, Mosse forthcoming.) In other words, by virtue of its capacity to mobilize resources, exert influence and arbitrate disputes, the project (and the Society it formed) rapidly became focal to the articulation of caste and political conflict locally. Moreover, it is known that the project too has its interests and will strike bargains. Thus Harijans have been careful to bargain the terms of their own participation (e.g. the contribution of their labour and financial resources) both with Mudaliars *and* with the project, as part of their long-term strategy for social and economic advancement.

The project team is an influential external agent operating at the centre of a delicate balance of interests and power in the village. If the project intervention is based too firmly on the existing structures, its new institutions will be perceived as serving limited élite (Mudaliar) interests, and subordinate (Harijan) groups are likely to withdraw their participation. If, on the other hand, the project overtly challenges the existing structures, key members of the dominant group are likely to withdraw, thus marginalizing the institution, confining it to a limited group and increasing dependence upon external support.[8] At the same time, project procedures of accountability, democratic decision-making and collective action may challenge existing styles of leadership and élite livelihoods based, for example, upon public works contracting. Key village leaders may choose to distance themselves from project activities, as the head of the statutory village Panchayat has done in Nallaneri. Such self-excluding élites can rapidly undermine new institutions, either directly or by engineering factional conflict internal to the new institution.[9]

In some situations threatening development institutions, while effective in one area (e.g. irrigation) can find themselves newly isolated from the key areas in village life where social standing is defined and challenged. In this way changes in social relations achieved in one institution need not be admitted in another. Would, for example, the admission of Harijans to the *pangu* system have any bearing on their admission to the temple? The manipulation of the 'spheres' of different institutions is important in managing changing power relations in participatory development, both by dominant groups hoping to diffuse change, and subordinate groups trying to generalize and legitimize situation-specific status gains.[10] It is certainly the case that the establishment of 'participatory' institutions brings with it a range of 'ritual' trappings (formal meetings, minutes, training programmes etc.) which create new types of belonging and symbolically separate these activities from other areas of village life. Whether this isolates or strengthens the members' position in the community will depend upon local circumstances.

Above all, it is obvious that participatory local institutions of any kind may serve a number of purposes beyond their stated aims. They may become vehicles for political ambition, contexts for leadership conflict, or bridgeheads for status change. These social dynamics (changing membership, leadership etc.) can have a crucial impact on the local outcome of participatory development efforts. While, as in the present case, these processes are beyond the project agency's control, through its attempts to manage shifting power relations *within* the community, the Centre for Water Resources (and the visiting professionals of the Ford Foundation, the European Community and the Public Works Department bureaucracy) become themselves part of local power relations.

Although the village tank society provides an institutional means for articulating *existing* processes of social change, it could not have emerged without the presence and intervention of project staff. Subsequent physical and institutional initiatives have also depended upon them. As with all local

154

institutional development there is, therefore, a risk of generating new forms of dependency which prevent institutional sustainability. In extreme (but not uncommon) cases local village societies become little more than mechanisms for the delivery of development benefits, or client institutions dependent upon the permanent presence (and patronage) of the promoting development agency. The greater the innovation, the faster the change, and the more complex the participatory institution created, the greater the continued dependence on outsider inputs and management support, and the harder it will be to transfer the full range of functions from the project to the village.

Conclusions

The argument of this paper has been that the management of natural resources is mediated by social institutions which are determined by changing configurations of power. In the 'community management' of irrigation tanks local social relations have always articulated with external agencies and powers - kings, bureaucrats, non-government organizations - in the definition, negotiation and challenge of rights in tanks and water. But through the intervention of external agents with resources, more than just water rights have been asserted or contested. Development interventions are about power as well as resources; contested rights are to social position, respect and influence as well as to water. Since village development organizations institutionalize power in new ways, they are often the focus for challenging or renegotiating public status and position. Indeed, much is at stake in gaining control of local institutions linked to external resources (or failing this, in ensuring that they are effectively obstructed).[11]

These issues suggest a need for field methodologies in development planning which build the social analysis of power into project processes (Mosse 1994d). More broadly an understanding of history and power suggests that present 'theories of participation' are overly functionalist and draw excessively on rational choice theories of collective action (classically stated in Olson 1971). Attempting to account for the strengths and weaknesses of institutions of common resource management in terms of the balance of individual costs and benefits gives little recognition to the fact that material interests are inseparable from social relationships, and that choices are mediated by social institutions involving shared assumptions about such things as justice, fairness and reciprocity (Spencer 1990: 98; Douglas 1986), and that the social and political meaning of 'common' or 'public' resources are constituted in culturally and historically specific ways (Mosse forthcoming).

While community institutions both inscribe social power and are subject to historical change, in popular (and populist) development thinking they are conceived in strangely apolitical and ahistorical terms. I have taken the use of the 'traditional community' as an *ideology* for participatory rural

155

development as an example of this. The image of working institutions of tank management in the past is as potent as the image of the ideal and threatened community of which it is a part. Just as 'community' is an ideal category invariably presented as loss (cf. Spencer 1990) and the goal of development is retrieval of this lost state, so tank systems will always be in decline and tanks will always need rehabilitation.

14. Institutionalizing adaptive planning and local-level concerns: Looking to the future

JULES N. PRETTY and IAN SCOONES

Despite decades of development effort, the number of people subject to extreme poverty is increasing. Many are now faced with accelerating environmental degradation, coupled with a growing immediate need to utilize natural resources to survive. Their livelihoods are complex, and have to be adapted rapidly in response to unpredictable environmental and economic change. Although our knowledge of these complex pressures and inter-linkages is extremely limited, we behave as if it were nearly perfect. This is because development practice has long been dominated by the positivist paradigm, in which we seek to discover the true nature of reality to predict and control natural phenomena. Knowledge about the world is summarized in the form of universal, or time- and context-free generalizations or laws. Technologies known to work under one set of conditions are applied widely, on the assumption that different receiving environments and economies will benefit too.

Yet it is impossible for such a reductionist analysis to account for the complexities of real world systems. No scientific method will ever be able to ask all the right questions about how we should manage resources for sustainable development, let alone find the answers. The results are always open to interpretation. All actors, and particularly those stakeholders with a direct social or economic involvement and interest, have a different perspective on what is a problem and what constitutes improvement in rural systems. As a result we are rarely able to predict the effect on a whole system when one part is changed. Impacts are often short-lived and bring unexpected failures. All too often, the only persistent element of a project is a heightened dependency on outside support.

If development is to be sustainable, planning will have to begin with the people who know most about their own livelihood systems. It will have to value and develop their knowledge and skills, and put into their hands the means to achieve self-reliant development. This will require a reshaping of both philosophies and practices associated with development planning. It will have to become much more adaptive to local needs.[1]

Adaptive planning

The debate about adaptive planning relates historically to the role of de-centralization in rural development, basic needs, and the requirements of integrated development with appropriate technologies. Current concerns about economic liberalization and reducing direct state control over development are also relevant. However recent concerns increasingly focus on the importance of participation in local planning and the need to institutionalize the attitudes and behaviour in the context of devolved and adaptive approaches to planning. Planning is often thought to be synonymous with intervention, and the starting of 'projects', implying the involvement of outsiders and external funding. The development aid business reinforces this with its concentration on discrete project identification and funding. This is a dependency that needs to be challenged and a wider, more flexible, process-oriented approach to planning evolved (Korten 1980, Goethert and Hamdi 1988).

Adaptive planning thus implies that local people participate in both agenda setting and resource allocating and controlling processes. In order for this to be achieved the acquisition of knowledge must occur through the use of an improved compendium of alternative planning approaches and systems of inquiry (Pretty 1994). The gathering, recording, analysis and use of information must be cyclical, with regular analysis, reflection and timely action. For effective planning, there must be active collaboration between disciplines and sectors in data collection and analysis. Information gathering systems and decision-making processes must therefore be local people-centred, site specific and must change according to external circumstances, requiring that the interests and activities of different formal and informal institutions are well co-ordinated.

The advantages of adaptive planning are most obvious when seen in the context of the drawbacks of normal practice. The blueprint approach to development planning remains the conventional wisdom. Those implementing projects select the most cost-effective designs for achieving outcomes based upon data derived from pilot projects and other studies. Implementing agencies faithfully execute the plan. Once implementation is complete, evaluators may measure actual changes in the local populations (or simply assess whether initial goals were achieved) and report actual versus planned changes at the end of the project cycle. The blueprints can then be revised before they are reapplied.

Normal land-use planning is thus flawed by many factors (Dalal-Clayton and Dent 1994). It focuses on a narrow technical view, rather than considering the social and economic complexities of farming and livelihood

158

systems; it is data hungry, with information needs being partly defined by availability of large quantities of money and partly by the apparent utility of sophisticated technologies, such as satellite imagery. These measure too few factors, become the domain of technically skilled outsiders, claim accuracy and are rarely grounded on truth. Outsiders tend to define local needs and develop technologies and innovations on research stations, so there is little use of local expertise, knowledge and skills. The results are often comprehensive maps and mesmerizing taxonomies that gather dust on shelves or need to be translated into another form before they can be used at the local level. Once land-use capabilities or classifications are completed, there is no room for adjustment or change in the face of local environmental, economic and social change. The response to these shortcomings has been the growing realization that local involvement is a vital ingredient in planning.

Participation in planning

There is a long history of 'participation' in development, and a wide range of development agencies, both national and international, have attempted to involve people in some aspect of planning and implementation. The terms 'people's participation' and 'popular participation' are now part of the normal language of many development agencies, including non-governmental organizations, government departments and banks (Adnan et al 1992). In conventional rural development, participation has often centred on encouraging local people to sell their labour in return for food, cash or materials. Yet these material incentives distort perceptions, create dependencies, and give the misleading impression that local people are supportive of externally driven initiatives. This paternalism then undermines sustainability goals and produces results which do not persist once the project ceases. As little effort is made to build local skills, interests and capacity, local people have no stake in maintaining structures or practices once the flow of incentives stops.

There is also a tendency for those who use the term participation to adopt a moral high ground, implying that any form of participation is good. But recently developed typologies of participation suggest that great care must be taken over both using and interpreting the term participation (Pretty 1994; Adnan et al 1992). It should always be qualified by reference to the type of participation, as most types will threaten rather than support the goals of sustainable development. A recent study of the views on participation of some 230 governmental and non-governmental organizations in Africa found that although participation in planning was relatively common, monitoring and evaluation is still largely conducted by outside organizations (Guijt 1991). Some organizations felt that participation simply implied local people doing what planners wanted.

159

It is also common for practitioners to assume that everyone in a community is participating, and that development will serve everyone's needs. The appearance of external solidarity, though, may mask internal differentiation – and understanding internal differences is crucial. Different livelihood strategies imply differentiated local knowledge systems, and these are easily missed by those who assume that communities are homogenous. This requires methodologies that are sufficiently responsive to such complexity, that can accommodate an understanding of agriculturalist – pastoralists' views, and the views of different constituencies (e.g. men and women, the old and young, poor and wealthy) and which can in turn reflect these in the responses made by development agents.

Where there has been the devolution of planning and monitoring to villagers, people in rural communities are no longer seen simply as informants, but as teachers, extensionists, activists and monitors of change. These specialists include village para-professionals, extensionists, game wardens, veterinarians and so on (Shah 1994). An emphasis on village specialists integrates marginalized groups more readily, so allowing their skills and knowledge to influence planning priorities.

Another difficulty with the term participation is that it may be used to accommodate a failed political process, where politicians may accept participation and its associated rhetoric, but not democracy, pluralism and accountability in planning. Effective participation implies involvement not only in information collection, but in analysis, decision-making and implementation – implying devolution of the power to decide. The political context of attempts at institutionalizing participatory planning is thus critical. Empowering people to take control at local level inevitably leads to conflict if external institutions are unwilling to give up some of their existing power. It should therefore be asked: how genuinely democratic and accountable are governments or non-governmental organizations promoting 'participatory approaches'?

Institutionalizing adaptive planning processes

Two approaches are crucial to institutionalizing adaptive planning processes. These centre upon improving accountability and increasing the number of stakeholders. It is generally felt that financial accountability, in the form of successful cost-recovery or cost-contribution, is a measure of the value that people put on an intervention or change. Support at the local level is seen as encouraging local autonomy and independence, but this may depend upon the degree to which these revenue-earning technologies are supported. Political accountability is important too. An important question arises: are non-governmental organizations concerned with accountability? Where there is economic and political liberalization, governments may be more concerned with accountability.

Who has a stake is also important. Local people could have an increased stake if they were empowered to make decisions; local governments could achieve developmental goals more effectively; donors could see a more efficient use of funds; but state-wide institutions, with competing interests, may be threatened.

It is essential, therefore, to sensitize bureaucrats to the needs of adaptive planning. In some cases they understand the skills and knowledge of villagers poorly. Many have only the vaguest understanding of informal approaches to participatory data gathering. They may lack local credibility, and may be restricted to establishing dialogue with 'traditional' authorities. Most importantly, however, they lack the political and financial support to gather and deal with new and sometimes sensitive information. Planners must be trained in the use of local level information. This will require linkages with the formal government planning system and methods of articulating local responses with sectoral concerns of line ministries/agencies as well as integrating conventional and new approaches to planning.

Support for change can come in several ways. There could be provision of appropriate training, better dialogue with non-governmental organizations and the creation of local pull on their services. In Kenya, the Soil and Water Conservation Branch of the Ministry of Agriculture has established participatory extension planning at the community level. Not only have agricultural yields, land prices and labour rates improved, but extension workers are enthused and rural people from these catchments have become more vocal in requesting support from the public service. More people now have a stake in a process of negotiation in which they may all benefit (Pretty *et al.* 1994).

Is adaptive planning capable of revitalizing the processes of government? Governments fearing loss of control are wary of flexible approaches, but such approaches do provide some solutions to many of the problems faced by ineffective centralized planning. Adaptive planning offers the opportunity for local-level negotiation on the sharing of the gains from the planning processes, and encourages an active bargaining process for external support. Expectations may be biased towards an approach to development which stresses service provision and projects on predetermined themes (agroforestry, soil conservation, water development and the rest). In addition, new organizational and management structures for innovative planning will be required for effective institutionalization.

Scaling up – scaling down

There are many local successes in community-based, participatory and adaptive planning (Pretty *et al.* 1992, Edwards and Hulme 1992, Pretty and Chambers 1993), but these have so far tended to remain local. A major challenge lies in widening the impact. This must go beyond simply replicating successful projects in different areas and move towards strategic policy changes. Projects are situated within wider policy frameworks and sustainable efforts may be reliant on strategic policy changes. How then can local-level successes be used to generate the capacity for strategic or regional change? A clear understanding of the principal advantages and disadvantages of both scaling up and staying scaled down is necessary.

At the local level, organizations can finely tune their strategies. Locally based organizations are also good at having an integrated view of problems, tending to have a power base with local links therefore receiving ready feedback. Their major difficulties, however, lie in commanding technical expertise, and the fact that diagnoses at a local level cannot solve problems arising out of the wider political context, such as product pricing and labour markets (Farrington *et al.* 1993). Disaggregated local institutions also find it difficult to influence state policies.

There are two approaches available for scaling up – either by encouraging federations and networks, or by making strategic change at the centre. In the first approach smaller organizations can federate to produce larger organizations, which can then have a regional lobbying role and can express political concerns to state level. In Ecuador, national non-governmental organizations such as CESA and FEPP maintain close links to the local level whilst co-ordinating regional and national research, as well as engineering formal and informal relationships with government departments. Scaling up does not necessarily have to imply institutional growth (which can be a threat in itself); it may simply involve spreading good ideas (or avoiding the spread of bad ones) through a region. Co-ordinating networks can perform an efficient scaling-up function, such as those at department level in Bolivia (Bebbington 1991).

A major advantage to local institutions of these scaled-up networks or federations is that they present a united front to donor organizations and governments. These create the opportunity for more efficient and more effective disbursement of funds by donors, with lower administrative costs. At this level organizations with greater membership, carrying greater political clout, can begin to influence state policy and are able to draw on technical expertise. However they also stand the risk of missing or misrepresenting local diversity and becoming less driven by local needs. Such organizations may not necessarily be representative of popular movements. Within non-governmental organizations an important distinction between accountable membership and non-membership organizations needs to be made.

The second approach to scaling up is to encourage change in strategic organizations, such as government departments, where there can often be many people who would like to innovate if they had the support and resources to do so. Sometimes strategic organizations can be as successful as local ones in picking up the local diversity and finely tuning approaches. Heterogeneity may in fact be greater than conventional planning approaches would have us think. For example in Kenya the District approach to planning has decentralized decision-making and allocation of resources to District Development Committees, on which sit representatives of various line agencies. Decisions are taken on the basis of available data, and inevitably, these committees have acted as if there is little variability in local needs from community to community, particularly within well-defined agro-ecological zones. However emerging evidence from the community-based planning by the Ministry of Agriculture shows clearly that there is a huge diversity in needs within these zones (Muya *et al* 1992, Mucai *et al* 1992). As extension officers are now working more closely with local communities, they are able to respond to these specific needs and, as a result, local planning has become more effective (Pretty *et al* 1994).

Governments and non-governmental organizations (NGOs)

There is considerable debate over whether only NGOs can be successful at adaptive and participatory planning, or whether more collaborative partnerships between NGOs and the public sector are the best way forward (Farrington and Bebbington 1994, Farrington *et al* 1993). Government institutions may be by-passed, either because they are weak, a trap for human capital, or simply repressive, and funds channelled to NGOs to create parallel structures. Creating parallel structures, though, is both inefficient and not likely to persist. The alternative is to work with governments, so that NGOs 'identify how best they might support but not substitute for what exists' (Roche 1991: 41). The principal objective must now be to foster change from within, not to threaten power but to put pressure on the system, and to support innovative individuals.

Governments are currently under wider political pressure, the result being an opening up of new opportunities for local-level grassroots approaches to be implicitly or explicitly supported. Participation, empowerment and increased awareness can create a pull on the public extension service, so increasing accountability and making the extensionist's job more rewarding.

It is important to draw attention to some further aspects of NGOs. There are significant differences between those in the North and those in the South, and between service and people's organizations (Fowler 1991). NGOs are successful at small-scale initiatives and, as they are locally based, may be a better defence against repressive states. However, where there have been transitions to elected democracies, 'NGOs are presented with the difficult fact that governments are to some extent popularly elected whilst NGOs are not' (Bebbington 1991: 72). Many NGOs, at least non-membership organizations, are not accountable, and just because they are

NGOs does not mean they are not subject to corruption. With increased access to donor resources in recent years, there is growing evidence of the wastage of funds and of rural people's time.

Opportunities exist for innovative work to catalyse change within governments, particularly under conditions of increased decentralization and participation in planning. An enormous amount of human capital and resources are locked up in government institutions and it would be foolish to ignore this. There is a danger of parallel structures evolving with the NGO sector being highly funded by donor aid, and at the same time being parasitic (for staff, technical support) on under-resourced government services.

There is a strong need for partnerships between institutions: these may be tripartite, such as between technical, intermediate and local institutions; or at community level but subject to implicit government rules. Partnerships either open up information flows or define the need for dialogue. In Mali, there is often a large difference between what local development committees think people want and what they actually desire – thus it is essential to keep the local committees informed in a continual dialogue (Roche 1991). These partnerships accept that 'in short, the aim is to change the state rather than simply criticise it' (Bebbington 1991: 73). There are obvious opportunities for joint funding and training activities between the government and NGO sectors.

Adaptive management and organizational structures

All of these desires, goals and objectives are rooted in the organizational and management cultures of governments, NGOs, communities and donors. Although there is a growing literature on organizational and institutional development and change, little has filtered through to have a significant impact on the development process. There are four central requirements: a need for new institutions to represent the user constituency better; a need to understand fundamental differences between commercial organizations (most management literature is about these), NGOs and governments; a need to identify pressure points through which change can be made; and the need to learn how to manage for innovation and experimentation in a turbulent environment.

Despite talk of decentralization, governments tend to retain bureaucratic power at the centre. Opportunities for organizational reorientation to develop a commitment to a listening and responding approach are missed, and the trend has been to rely on the non-government sector for adaptive approaches. However, the post-adjustment 'culture of government' should evolve towards rewarding enterprise, innovation, good governance and self-reliance. Governments need to become responsive and enabling institutions, rather than merely service providers.

Caution is required in the establishment of new local institutions, in that they may depend on transitory external funding and not be sustainable. They may lack accountability and popular support and so may be inappropriate channels for local concerns, but in many cases they have been successful in giving a voice to their users. By participating in technology generation, adaptation and extension they create new demands on the research process. These new institutions include innovator workshops, producer organizations, group workshops, options-testing groups, farmer networks, functional groups and village fora (Uphoff 1992; Pretty and Chambers 1993).

For change to be fostered in current organizations there are several factors that determine the different organizational and management demands on institutions. These are connected to the different ways organizations relate to clients, to the rest of the outside world, the sources of resources, and the controls over performance (Fowler 1992). Commercial organizations have simple and short transactions with clients – they sell an obvious product. Governments supply services and goods, and have permanent and obligatory relationships with people, whilst NGOs have no authority, and so can only extend their influence through dialogue and negotiation. In the end 'rural people must own induced social development processes and benefits if they are to be sustainable' (Fowler 1991: 77). Governments regulate and control, whilst NGOs must negotiate to integrate. Commercial organizations are paid by clients for their goods and services; governments get taxes and payments; NGOs rarely have a financial relationship with clients, their resources coming mostly from donors of one type or another. The final differences relate to the feedback received on performance. For example: a drop in sales tells a commercial organization they are performing badly and the feedback is therefore rapid; governments get indirect and delayed feedback from elections and tax evasions; NGOs rarely receive feedback to influence their performance, especially if they are based far from their clients.

These factors imply a need for new methods and a more structured approach. Leaders have a responsibility to offset bureaucratic stresses by adopting new methods for managing in a turbulent environment, staying in touch, and ensuring a steady two-way flow of information in an informal fashion. There must be the flexibility and capacity to allow adaptation and change, in which management is responsive and enabling. Incentives to innovate and experiment, rather than accepting the status quo, are needed, along with non-hierarchical structures that do not inhibit creativity and dynamism. Too often rural people, their knowledge and perceptions, are seen as a nuisance whose unpredictable behaviour inhibits the success of carefully made strategic plans. For problem identification, as well as monitoring and evaluating, there is a need for new information systems that are adaptive, flexible and people-oriented to provide steady flows of relevant information.

165

Training strategies for human resource development

An important strategy for change clearly rests on training and human resource development. Training must be targeted at key people so as to create a critical mass within an institution. Training processes are threatened by postings and poaching, but nothing can be done about this save for more training. The approach must be multi-level, especially to create an understanding in senior staff – get them in the field – and put field staff more at the core rather than at the periphery.

Recent years have seen a remarkable expansion in participatory learning in rural development planning, management and monitoring. Most common are the approaches of Participatory Rural Appraisal (PRA) and Rapid Rural Appraisal (RRA), which have strong methodological and conceptual similarities with a variety of other approaches (Mascarenhas *et al.* 1991, RRA Notes 1988–1994, Cornwall *et al.* 1993, Pretty 1994). These grew out of dissatisfaction with two common modes of investigation – formal questionnaire surveys and rural development tourism (Chambers 1983, KKU 1987). Questionnaires tend to be long, costly and prone to distorting non-sampling errors, while the short and often rushed visits to field sites by consultants, officials and researchers are characterized by haphazard data collection and superficial contact with local elites. The methods of Rapid Rural Appraisal, and lately of Participatory Rural Appraisal, emerged in the 1980s as alternatives to these two common approaches. They now comprise a rich menu of visualization, interviewing and group work methods that have proven valuable for understanding the local functional values of resources, for revealing the complexities of social structures, and for mobilizing and organizing local people.

The above methods are based on principles aimed at offsetting the deficiencies in the former investigative approaches. First, professionals work in multi-disciplinary groups, adopting sensitive attitudes and devolving the analysis to local people. Thus learning is from and with rural people, as professionals explicitly recognize the need to understand local knowledge, skills and practice. Learning is also rapid and progressive, as sequences of methods are applied iteratively, rather than in a fixed blueprint style. The range of conditions and extremes are sought out through purposive sampling to ensure that action is based not solely upon averages. Finally, probing and triangulation of methods and sources of information ensures rigour, reliability and trustworthiness (Pretty 1994).

The success of Participatory Rural Appraisal and Rapid Rural Appraisal in a wide range of development contexts is derived from their discrete and easily applied methods, the appropriate attitudes of both technical and social science professionals, and the shared analyses between disciplines and between professionals and local people. Where these elements are present, then participatory methods can be more cost-effective in both time

166

and money than the more conventional approaches to surveying and mobilization (Gill 1991, Inglis 1991, Chambers 1992).

A great deal is now known about the potential value of these methods. In some contexts their use has long been proven to be successful. One such success story is Planning for Real in the UK (Box 1). Less well understood or institutionalized are the methods for training. Conventional training or teaching does not necessarily imply learning, nor learning to learn. There is

---

Box 1. Planning for real: adaptive planning in urban Britain

At public meetings and consultations, local planners and other outsiders sit on a platform, behind a table, maintaining their superiority. When only a few people turn up, and only a few of them speak up, they blame local indifference. Planning for Real attempts to bridge this gap by focusing on a model of the neighbourhood. Unlike an architect's model, these should be touched, played with, dropped, changed around. At the first meeting the neighbourhood model is constructed, using houses and apartment blocks made from card and paper on a polystyrene base. The model then goes into the community, to the launderette, the school foyer, the fish and chip shop, so that people see it and get to hear of the second consultation.

At the second meeting the objective is to find out whether the planners have got it right. There is no room for passivity, not many chairs, no platform, with the model in the middle of the room. People spot the landmarks, discuss, identify problems and glimpse solutions. They are permitted to put more than one solution on the same place – so allowing for conflicts to surface. Often people who put down an idea wait for others to talk first about it. The process permits people to have first, second and third thoughts – they can change their minds. The model allows people to address conflicts without needing to identify themselves. It depersonalizes conflicts and introduces informality where consensus is more easily reached.

The professionals attend too. These local planners, engineers, transport officials, police, social workers, wear a badge identifying themselves, but can only talk when they are spoken to. The result is they are drawn in, and begin to like this new role. The 'us and them' barriers begin to break down.

Priorities are assessed, and local people involved in local skills surveys. The human resources are documented, and planning can then capitalize on these hitherto hidden resources.

Source: Gibson 1991: 29–30.

167

a need for training styles and programmes that are experiential and emphasize attitude forming. The basic precept of such training implies practice of the methods, reflection, and more practice, rather than teaching of information. It is more than simple skills-training.

The experience of using these methods can promote understanding of the underlying principles and lead to attitudinal change. An important facet of these methods that can foster this process is that they are neither value nor ideologically neutral. Evidence suggests that, although many can be used simply for data collecting, their use does actually provoke individual and institutional change. It is not necessary to understand all the principles underlying the methods before using them and in some circumstances this may be seen as a disadvantage or threat. However, there is no necessity for the methods to be promoted as provokers of attitude change. Training should thus be action based.

This has important implications for the site of training. Hitherto conventional training and educational institutions, such as agricultural universities, have largely failed to supply technical graduates capable of understanding the complexities of rural people's livelihoods. The maize agronomist, for example, is not encouraged to think beyond maize – which is simply a small subset of any rural livelihood system. Such institutions could be challenged by adopting participatory approaches. Only with effective training throughout the educational system can the appropriate attitude changes be enhanced; single one-off training exercises will inevitably have a lesser impact if the educational and professional culture remain unaltered. Most educational and learning innovation does not, however, occur in core institutions, and progress is unlikely to be quick.

There are major changes necessary in development assistance agencies. Many are strong on rhetoric, but find it difficult to be client-led when they are supposed to take a strategic focus. There have been many cases of community-based, people-based and process-based development projects, but relatively few documented successes. Evidence does, however, suggest that adaptive planning and implementation can result in increased productivity (food, health, trees etc.) at the local level on a sustainable basis, and that this represents a more efficient investment. Although potentially more expensive to administer, the feedback and community base mean fewer mistakes and greater effectiveness.

Conclusion

It has long been clear that those people directly involved are best placed to manage their environments and resources. Policies must support the resourcefulness of local people. Such development requires that they control their own resources. A major challenge for policy formulation, therefore, is to find the economic, institutional and legislative measures to support sustainable development at the local level. These changes must be combined with changes in the way the professionals who are involved in planning think and act.

All this must mean the relinquishing of some power to local people; and it is over power issues that the greatest threats lie. In a new context of participatory and adaptive planning, it will be important to keep track of who are the winners and who are the losers within communities. Any pretence by development professionals that participatory planning is occurring, whilst continuing to mask conventional practice in rhetoric, will simply lead to greater conflict. On the other hand, where there is institutional, attitudinal and policy change, then adaptive planning to support local concerns could succeed in unlocking enormous potential.

Acknowledgements

This paper emerged from the discussions at a two day workshop held in London in December 1990, entitled Local Level Adaptive Planning. An earlier version of this paper appeared in *RRA Notes* vol. 11 (191), pp. 5–21. This issue of *RRA Notes* contains 15 articles on various aspects of adaptive planning, and is available from IIED, 3, Endsleigh St, London WC1H 0DD.

15. Participatory ideology and practical development: agency control in a fisheries project, Kariba Lake[1]

KARIM HUSSEIN

Most development agencies are centers (sic) of power which try to help others change. But they do not themselves change. They aim at creating awareness among people yet they are not themselves aware of their negative impact on those they claim to serve. They claim to help people to change their situation through participation, democracy and self-help and yet they themselves are non-participatory, non-democratic and dependent on outside help for their survival (Nyoni in Gezelius and Millwood 1988: 5).

'Participation' has become the dominating ideology in contemporary thinking in both non-governmental organizations (NGO) and governmental/ inter-governmental agencies (Cernea 1985; Poulton and Harris 1988; Oakley *et al* 1991), where it broadly refers to 'the involvement of a significant number of persons in situations which enhance their well-being e.g. their income, security or self-esteem' (Cohen and Uphoff 1980: 213). However, it has been noted that development practice lags behind the elaboration of this ideology and that 'participation' is a multidimensional concept meaning different things to different people (Cohen and Uphoff 1980: 213; Oakley and Marsden 1984: 32). This chapter identifies key paradoxes in participatory approaches to development. These largely result from an inherent conflict between the power held by outsiders[2] over financial resources and stated objectives of 'empowering' the intended beneficiaries of development programmes. My case study[3] is a rural development project in Zambia involving The Gwembe Valley Agricultural Mission (GVAM),[4] which, it was claimed, was following a 'grassroots bottom-up approach to development' (Wood 1987: 13). I will examine GVAM's recent venture, a commercial offshore, open-water fishery to offer a constructive, critical appraisal of the gap between an ideal of participation and development practice.

Case study context: the need for outside resources

GVAM is involved in an integrated rural development project in a remote region covering about fifty square miles inhabited by approximately 10 000 people on the Zambian shore of Lake Kariba (Scudder 1990: 11). It works

170

with the largely Tonga people indigenous to Gwembe Valley who were forced to relocate from the shores of the Zambezi river as a result of the construction of the Kariba Dam in the late 1950s (Colson 1971; Scudder 1985). This rupture, in addition to the collapse of the Zambian economy and the Zimbabwean war of independence, necessitated changes in Tonga lifestyle as higher population densities and lower quality land rendered their previous mode of living more precarious (Wood 1987: 6), even unsustainable.[5] A combination of these factors led Scudder *et al* to conclude that development in the Gwembe region would not be possible without international help and resources.

Since the commencement of the project in early 1986, GVAM has established the following aims: to raise farming above subsistence level; to improve nutrition and general health, as well as to provide adult literacy and numeracy. The overarching aim is to develop the ability of the Tonga people to 'sustain their own development without outside aid' (Harvest Helper No. 11, June 1988: 3). These aims are to be realized through a network of multi-purpose co-operative societies run by their Tonga members.

Commercial fishing of kapenta (a non-indigenous pelagic sardine – limnothissa miodon (Scudder 1993: 147) – introduced into Kariba Lake in the 1960s) was begun in 1989 with the belief that it was central to the whole project's sustainability and to its 'essential purpose. . .to enable the lakeshore communities to take advantage – for the first time – of this gigantic lake' (Harvest Helper No.12, September 1988). Scudder wrote that 'the harvesting and marketing of kapenta more than any single activity will provide the project, and eventually the co-operatives, with the funds necessary to meet capital development costs and recurrent expenditures (i.e. health and education services)' and it has already 'helped the project deal with cash flow problems and inadequate funding' (1990: 16).

The importance accorded to the development of the kapenta fishery by GVAM is evident in the substantial resources allocated to it compared to other components of the project: the initial outlay of £44 723, amounted to 35–40 per cent of total annual project expenditure in 1989 (Harvest Helper No.20, September 1990), and for the period 1991–95 it was projected to absorb £129 250, or 11 per cent of total funding. These large outlays were made with the expectation that the fishery would soon be self-financing (Harvest Help 1990).

Gwembe Valley agricultural mission's ideology and the broader participatory ideology

In its publicity material GVAM stresses beneficiary participation at all stages of the development process (Scudder 1990: 10), from initiating and planning to contributing resources and knowledge. However, this must be understood within the context of GVAM's central goal of the project's long-term economic and social sustainability, implying the eventual self-reliance of project participants. As is the trend among non-governmental organizations, GVAM sees itself as a partner and catalyst to development, introducing but not imposing ideas, helping communities to perceive and face up to their problems (Harvest Help 1990; Wood 1987: 1, 9–13).

If we distinguish between a conception of participation used as a *means* (i.e. as a functional element to achieve overall project objectives) and/or as *an end in itself* (i.e. as the fundamental dynamic of the project, Oakley and Marsden 1984: 27–9; Oakley *et al* 1991) then it would seem that these elements of GVAM's approach conceptualize participation as both a means to achieving sustainable development and as an end in itself. However, the latter is stressed in GVAM's project literature, approximating the ideal approach set forth in Oakley and Marsden (1984: 29).

Such an approach stresses empowering the people to take active control in their lives (Oakley and Marsden 1984: 66–7). The outside organization acts as a catalyst, often setting up the organization of the supposed beneficiaries (Oakley *et al* 1991: 189–190). It is commonly assumed that such organizations will function as a means by which people are encouraged to participate in the development process. However the introduction of an external mode of organization as the sole instrument of project implementation, even if directed by some of the local beneficiaries, merely gives some beneficiaries a voice in development programmes and does not generally lead to meaningful (i.e. empowering) participation (Oakley and Marsden 1984: 29).

A review of the literature on participation[6] gives us a broader overview of participation, providing a set of guidelines by which to assess the extent of GVAM's participatory practice. The first question to ask is *who initiates action*? Who formulates aims and chooses needs and priorities? Who designs project plans and whose knowledge is used? Who implements the plans, who monitors and evaluates? Finally, who benefits and keeps overall control? The second question is *what kinds of participation are there*? Who contributes, who controls resources and aims etc.? The third question is *how does participation occur*? Is it voluntary or coercive, continuous or on an *ad hoc* basis? Are we referring to the participation of individuals directly or through an organization, and if the latter, an imported or indigenous one? Fourthly we must ask, *why is participation used*? Is it simply intended to facilitate the implementation of pre-planned activities (participation as means)? Or is it intended to begin a far-reaching process of structural change empowering the poor in a society (participation as an end)? The fifth point to consider is, *what are the constraints placed on participation by the social and cultural context*? Sixth, we must consider *what kind of impact does the project have*? Seventh and last, we must question *whether the project will be sustainable*.

172

This paper will use these questions to analyse participation in GVAM's kapenta fishery project.

Paradoxes in the participatory approach

. . . participation in rural development programmes is more myth than reality (Cernea 1985: 10).

GVAM did make participation of some kind an important aspect of its project. However, there are often contradictions in the practice of participation by outside organizations who control funds for development projects.

First, from the start GVAM has held the initiative in all the key areas of decision-making, planning, institution formation and implementation. Tonga participation was largely non-existent in the first two stages and purely functional in the institution-building and implementation stages.

GVAM was asked to begin a project by Chief Simamba and some headmen from an area of the chieftaincy called Munyama, who had been impressed by GVAM's work to increase agricultural yields among the plateau Tonga and certain participatory characteristics of their approach (Wood 1987: 6). After carrying out a preliminary survey and discussions with villagers, GVAM staff did wait for the communities to organize themselves, decide their priorities and present a written request for GVAM to move in (ibid: 9). However, it was the GVAM team that chose the site of their base on the lakeshore of Lake Kariba, which they saw as having the greatest potential for development.

Likewise, the overall approach to development was decided by GVAM. When communities were asked to draw up their own priorities of needs, their highest priority was for medical services followed by improved access to basic consumer goods and agricultural inputs, and improved communications links with the nearest town, which has an all-weather road to the capital, Lusaka (Wood 1987: 10). Although GVAM did begin working with the central concerns of health, and later with education at the request of Tonga communities, they decided the first priority was to stimulate economic innovation and development. Economic growth, they reasoned, would provide resources for improved services.

The GVAM team, and in particular the team leader, saw the fishing venture as the most viable way to supply local funds to realize the community's goals (op. cit.). GVAM felt that in order to encourage beneficiaries to innovative new economic developments, it had to initiate them itself. This is often seen as a necessary paradox in the literature on participation. Freire (1972) saw conscientization of the masses by outsiders as essential to awaken beneficiaries out of the 'culture of silence' brought about by their circumstances of underdevelopment (see also Oakley et al 1991: 3). The decision to begin a kapenta fishery was made in 1988 in

173

consultation with Harvest Help (UK), and on the basis of the available research (e.g. Mabaye 1987; Ramberg *et al* 1987; Scudder 1982). These pointed to the economic viability of a move into kapenta fishing. Critical to the timing of the move was the sudden availability, at a comparatively low price, of five fishing rigs, a sizable stretch of land on the lakeside in the project area and extensive fish drying facilities through a relation of the project leader (Harvest Helper Nos 12 and 13, September 1988 and January 1989). It appears that GVAM and Harvest Help decided to prioritize this purchase without consulting the co-operatives. Not possessing the required £37,000 the Tonga communities obviously could not have made such a choice.

Not only did GVAM's command over project resources confer control over the process of initiation, but it also allowed them to control vital aspects of decision-making. The Tonga did not control the operation or profits of the kapenta business. Tonga participation was limited to implementation. Originally, GVAM planned to employ local Tonga on the rigs. In addition, it would hire people to dry the fish (Harvest Helper No.12, September 1988). In a second stage of the fishing operation the co-operatives would be involved. This involvement was to be planned and managed by GVAM in consultation with co-operative members. However, in the initial stages GVAM decided that the co-operatives would be firmly under an outside manager's supervision. Subsequently, the GVAM team took over the fishery's management. This remained the situation until 1990 (Scudder 1990: 16) and was expected to remain like this until GVAM decided that the Tonga were ready to sustain it (op. cit.; Poulton and Harris 1988: 9, see note 9). Thus, participation became merely a means subordinated to the end of producing a profitable business.

Hence, while GVAM wants the people to run their own development, and participate in the initiation and organization of new activities, it is assumed that they cannot do so effectively in the beginning. Further, the organization of such non-governmental organizations makes concerns with efficiency, value-for-money, avoidance of 'waste', providing evidence of tangible improvements in the living standards of intended project beneficiaries and sustainability more important than participation. They are, as a result, reluctant to give up real power e.g. power over resource allocation. However, without a conscious effort to share this power from the very beginning, the intended beneficiaries will only ever participate in a functional sense.

This problem was recognized by Harvest Help's project officer. He pointed to the danger that 'lacking direct involvement from the outset, members of the co-ops will feel alienated from the project team' (Harvest Helper No.13, January 1989). However, GVAM still decided that it was better to simply 'explain the plan' to the co-operatives. The longer term plan was gradually to hand over control over the kapenta fishery. Rigs would continue to belong to GVAM and would be hired out to the co-operatives, selling fish through the base co-operative (Harvest Help 1988). Control, however, continued to rest in the hands of the innovator and capital supplier.

The mode of on-going project monitoring used by GVAM also reflected this control. It did not seek actively to involve all Tonga people, but only to involve passively some carefully selected households in the area of each co-operative, using carefully targeted questions set by outsiders (Scudder 1990: 37). Also, evaluation has always been commissioned from outsiders who, although careful to conduct interviews with Tonga people and present their views, cannot take the place of a broadly-based, on-going process of evaluation.[7] The type of evaluation systems used are geared to helping outsiders and managers make efficient and 'effective' decisions about resource use. The need to control expenditure does, then, tend to lead practitioners in rural development programmes to focus on implementation, rather than in facilitating participation in decision-making (Cohen and Uphoff 1980: 220).

Also, when the funding agency sees it necessary to introduce economic innovation into a society, it is likely to select a technology that conforms to its criteria rather than use local, existing knowledge. This is clearly the case in regard to GVAM's fishery. The fishing rigs required strong powered lights necessary to attract kapenta at night and were due to be motorized. They are a technology to which the Tonga previously had little access due to lack of capital (Scudder 1982). While they were not difficult to operate, the technology came from 'outside' and this would automatically limit participation to the functional: i.e. training in how to operate the rigs. Further, control over the rigs would not be given up to co-operatives until GVAM was sure the crews were highly competent. This was expected to take 'many weeks or months' (Harvest Help 1990, see note 9). This revealed a protective and paternalistic approach to rural people's participation characteristic of many developed country aid organizations.

The decision to motorize the rigs was taken by GVAM to maximize catches by getting further out onto the lake (Harvest Help 1990). However, the use of motors on the rigs would require maintenance, spare parts and fuel. This would not only be a threat to technological sustainability, but also to participation. By using one type of engine, and by setting up a training workshop to train apprentices and service the motors, GVAM hoped to maximize technological sustainability. However, the move to engines necessitated a reliance on fuel which militated against self-reliance (Scudder 1990; Oakley and Marsden 1984). The need to use lights only added to this decreasing self-reliance.[8]

Scudder proposed dealing with this problem by involving the fisheries department of the Zambian Government in the project region to provide Tonga with advisory services in the long term (1990). Although a seemingly far-sighted proposal, it might not have been necessary if there had been greater participation in the choice of technology (and, indeed, the activity itself). A smaller rig would have better suited Tonga culture (where productive activities are organized at a household level) and would have been easier to provide credit for, but it appears that none had been developed. GVAM did consider focussing their expenditure on developing a smaller rig, but in the context of the sudden availability of commercial kapenta rigs and licences, GVAM made a pragmatic choice for an income-generating kapenta fishery.

If the use of technology is initiated, planned and closely guided by the outside agency through which funds are channelled it lowers the level of participation. This may also lead to unsustainability, which ultimately undermines participation as an end. However, if the alternative is the continuation of poverty for a marginalized people, then functional participation may be preferable. In this case, non-governmental organizations should be honest and modify their ideologies accordingly. This may not be easy, however, as non-governmental organizations are bound by their lifeblood: their sources of funds. If an important member/donor is in favour of participatory ideology, the non-governmental organization is likely to retain that ideological stance in their fund raising literature, while still being pragmatic in practice. Alternatively, a non-governmental organization may retain a rigid ideological stance which it knows to be unrealizable in order to educate its members/donors. For example it may try to change paternalistic attitudes of giving 'charity' to weak people unable to help themselves, to those of providing resources to allow poor people to themselves overcome barriers to their own goals and aspirations. In the case of GVAM it may actually be a complex mix of these two that prevented an overt acknowledgement of the limits of the participatory ideology and the need for pragmatism in practice.

Outside agencies may believe that the 'consciousness' of rural people must be raised before they can be ready to participate fully in their own development. Some stimulation may be necessary to encourage truly participatory development with a marginalized displaced population such as the Tonga. However, this outside intervention has to be minimized – people must be allowed to develop their own thoughts and knowledge, based on critical reflection on the material realities of and constraints on their lives (Freire 1972). The latter is the essence of an empowering approach to development (Oakley and Marsden 1984; Hedenquist 1989). However, 'consciousness-raising', like institutional development, can be a means to ensure that participation occurs only on the non-governmental organization's terms.

Lastly, if development is centred on an organizational framework designed by the non-governmental organization, this fails to empower rural people. GVAM had preconceived an overall plan and approach to development on the basis of their previous experiences (Scudder 1990: 10).

Thus, GVAM made organization central to the project, requiring Tonga communities first to organize themselves to request assistance. Then, the choice of base site complemented the overall pattern of development that GVAM envisaged. Numerous small multi-purpose co-operative societies along the lakeshore were supposed to provide a channel by which GVAM could provide advice, skills training, loans and services. Eventually, these co-operatives were to become the focal point for income-generating activities. This reflected GVAM's preconception that successful development would require the 'building up of a co-operative spirit among each community' (Harvest Help, no date) through which they could tackle and solve the problems facing them together (Wood 1987: 9–10). The co-operatives were also intended to soften the impact of developmental change on traditional Tonga coping strategies, providing a forum for mutual support as traditional ways of living disappeared, whilst being primary vehicles for integrating a fairly recently monetized culture (Colson 1960: 37) into the wider economy via the purchase and sale of produce (Wood 1987: 3).

Co-operatives were intended to be institutions through which the people could participate in the development process. However, since these institutions were introduced from outside with the aim of changing the traditional egalitarian and individualistic social organization (Colson 1960; Scudder 1990) they could constitute a hindrance to fuller Tonga participation. While there was some room in GVAM's plans for Tonga people to develop their own forms of social organization at the stage of requesting assistance, the Tonga did not take full advantage of this. When the project commenced GVAM's role was more akin to the social engineer with a blueprint for social transformation:

> While it was recognized that in theory the project wished to respond to the requests of each community individually, it was also recognized that a standard model of project activities would need to be developed to allow [GVAM] to cope with the number of communities from which it expected requests (Wood 1987: 10).

Although co-operatives have been chosen as the primary institutions for development in various developing countries for ideological reasons, they have generally failed to stimulate development where they have not arisen out of the desires and social structures of the people concerned (UNRISD 1975: 20). Indeed, an uprooted people is likely to be even more tentative in accepting new forms of social organization (Colson 1971: 2). Scudder warns of past failures of co-operatives in Gwembe Valley. Many of the members of co-operatives (amounting to only 5–10 per cent of project area population) did not feel the co-operatives belonged to them, but to GVAM (Scudder 1990: 19–32; see also Harvest Helper No.21, December 1990).

GVAM's initiation of the co-operative structure conditioned the types of participation that could be achieved such that participation occurred largely on GVAM's terms. However, co-operatives contained at least some aspects conflicting with known characteristics of Tonga culture (e.g. envy; productive activities normally being organised at the household level).[9] Participation tended to the functional: e.g. the communal building of a structure for a clinic and co-operative activities. The establishment of the kapenta fishery by GVAM can then be conceived as necessary to provide the Tonga with the surplus resources required for the outsiders' participatory vision (co-operatives) to survive, in which 'the common good is given priority over individual interests' (Wood 1987: 13). This approach to empowerment is gradualist and paternalistic.

In this way, the non-governmental organization went beyond its stated role of catalyst. It took the initiative in designing an overall development strategy. It pursued a directive rather than 'dialogical' approach to conscientizing the rural poor (Oakley and Marsden 1984: 77 ff). This was likely to limit the intended beneficiaries' future participation to a means rather than as an end in itself. While we may accept the paradox that 'promoting bottom-up development often requires some top-down efforts' (Uphoff 1985: 389), the problem is knowing when the latter begins to undermine the former goal.

Conclusions

GVAM's actual approach to participation in the kapenta fishery development was to attempt only what it perceived to be possible. Thus, the project can be broken down into three stages. During the first stage, lasting two years, Tonga were involved in implementation (employment) and as the objects of training. GVAM controlled both the project and funds. During the second stage, projected to last ten years or more, Tonga were to lease rigs from GVAM through the co-operatives and sell fish through the GVAM based co-operative. GVAM would retain overall control over the fishing operation and continue to supply funds. In the third and final stage, it was intended that Tonga co-operatives would own and operate their own rigs and market their own fish. At this stage only Tonga would control the fishing operation, via co-operatives, and become self-reliant. This stage would take 'a long time'.

I would suggest that the paradoxes in the participatory approach noted in this paper made it very difficult to ever achieve the third stage to the satisfaction of the non-governmental organization. Indeed, this has been confirmed as the kapenta fishery has since been abandoned by the Tonga, while retained by GVAM only as an income-generating activity (James Copestake, personal communication).[10] The declared goals of social sustainability and self-reliance are likely to be undermined by the paternalistic approach pursued by GVAM. Further, 'even in the best intentioned programmes of development control from the outside may appear locally as a

178

new form of alien domination discouraging participation' (UNRISD 1975: 20).

At another level, the problem may be that many rural people do not actually want to participate more comprehensively in development projects. In this case they may be satisfied by an outside organization involving them only in the functional ways described here. This paper, however, is not assessing the *effectiveness* of the participatory approach so much as whether the ideal matches practice. Activities involving functional participation at best may result in profits and improved living standards, but they will not promote participation as an end in itself. They may also not be sustainable without the continued presence and funds of the outside organization. These failures contradict the stated aims of many non-governmental organizations.

The practice of participation by the non-governmental organization under consideration here has been pragmatic and gradualist. Using its access to outside resources it has simultaneously acted as a capitalist entrepreneur in addition to catalyst. It has been juggling with conflicting commitments to participation, efficiency and the achievement of concrete improvements in living standards. Its actions show that it believes there are limits to participation's usefulness in a development project, at least in the early stages. This means that what is called participation can in fact be very close to a 'blueprint' approach to establishing a development activity. Treating participation as an end would have led to the adoption of a 'learning process' approach, where a priority would be the sharing of the complexities of decision-making and power, even over outside resources, from the beginning (Hedenquist 1989: 4). The gradualist approach to participation is not consistent with the empowering participatory ideology adopted by many non-governmental organizations. In fact it is likely to inhibit beneficiaries from ever reaching the last stage of empowerment, that of control and self-reliance.

The general conclusion that we can draw from this case is not that GVAM's approach was wrong *per se*, but that it is important to grapple directly with the real and problematic paradoxes in, and limits to, participatory approaches to development. These arise essentially as a result of the control a non-governmental organization has over funds. A central question regarding empowering participation is: how quickly and to what extent is an agency prepared to yield to beneficiaries control over decisions concerning the use of funds? This is rarely considered seriously as it implies a real shift in decision-making power between giver and receiver.

This does not negate the value of the services (e.g. injection of resources, education, health care, expert advice etc.) a non-governmental organization can provide to poor people. Indeed, the intended beneficiaries of aid projects may prioritize such services, as did the Tonga. However, realistically a service oriented approach is likely to limit participation to the functional (participation as means) in the pursuit of these specified material ends. A lack of empowerment, amongst displaced populations in particular, has been identified as an important constraint to successful development (Scudder 1993: 149). However, the need to uphold participatory rhetoric can prevent an organization from carefully assessing when and in what activities functional participation or radical empowerment is appropriate.

16. Non-governmental organizations and participatory development: the concept in theory versus the concept in practice

JACQUELINE LANE, Charities Aid Foundation

The role of non-governmental organizations (here after referred to as NGOs) involved in Third World relief and development work has received increasing attention in recent years, to such an extent that the 1980s has been termed 'the decade of the NGOs' (Bratton 1989: 569). This reflects the current opinion that NGOs are in some way better at relief and development work than official bilateral or multilateral aid agencies.

Two factors contribute towards this view. Firstly, a general dissatisfaction with official aid policies has prompted both governments and public alike to view NGOs as alternative development channels. Secondly there has been a paradigm shift in development thinking, stressing the active participation of local people in the development process, an approach traditionally characteristic of NGOs. While inter-governmental organizations are adopting the rhetoric, it is still argued that NGOs might be better at participatory development in practice.

A fundamental problem in critically assessing the experience of Northern NGOs with participation is that the concept is unclear in practice. What is participation and what are we trying to achieve in promoting it? Are NGOs successful in its practice? This paper attempts to answer these questions with reference to the experience of Northern NGOs in Africa. It will be seen that both the theoretical concept of participation and its association with the Northern NGOs is both ambiguous and controversial.

The NGO community and participation

The term NGO is not very helpful as a starting point for an analytical discussion since it is an umbrella term covering a wide range of organizations from household names such as Oxfam to small peasant organizations in rural Africa. In this paper I am focusing primarily on the experience of the group of 'international NGOs' which are concerned with African development issues, rather than the very large and diverse group of 'indigenous NGOs' originating locally. However I do attempt a brief comparison at the end of the paper.

Analyses of Northern NGOs have identified several reasons why it is thought that NGOs might be better able to put participation into practice.

181

Firstly NGOs claim to be innovative, flexible and not weighed down by bureaucracy. These advantages, plus their ability to rely on voluntary and committed staff, may allow them successfully to follow risky and non-conventional policies, whereas governments and official aid agencies may be more constrained and restrained. The second comparative advantage claimed is independence and autonomy which, it is argued, enable NGOs to remain free from political pressure and to by-pass inefficient and corrupt government structures and local elites. However the increase in official funding of NGOs may challenge this independence at one level.

A third claim of NGOs is that they are already operating at the grass-roots level, close to the poorest of the poor. This 'people first' orientation stems partly from the ethical position of many NGOs, and also from the nature of NGOs as small resource constrained organizations, dependent on uncertain funding. Resource contributions from recipients are therefore often required, and greater responsibility is more likely to be delegated by necessity than would be the case in official agencies (Brodhead 1988: 6).

These three areas of comparative advantage suggest that an NGO approach fits naturally with a stress on participation. However as Judith Tendler (1982) notes in her much quoted evaluation of American NGO experience, it may be more appropriate to label such self descriptions as 'articles of faith' rather than accurate representations of NGO activity. In order to move towards a more systematic evaluation we first need to define what we mean by the term participation.

Participation defined: a framework for analysis

Participation is a very broad concept, and when the term is used in the context of development the first question to answer is exactly what type of participation we are talking about. Participation in the construction and implementation stages of a project is now very common and often involves the beneficiaries contributing resources. Here participation is equated with co-operation and incorporation into pre-determined activities. However this is only one stage in the development process, and we must also consider participation in decision-making, in implementation and maintenance, in benefits, and in evaluation of both successes and failures.

The second dimension of participation is who should participate? In a truly participatory approach we might expect all those affected to have a role to play at all stages of the development process. This highlights the fact that certain groups (for example the poorest and women) have been by-passed by previous development and should now be included, or even 'put first'.

Once we have decided the scope of participation and who is to participate, we need to consider how this is to be achieved in practice. It is

182

important to make a distinction between voluntary and coercive participation, however in practice this may not be easy, particularly when extensive material incentives are employed to ensure co-operation.

In his World Bank Discussion Paper, Samuel Paul identifies four methods of participation: information sharing, consultation, decision-making, and initiating action (Paul 1987). The latter indicates participation of the highest intensity. Each level of participation is characterized by a different relationship between the implementing agency and the beneficiaries. *Information sharing* participation refers to a process where the agency informs intended beneficiaries about the project, and so flows of information and control are both in a downward direction. In a process involving *consultation* information flows are more equal, with the agency often making use of local knowledge, however control is still from the top down. In *decision-making* participation beneficiaries have some control over the process. Finally where participation has advanced to the stage of the beneficiaries *initiating action* both information and control flows are primarily upward, from the beneficiary group to the agency, but the donor agency retains some degree of control.

The mix of how and what in a particular situation is basically determined by the answer to the final question – what is the purpose of participation? Is it 'participation as an end' or 'participation as a means'. Participation may be a *means* to improve project effectiveness through the use of local information to specify correctly problems and needs, improve solutions, avoid misunderstandings, and enable the NGO to reach more people. Project efficiency may be increased if participation involves the beneficiaries' contributing labour and other resources. Finally if participation develops a commitment to the project and local self-reliance this may promote sustainable development. In all these situations participation is seen as an input into development projects, and many writers are optimistic about the link between project success and the extent of participation involved.

Participation may however be seen as an end itself. It may have an intrinsic merit, if it increases self-esteem, confidence, and the individuals' sense of power. It may also be seen as a basic human need, in which case we would be concerned with participation as an ongoing process. This suggests a wider scope and greater intensity of participation than where participation is viewed as a predetermined input. The fact that participation has a variety of meanings suggests that we should be wary of approaches that use the term uncritically or view it as unequivocally good.

Participation in practice

Moving on to look at NGOs' experience in the practice of participatory development, there is remarkably little information and systematic evaluation of actual cases. The evidence which does exist seems to be contradictory, and the only consensus in the literature is on the need for more information. In one general survey that does exist Brodhead (1988) estimates the degree of participation in 51 Third World development projects as follows:

- o 22% – no participation
- o 24% – low participation
- o 36% – moderate participation
- o 18% – high participation

It is however very difficult to make general statements about the character of the organizations referred to as the Northern NGO community owing to the heterogeneous nature of the group. David Korten proposes that there is a pattern of evolution away from traditional relief activities, towards acting as a catalyst for development more widely defined (Korten 1990). In what follows I will divide the NGO community initially into four groups: 'relief and welfare', 'modernization', 'community development', and 'institution building', the latter three collectively being called 'development NGOs' and outline the type of participation (in terms of scope, intensity, and purpose) which occurs in each group.

Relief and welfare NGOs arise out of a long history of international voluntary action to assist victims of war, drought, poverty etc. and in the United States today many NGOs (63 per cent according to Smith 1987) still rely predominantly on material aid. Whilst in other countries the proportion of resources devoted to relief and welfare appears to be smaller, the recent succession of natural and man-made disasters has emphasized the role of relief work, and new NGOs such as Band Aid have sprung up in response to specific crises.

What can we say about relief and welfare NGO experience with participation in development? Many of these agencies see their most important goal as 'immediate alleviation of suffering' (Smith 1984: 118) and aim to meet immediate needs wherever they are visible, by the provision of goods and services. Recipients are often seen as an undifferentiated passive group with no control over their own lives. The agency on the other hand is active and its ability to claim to be doing something is the basis of its fundraising activities at home. Resources and information flow down from the agency to the recipients taking little account of variable local conditions. This type of intervention can be characterized as top-down, militaristic and paternalistic, where the agency retains complete control and the only constraints are seen as logistical. The only 'participation' expected is the receipt of aid by the intended identified beneficiaries.

A second major group of NGOs can be called 'development NGOs'. The main distinction between this group and relief and welfare NGOs is their aim to initiate long-term change and increase the capacity of people to meet their own needs. This group of NGOs is the largest in the Northern

184

NGO community, except in the US. For example Canadian NGOs covered by Brodhead's survey (Brodhead 1988: 14) allocate an average 58.9 per cent of their total overseas expenditure to development projects, compared to 18.5 per cent to relief and material assistance. Given the abundance of theories of development, it is not surprising that the development NGO group is varied and complex, with different sub-groups corresponding to different theoretical positions.

One of the earliest types was that which adopted a *modernization* approach: the dominant perspective in the 1960s. Many NGOs shared the view that economic growth along the path already travelled by Western countries would lead to development. It was thought that transfers of material resources and technology could fill identified 'gaps' up to the point where the economy could take off into sustained growth and so many agencies in the 1960s originated to transfer credit, technology and training to microenterprises in the Third World (Gorman 1984: 122).

For many of the early technical assistance NGOs, participation meant participation in implementation of a project, amounting to the acceptance and efficient use of transferred resources and new technology. Non-participation was seen to be due to backwardness, ignorance and laziness, and evidence of the need to 'educate people out of ignorance'. This paternalistic and superior attitude implies a very limited view of participation, one based on information receiving and implementation, and calls to increase participation may simply be made in order to increase coverage or efficient use of resources.

Some technical assistance agencies do stress a participatory approach. Literature from Oxfam and Technoserve illustrates recent shifts in the attitude towards technological assistance, where the value of indigenous knowledge and use of appropriate technology are increasingly stressed, and the argument that the technical nature of assistance limits participation is increasingly discredited. However whilst the rhetoric surrounding technical assistance has changed, it is not clear how indigenous knowledge can be discovered and incorporated, or how marginal groups will benefit. For example the transfer of agricultural technology is only likely to benefit those with sufficient land to use it efficiently, not subsistence peasants or landless labourers. Despite the rhetoric, the nature of technical assistance is likely to limit participation to the few who already have access to a certain level of resources, and the participation of those few may be limited to participation in benefits and implementation. This is not to say that this type of participation does not have a valuable role to play, simply that the only route to the full participation which the agencies claim to be pursuing may be to move on from the technical assistance mode of operation.

A second group of development NGOs, which can be called the community development group, concentrates on 'developing the capacities of the people to better meet their needs through self-reliant local action'

185

(Korten 1990: 118). The theoretical basis can be found in the Basic Needs theory of the 1970s. Whereas to the technical assistance NGOs participation was simply a means to improve effectiveness and efficiency, to the community development NGOs it is a central concept . Poulton and Harris (1988) have proposed that the approach can be written as:

Basic Needs + Participatory Development = Community Development

There are good reasons for the close association of participation with a community development approach. First, the aim to meet basic needs obviously requires the participation of all in benefits. Second, participation in implementation improves efficiency through the mobilization of local resources. Third, the development of a community's capacity to plan and implement change will require greater intensity and scope of participation as the project proceeds.

A review of various community development projects reveals a mixed experience with participation. In some projects, for example community health care, community involvement and training are actively promoted to develop commitment to the project. However there is often a notable absence of participation in the early stages of the project, in decision-making and design. Furthermore the participation which does occur is of a low intensity, and based purely on information received from external sources. The aim is usually slowly to mobilize local funding and release control to beneficiaries, but in most cases agencies involved in community development retain the control of resources and decision making processes. It seems unlikely that this type of participation will promote self-reliance.

Judith Tendler (1982) characterizes this model as 'enlightened top-down', and points out that this can be very effective in achieving agency objectives. However there remains an inherent contradiction between operating at the periphery whilst maintaining control from the centre, since the lack of participatory decision-making may create dependency on the external agency. Only the development of more genuine participation will enable the incorporation of local knowledge and the development of local commitment necessary for sustainability and self-reliance. This implies that in the long-term the only viable strategy for project success is one involving a considerable degree of participation.

One important theoretical development of the 1980s has been the recognition of the fact that any development takes place within a particular structure of social organization. As a result of this we can see the emergence of a third subset of development NGOs, 'institution building NGOs', who see the development of participatory local institutions as a necessary vehicle through which development can occur.

Institution building may involve setting up new institutions from scratch with the specific function of implementing projects. In the short-term the organization is a means to improve efficiency and effectiveness.

Participation of a functional nature is expected when operating externally devised projects. To meet long-term goals of self-reliance and sustainability, control and decision-making power may gradually be released to the local organization; however, in practice problems often occur: African counterparts may be inadequately trained, and the organization may remain dependent on outside support.

A viable alternative may be partnership with indigenous organizations. Brodhead (1988: 133) reports that 53 per cent of the projects he surveyed aimed to strengthen local voluntary organizations but in practice the impact was limited. There may be a tendency for new groups to grow up around new activities in competition with weak traditional institutions. Even where well developed organizations do exist this is no guarantee that they will be effective channels for active and full participation by their members. Local organizations are often open to influence and control by local élites who will then continue to make decisions in their own interests under the cover of a participatory organizational structure.

From a brief review of the extent and nature of participation achieved by Northern NGOs in development activities it seems that at best we can agree with Brodhead that 'NGOs' efforts at instituting participatory development processes have been uneven'. (Brodhead 1988: 126). Over time the NGOs' interest in participatory development has increased, as has the likelihood of achieving at least some degree of participation in practice. In the first group, the relief and welfare NGOs' participation was a means to ensure effectiveness in meeting immediate needs but both the identification of these needs and their solution were seen as the responsibility of the agency. As the development group evolves participation becomes increasingly central as a means of ensuring efficiency, reducing costs, and promoting sustainability. However where participation does exist it seems to be tacked onto existing styles of operation: participation is a means to an end which is predetermined by the external agency.

African NGOs respond

The view of participation seen so far contrasts sharply with a view from Africa itself, the clearest exposition of which comes from the United Nations' Economic Commission for Africa Conference (UNECA) in Tanzania in 1990. For this Commission, Paul Wangola (1990) traced the history of participation back to the beginning of Africa's contact with the West, arguing that the African people have obviously participated in a development process, but they have not directed it or reaped the benefits. This form of participation has been exploitative and disruptive, only possible because participation has not been voluntary.

At independence there was great optimism that all this would change, however many of the new governments pursued policies of 'departicipation', for example the dismantling of participatory structures hastily installed by the departing colonial authorities, such as elections, local government and trade unions. Where governments have claimed to promote participation, in reality this has often amounted to a process of incorporation. The masses have been forced to acquiesce to development initiatives which have benefitted others.

Inadequate participation at all levels in this sense arises from the unequal distribution of power between individuals and social groups. If participation is defined as the ability of a person to control and influence his working environment the essence of the participation debate is how to return power to the African people. Participation is now no longer just the means to some predetermined end, but the most important end in itself. Once people are able to meaningfully participate in all spheres of life, including the political process, they will be able to take control of their own development and challenge existing structures which have not worked to their advantage.

From this we can conclude that when African NGO leaders call for participation they have in mind a very broad concept, which can be called empowerment. This refers to the ability of individuals to influence all decisions taken at all levels and in all spheres which affect their lives, and their capacity to initiate action to enhance their quality of life. This participation must be voluntary and must include the ability to change the existing environment.

An African view, thus characterized, contrasts sharply with the functional view of participation which many Northern NGOs seem to have adopted. Rather than being a choice at the level of inputs to discrete and well-defined development projects, participation becomes a fundamental right and a basic need of individuals, and hence of society as a whole. It is therefore the most important objective of the development process. However, we see from Smith's survey that few development NGOs ranked 'empowerment of the poor to challenge and change the dominant political and economic structures in their environment' as an important goal and some explicitly rejected it (1984: 125). Here we come to the crux of the debate about participation and NGOs: empowerment of the poor is what African NGOs understand by participation; yet many Northern NGOs consider it either unimportant or irrelevant.

Participation as empowerment

In recent years a small group of Northern NGOs, which can be termed the empowerment group, have adopted an approach to development close to that expressed by African NGO leaders. The rhetoric of empowerment is prominent in their projects and policy statements as a result of ideological commitment as well as in response to the perceived limitations of development NGOs.

188

The essential difference between the modernization and community development NGOs and the empowerment NGOs is the underlying view of the latter that development must be a process which is carried out from within. A fundamental prerequisite for this is a distribution of power which allows individuals to influence all decisions affecting their lives. The Northern NGO should therefore aim to facilitate meaningful participation of individuals and groups in all stages of the development process including that of initiating action.

The question of how to undertake an empowerment approach in practice is far from a simple one. Here I can only suggest three initial changes required of Northern NGOs. First they must recognize and support the competence of Southern NGOs to direct their own development, through the transfer of resources and creation of a favourable institutional and political environment.[1] Second they must see development as an ongoing process rather than a series of discrete projects which are designed and controlled by the Western agency. Third, they must accept an international division of labour between NGOs where the Northern organizations increasingly withdraw from 'doing', focus on education and advocacy in the West, and leave the initiation, design, and operation of the process of development to African people themselves.

To what extent is the rhetorical shift in Northern NGOs' language matched by a shift in practice? Again generalization is difficult but there are some NGOs or areas of NGO activity which can be accurately placed in the empowerment group. First, for example, some large organizations in the UK, for example Oxfam and Christian Aid, place considerable stress on empowerment, adopting a new approach which focuses on increasing the scope and intensity of participation (in particular involving beneficiaries in strategic decision-making) and relinquishing power to the field. Second there are now several organizations which exist purely to channel resources. Organisations such as Comic Relief fit into an empowerment framework since they have taken a step back from development activity, leaving other organizations to act in the field. Third there is a growing group of co-ordinating NGOs for example Partnership Africa-Canada (PAC) and ACORD (a group of European and Canadian NGOs) which aims to promote local institutional development in Africa.

However the fact remains that NGO projects in general do not guarantee either the high intensity or wide scope of participation implied by the empowerment approach. Most Northern NGO activities can still be classified in the relief and welfare and development groups, and many organizations have not undertaken the changes in operation suggested as necessary for an empowerment approach. In fact it may be the case that the great need for emergency aid during the 1980s has stimulated a shift in the opposite direction – from functional back to passive participation, with a

189

stress on meeting immediate needs. We are left with a serious contradiction between rhetoric and reality.

This currently observed contradiction may only be a temporary feature of an NGO community in transition, rather than a permanent contradiction, however two obstacles stand in the way. First it seems that NGOs are unsure how to translate the rhetoric of participation into practice. On the ground participation can mean very different things to different people. NGOs need to work out exactly what they are aiming for in each situation and how this is to be achieved.

The second problem is that even if NGOs are able to address successfully the issues outlined above there are several internal and external constraints remaining. Within the Northern NGO community there is a strong preference for a project approach to development within which empowerment does not easily fit. Neatly packaged projects which can produce quick results are the most effective way of raising funds, and also suit the bureaucratic structures of many of the larger NGOs. This implies that it will be difficult to adopt the risky open-ended funding of development processes through local organizations which is a crucial part of an empowerment approach.

Even if the internal constraints can be overcome, there is still a major external constraint that empowerment is overtly political in the sense that it sets out to challenge existing power structures. This may result in attempts to control the activities of the NGO, both at a local and international level, especially where a significant amount of official aid is involved.

Conclusion

As the notion of participation has become widely accepted in donor circles, NGOs have found themselves thrust into centre stage, channelling a greater proportion of official aid and increasing voluntary contributions. However, the above discussion highlights the fact that both 'NGO' and 'participation' are dangerously close to becoming buzzwords, rhetorical terms without theoretical clarity or practical content.

Whilst it is clear that much Northern NGO rhetoric has moved on to endorse a participatory approach, different groups of NGOs mean very different things by participation, ranging from increased coverage of passive beneficiaries to functional involvement in project operation and finally to empowerment of the poor to challenge the factors which govern their lives. A basic division seems to be between those who see participation as a means to improve the effectiveness and efficiency of externally determined projects, and those who see it as an end in itself. For the former group, participation in practice tends to be limited in scope. The agency retains ultimate control, with the mode of operation being characterized as 'enlightened top-down' rather than meaningful control from the grass-roots.

There is little doubt that participation of this sort can have positive effects in terms of project success. However, in the long-term there is a contradiction in an approach that only allows participation in externally determined projects. The only way to ensure that individuals have the power to attack the root causes of underdevelopment is to enable them to influence all decisions, at all levels, that affect their lives. This implies a very broad concept of participation, where participation is seen as an end in itself, and all control of the development process is devolved to those who are affected by it.

This paper has highlighted many of the issues to be considered in the participation debate and we can conclude that a large gulf remains between participation in theory and current practice. This observed contradiction may only be a temporary feature of an NGO community in transition and there is evidence that some organizations are successfully redirecting their approach. What is clear is that NGOs will not achieve a smooth transition to truly participatory development if they remain unsure about the real meaning of the participatory rhetoric.

17. Popular participation in aid-assisted projects: why more in theory than practice?

ROSALIND EYBEN and SARAH LADBURY

The concept of participation in development is far from new. Indeed, it was part of the rhetoric of the New Deal in the 1930s. The recent revived interest, linked to concepts of good governance and democracy, post dates years of low key but significant attempts by development agencies (particularly non-governmental organizations) to enhance beneficiary participation. In the Overseas Development Administration (ODA) also we have been exploring for some time the extent to which popular participation in project activities is feasible and appropriate.[1]

Our primary intention in this paper is to clarify and itemize some of the advantages and disadvantages (to all parties concerned) of collective participation in a development project and to seek to determine whether the nature and extent of participation will be contingent, *inter alia*, on the type of project funded. Many of our examples come from the health sector, including population planning. This is because of previous work one of us has done on this sector and because it became apparent that, compared with other sectors, collective participation around some health services may be particularly problematic. We hope that this chapter will stimulate further enquiry and research.

Our approach – and analytical tools

Rather than discuss the assumed advantages of community (or people's, or popular) participation for beneficiaries, governments or donor agencies we will focus on why there is relatively little participation in aid-assisted or government-funded development projects even, sometimes, when attempts are made to encourage it. Note that we are not assuming that it is simply a case of communities not being given the opportunity to participate by governments and aid agencies. This is undoubtedly a problem in some situations and examples are well documented. But this chapter is interested in what is going on, within communities and within different projects, which makes participation unlikely or difficult.

We use a definition of participation similar to that used by the World Bank's Popular Participation Learning Group (1991) namely a process whereby those with legitimate interests in a project influence decisions which affect them. What sort of decisions? Let us suppose it is a population planning project. Here we might expect participation to mean that

192

potential users of the service get involved in decisions in the following ways. They would be involved in deciding the type of service offered (e.g. a choice of family planning methods); making choices about who delivers it (e.g. women from the community? traditional birth attendants?); when and where it would be delivered (clinic opening hours, outreach visiting times, siting of the clinics) and whether the service would be community-based as against clinic-based. Local residents would be consulted on policy matters such as whether depo provera should be offered, and financing issues such as whether or not provision of contraceptives should be subsidized or free.

Our definition of participation does not distinguish between individual and collective influence on decision-making but all the examples we have given would normally imply some kind of group or majority voice, if the potential users are to be involved in reaching the decision. When we refer to participation there is an assumption of collective action.

Community participation: why doesn't it happen very often?

From the development literature, and our experience, we have identified four main reasons why beneficiary or user populations participate relatively little in development decisions which affect them: economics, politics, professionalism and the nature of the product.

The economic argument for non-participation is that sustained collective action will only be achieved when beneficiaries perceive that the opportunity cost of their participation is more than offset by the returns brought by the project. The benefits, in other words, must be greater than the costs of participating. Whereas an anthropologist might argue that sociality is an innate characteristic of humans, and participation can therefore also be induced by other social and cultural forces,[2] an economist might argue that people will only co-operate in groups when there is an economic pay-off for the individual. We call the latter the rational free choice model. Ignoring social relations and norms it assumes that people will only chose co-operative action when it is inefficient to be non-cooperative. In this view, it is assumed that if agents keep to an agreed assignment of actions, the individual pay-offs will be greater than if they do not co-operate (Kanbur 1992).

Most economics also recognize that 'market forces' are not the only determinant and do not preclude the independent presence of society (Platteau 1991). Development anthropologists would be sympathetic to this latter argument, recognizing that unequal power relations and differential economic and social status will shape the way in which communities will respond to, and become involved in, development projects.

The danger for some aid workers, including some anthropologists, who have not integrated the complex issues of the market, social relations and norms into their analysis of participation, is to go down the road of normative wish-fulfilment giving absolute value to collective action as an end in itself. They would argue that community participation should be desired and is achievable in all projects.

One reason for emphasizing collective action as an end in itself is the use of – and our understanding of – the idea of 'community'. For most people, community is a word which generates good feelings. Unlike other terms of social organization (state, nation) it is rarely used unfavourably. There is an element of nostalgia to the word, symbolized by the concept of the district nurse cycling around the parish. This idealized view of community particip-ation relates back to the division, postulated by nineteenth century econo-mists and sociologists, between 'traditional' (non-market) and 'modern' (market) societies. In 'traditional', pre-market societies people are seen to make collective decisions based on commonly held norms or values. Since such societies were thought to be undifferentiated, it followed that people shared common interests (typified by *gemeinschaft* or community) as dis-tinct from modern social organization characterized by a high degree of individualism, impersonality and self interest (typified by *gesellschaft*). This distinction between the two types of society has, as we know, formed the basis for much of classic development theory. Development implied pro-gress from *gemeinschaft* to *gesellschaft*.

In the world of development practice these classic concepts have become part of the conventional wisdom of the aid profession: community action is linked to the small-scale 'traditional' village society where people are not self-interested individuals nor members of socially differentiated catego-ries. Homogeneity is assumed and along with it a population's structured capacity to co-operate with those designing and implementing a project. In our view this idealized notion of community is a real barrier to understand-ing the dynamics of participation and explaining the circumstances in which participation does, and does not occur.

We argue that there is often a strong individually-based economic ra-tionale for collective action, even in 'small-scale', culturally and econom-ically homogeneous communities. Conversely, there may be possibilities for collective participation, leading to greater project sustainability or effectiveness in a whole gamut of projects where we would not normally look for this. The basis of such participation may, in some circumstances, be what people perceive as commitment to the greater good of the society as a whole.

The political explanation for non-participation is that participation is going to be limited and/or the participators will be unrepresentative if the beneficiaries lack the power to organize and get themselves fairly repres-ented. An alternative way of phrasing this would be that participation of all or some of the beneficiaries may not be in the political interests of other actors in the project.

Does collective action fail because, as Sachs (1987) made clear 'participation is more frustrating than it is advantageous for those who are powerless? In community-based health and population projects women are often the principal agents and beneficiaries, yet collective participation has been difficult to achieve. Poor women receiving contraceptives lack the power and skills to participate in collective decision-making. The existence of participatory channels does not help the situation if these comprise committees of high-status men who themselves use private medical services and who fail to inform, let alone consult with the project's principal clients. In such a case, which is not uncommon, little or no real participation by beneficiaries is possible.

This problem of high status interest groups monopolizing the participatory process is recognized by social development specialists but rarely addressed by development projects. This is because most aid-assisted projects have tended to focus on what Moser (1989) has described as women's practical gender needs, for example, delivery of contraceptives. Project designers may recognize that if strategic needs are not simultaneously addressed then a participatory approach to health care cannot succeed. However, they may be unwilling to address strategic needs in project design because of possible political opposition (Askew 1988).

The approach of donor and lending agencies to participation is therefore somewhat paradoxical. For example, the World Bank's Learning Group on Participation stresses the importance of empowerment which entails sharing power and raising the level of political awareness and strength for disadvantaged people' (Paul 1986:) However, many aid agencies, not least the World Bank, have difficulties with this as an explicit project objective. It is part of the paradox of aid agencies. They exert influence while desiring to build up local self-capacity and participation. In the final analysis they are understandably reluctant to use the final leverage of financial assistance to exert political influence. Because of pressure to speed up implementation, donor agencies may find it difficult to encourage greater consultation with project field staff, let alone to further collective action by beneficiaries.

Participation by (disadvantaged) beneficiaries may be discouraged not only by the more powerful sections in a local community but also by the principal implementing agency, a line ministry for example. This resistance is often due to a concern that existing hierarchical management structures will be challenged. A common occurrence is that, under donor pressure, the implementing agency establishes user groups or village-level committees of project beneficiaries. No feedback is provided for senior management because the local-level, community-based workers are actively discouraged from being themselves involved in project decisions. Health systems, in particular, are traditionally hierarchical structures and there may be few channels for field staff to convey ideas and opinions (rather than just quantitative information) to those above them. Moreover, compared to agricultural or forestry projects where men are employed at all levels, there tends to be a gender division of labour in the health sector with male doctors at the top and women health visitors in the field at the bottom and little dialogue between them.

Even when all those with legitimate interests in a project – funders, managers, workers, beneficiaries – are in favour of beneficiary participation they may have different objectives. In a study on community participation in south Asia for the International Planned Parenthood Federation, Askew (1988) found five different objectives put forward for community participation by actors in the same project. This is not uncommon. To a donor agency, community participation might represent a mechanism for increasing effectiveness and making the input more organizationally sustainable; to project management it might indicate voluntary (cheap) labour; to local women it might be the chance to have a voice for the very first time. While these objectives do not conflict, they do not completely coincide either.

Professionalism is also put forward as a reason for non-participation because the professional training and culture of some sector specialists mitigates against an emphasis on participation. For example, in the health sector, beneficiary participation (or lack of it) could be due to the fact that health professionals have traditionally tended to take a more top-down, authoritarian (doctor knows best) approach to their clients than have most other technical specialists, for example agronomists.

An additional reason why beneficiaries might have little influence over project decisions is that professionals assume the role of identifying beneficiaries' needs and of finding solutions. The greater the assumed knowledge gap between professionals and beneficiaries, the more likely it is that this will happen. Individuals are content to rely on professional judgements in any country, as long as the service is relatively equitably distributed in a way which makes sense to them. Most people in the UK would not expect to be consulted about the width or depth of a mains sewerage pipe put down in the road outside their home; the same goes for similar technical decisions in developing countries. The problem however, is that the line between what people want and need to know and what they don't tends to be drawn by the professionals, not by the general public. The following example illustrates this point.

A health profile of a village will indicate to health professionals (technicians, managers, planners, policy-makers) where priorities lie and which services are likely to improve the health status the poorest. However, while the combination of health services offered in a locality may not be an issue for public debate there may be other issues about which people have a valid opinion and about which they want to be consulted: where the dispensary should be sited, who should be chosen from the village to be health visitors, what additional community development activities are needed etc. It is when participation on these issues is not facilitated and encouraged that professionals and 'professionalism' become a barrier to participation.

The fact that people do not always want to participate, or do not want to participate at the level considered 'right' by outsiders must also be considered. A recent Overseas Development Administration-funded study sought to determine the extent to which community members were prepared to participate in family planning programmes. The conclusion was that while programme managers and staff felt that community members should be involved in the planning and implementation of programme activities, those at the community level felt that these functions were primarily the government's responsibility. They were unwilling to suggest that they themselves should be involved in carrying out specific programme activities and preferred to participate passively and/or through their community leaders. As noted above, participation has an opportunity cost and in this case the benefits of participation were not considered to off-set the costs.

Attempts at organizing collective decision-making or action may exacerbate existing conflicts and structural tension within and between households. One of us evaluated a rural community-based health and water supply project in Sahelian villages which were divided into discrete residential quarters or wards. There was to be only one well and health post per village but the ward leaders insisted that the location of this infrastructure be made by project management perhaps because they feared that any attempts to make the decisions locally would have exacerbated internal divisions. The disinterested professional was the appropriate person to decide.

Lack of community participation in projects can therefore be the result of professionals' assuming the role of knowledgeable specialists who do not take users' views into account because users do not 'know enough' to make decisions. However sometimes users themselves hand over their participatory rights to professionals – thereby saving themselves time, energy and, in some instances, conflict.

The last argument is one which relates to the nature of the product. It can be argued that the degree to which participation can be achieved will depend on the nature of the product (project output), and in particular whether its delivery brings people together in a way that they can, or must, develop common interests. This wholly depends on the type of project; if it is something which benefits individuals, as individuals, rather than as members of communities, then there will be less chance of collective participation. It is clear that the desire to participate is likely to depend on the 'product' offered as much as on the development of channels and structures to make participation a practical possibility.

A World Health Organization report (1988), discussing the implications of the Alma Ata declaration, identifies community participation as one of the five interdependent blocks in district health systems. However, the report makes it clear that for the most part the theory of community involvement in health is far ahead of practice. A rapid desk review of Overseas Development Administration-funded health projects in Asia indicated that there were fewer examples of successful community participation than in sectors such as agriculture, forestry, water supply or slum upgrading. Participation around a productive resource (forests) or community consumption (water supply) may be more welcome than that focused on an individual benefit such as education or health. Even education is delivered to a group of children in a single time and space. Parents can organize themselves around the delivery of this product and may be prepared to contribute to the costs of the teacher's salary. By contrast there is often a marked reluctance in a community to pay the salaries of health workers.

Is this then only a problem for health and population projects? In general, and with the exception of mass campaigns, health services are delivered to individuals as and when they are needed. 'Need' is *ad hoc* and usually, does not involve regular visits or user relationships. Family planning is even more private, more individually-based and it is focused on women. Generally health services can be dispensed and individual needs can be met without conflict between groups of beneficiaries. There is no zero sum game involved. Most of the time health interests are likely to become public only if a new health clinic or other physically located service is to be provided. At that moment participation becomes more likely because the interests of different groups may conflict (as to where it is sited, who provides the labour etc.). Ironically then, it is potential situations of public conflict which give participation is motivational force from the community's point of view. Where the product offered benefits individuals or is likely to benefit all equally, there is much less need to get involved.

Conclusions

The World Bank Learning Group is using a schema measuring the intensity of participation. Their four levels of intensity of participation relate to information sharing, consultation, decision-making and initiating action. The first, information sharing, occurs when information is shared with project beneficiaries about the aims of the project and the way it will affect them. It puts people in the picture and can help facilitate individual and collective action. The second, consultation, means that people are not just informed but consulted on key issues. Local people may provide feedback to project managers who can use this to influence the design and implementation of future phases of the project.

Third, decision-making, occurs when people are involved in decision-making about aspects of projects, including project design and implementation, from the beginning. They are able to influence the present, not just the future. Finally, initiating action takes place when people feel confident enough to propose action and to initiate it themselves. Proposals are community-based, not assigned by outside agencies.

This scheme could seem to imply a preference for 'initiating action', but no such hierarchy is intended. The appropriate level of participation depends on the type of project and the socio-economic environment in which it is being implemented. An aid agency encourages the project authorities to foster beneficiary participation on the grounds of enhancing efficiency, effectiveness and sustainability. This happens because local knowledge contributes to the planning process and there is a greater chance of outputs and objectives being relevant to perceived needs. Participation ensures that officials and contractors are more efficient (and honest) because they are under public scrutiny. It is hoped that community-based organizations will sustain project impact and help maintain services/infrastructure when the official project is over. Sometimes, communities may even decide to contribute to the costs of a project or fund additional activities.

It is clear from our desk review of Overseas Development Administration-funded health and population projects that the presence of certain elements in project design and implementation could contribute to enhancing participation without necessarily requiring an unacceptable level of sustained collective responsibility from the point of view of the clients. The elements we have identified are as follows. Firstly the type and nature of participation needs to be determined during project appraisal and clearly spelt out in the project document. On-going participation of beneficiaries during implementation will require a process approach with regular updating of project outputs. Second, all interested parties – project management and workers, donor agencies, non-governmental organizations, external consultants – need to have a clear understanding of the role of participation in any one project. Third, most users (clients) in any country do not want to influence decisions about issues they know little about. They see this as the legitimate role of professionals. It is therefore necessary to make a clear distinction between issues about which the users will have a valid and useful opinion, and will therefore want to be consulted, and those on which they will not. Distinguishing these is a priority task for a project at the start of implementation and should be identified as a project output.

Fourth, there needs to be communication channels which facilitate participation enabling those with least access to decision-making to be heard. They may want and need to be targeted separately, as well as receive training in communicating. This is likely to encounter resistance within the established power structure with which the project will continue to work. Trade-offs have to be negotiated (Chambers *et al* 1989).

Fifth, project design needs to ensure that approaches developed at the local level, and the experiences gained, are fed back up into regional and national planning and policy. This is because recipient governments and donor agencies often question whether the time and resources put into a locally specific participatory project bring a sufficient return on the investment. Project achievements need to be generalized and lessons learned need to be replicated nationally.

Lastly, the type of product offered to a community will determine the motivation of its members to participate in decisions about it. Better to realize this and not spend time attempting to organize participation at community level where there is no call for it. This does not mean that beneficiaries do not need to be consulted about the type of product offered or mechanisms for its delivery; rather it indicates that more individual methods may be necessary to elicit beneficiary opinion.

Notes

CHAPTER 1

1. Although the views expressed in this chapter are our own, we would like to thank members of the Social Development Department of the Overseas Development Administration for sharing their current thinking with us on a number of occasions, as they formulate their approach to and procedures for participatory development. We are grateful to Judith Turbyne for generously letting us see draft chapters of her thesis on empowerment and to Maitrayee Mukhopadhyay for sharing her understanding of trends in development. We thank Janice Baker, Robert Chambers and Emma Crewe for very helpful comments on an earlier draft.
2. One direct link is that 'Stakeholder' was introduced from 'new management' into World Bank thinking by the 1993 Wappenhans report on portfolio management.

CHAPTER 2

1. I thank Susan Wright, Olga Nieuwenhuys and Karin Willemse for their stimulating comments and criticism to an earlier draft of this chapter.
2. Although de Josselin de Jong (1977) turned 'the people in the field' into active subjects, he did not explicitly problematize the power relations reproduced and constructed during the research. Thus the 'anthropological gaze' (Marcus 1992) remained focused onto 'the other', and the researcher continued to be the invisible producer of knowledge.
3. In Sri Lanka, the Muslims, or Moors, see themselves as a distinct ethnic community, and are classified accordingly.
4. I worked together with research assistants who asked me not to mention their names, and to whom I am deeply grateful.
5. They belonged to the University Teachers for Human Rights. By regularly bringing out their reports these activists are under constant threat from both sides. Dr. Rajini Thiranagama, a woman activist and one of the founders, was killed in Jaffna on 21 September 1989.
6. Inspired by the protesting group on the street refugees in another camp suceeded in postponing the date of closure at least until after the school exams. In mid 1994 their camp was still there.

CHAPTER 4

1. This account is based on the early years of Mass-Observation. It should be noted that in its revived form from 1981 onwards, Mass-Observation only consists of participatory observers who respond to directives and keep diaries.

CHAPTER 5

1. The *ONI-yô* was the traditional marriage dance of the Bobo. The *ONI* is the gourd harp (kora) on the bell of which the drummer taps his rhythm, while the player calls out his words of guidance for the newlyweds. The player should be

an initiate, and they are few these days. Christian missionaries campaigned actively against the use of sacrificial *ONI* and the *ONI-yô* (a men's dance) has now almost disappeared in favour of the imported balafon (xylophone) dance-music. The balafon musicians, who are *griots*, have to be paid and this is taxing the farmers' families, although providing vital income for the *griots* themselves.

2. The Forestry Department in particular imposed fines for unlicensed cutting of trees, even on the villagers' own land, and other contraventions of forestry regulations. The whole community was responsible for these sometimes extortionate fines, from which the officer took a percentage commission.

3. In March 1991, the unpopular 23 year old regime of Moussa Traoré was finally toppled. Even before the coup, there were signs (demonstrations, burgeoning critical press) that the President's hour had come. In this climate, some officials welcomed an opportunity to show that they were on the side of the people. However, when the Embere'ui performers were rehearsing their play about the forestry service we briefed the project management who asked us to prevent its performance as it was considered dangerously contentious. In the event, the play went ahead with the sequel described but the incident was a reminder of unspoken limits to the Drama Unit's mandate to promote open communication.

4. The Drama Unit consisted initially of an expatriate theatre worker (Alex Mavrocordatos), later joined by a national counterpart. Bianivo Munkoro took over management of the Drama Unit after two years, later supported by Zoumba Dabou, himself of griot extraction. Both men originally came from villages around the project area.

Most of the material used in this paper is drawn from the first two and a half years of the Drama Unit's work, in the absence of detailed material for the later period. The Drama Unit's status in relation to the main project remained ambiguous. The Drama Unit was to be merged structurally into the main project. The longest serving theatre animator, Bianivo Munkoro, has left to pursue further studies in Europe.

SOS Sahel can be contacted at: 1 Tolpuddle Street, London N1 0XT.

CHAPTER 8

1. Thanks are due to the British Economic and Social Research Council for funding both pilot and main projects, and to both the Colegio de Michoacán, Mexico, and the University of Durham, England, for generous support with facilities. We are deeply grateful to the communities and municipal authorities, and above all to the pioneer women who contributed so unstintingly.

2. Shortly after our fieldwork, the Mexican Constitution was changed to make it possible for *ejido* land to be privatized by agreement of the members. The future of the Women's Units remains unclear in 1994.

CHAPTER 9

1. IRES-Piemonte was closely linked to the local authorities. During this period, a sociologist from IRES-Piemonte attended the meetings as an observer, and afterwards edited the research report for publication. He later took part in the other IRES-Piemonte research project on the attitudes of Piemontese towards the new immigration.

2. Being British did not, in the eyes of the group, make me an immigrant, though British and European citizens in Italy, especially women, may have some of the

same experiences as non-European immigrants. French and British residents are more numerous than any non-European group in Turin.
3. When the research eventually passed under the aegis of IRES-Piemonte, who also financed it, the formal and financial structure of the group took on an hierarchical aspect. There were three 'scientific advisers' – myself, F, and the Rwandan 'professor' – who were paid an annual sum, while the research workers were paid on a piece-work basis according to the life-histories they produced. F's payment went to the trade union body which hosted our meetings. My 'salary' was entirely redistributed among the research workers, after deductions for tax purposes. Since I was already salaried as a lecturer at the University, I felt this gesture to be necessary for the sake of coherence, but I was also anxious for the research to go ahead and for the research workers to feel able to give it more time.
4. This position has been made explicit by Arab intellectuals such as Mohamed Shakhr as recently as 1987. 'Whatever culture is, it is, he thinks, embodied in language; it cannot be acquired. He calls it inborn, though a little later he says that it is properly acquired in childhood . . . so to talk about or in Arabic effectively you must be an Arab, and to talk about Islam you must be a Muslim', (Daniels, 1990: 17). Eickelman (1989), in contrast, quoting Moroccan historians and anthropologists, points out that the idea that scholars of certain countries or religions are particularly capable or should even have the monopoly of dealing with specific subjects seems to have fallen out of favour.
5. Especially Mitchell (1969; 1987), Van Velsen (1967), Cohen (1974), Mayer (1962) and Eades (1987).
6. This concept is drawn from Turner (1968; 1969).

CHAPTER 10

1. The observations upon which this paper is based were made during consultancy and training visits to Nigeria in 1991/2 with field study in Kano, Katsina and Kaduna States, as part of the Development Administration Group (University of Birmingham)/ Institute of Administration (Ahmadu Bello University) project on in-service training for Local Government, which is funded by the British Government, Overseas Development Administration.

CHAPTER 11

1. The Forest Department does not have the authority to prepare forest management plans and carry out silvicultural operations.
2. At this time the village panchayats were the focal point of community forestry activities. Although forests are now handed over to user groups the programme is still referred to officially as the Community Forest Programme.
3. Community Forestry Management Workshop: attended by professional foresters, policy makers and aid agencies.
4. Master Plan for the Forestry Sector Nepal, Interim Legislation on User-Groups and Operational Guidelines for the Community Forestry Programme (HMG 1990)
5. Few aid projects have real expertise in participatory learning methods; District Forestry Officers' requests for 'start-up' workshops are often not met.
6. Changing bureaucratic structures, practices and value systems may be particularly difficult in Nepal, as a recent analysis entitled *Fatalism and Development* has shown (Bista 1991).

7. The description of user-group organization that follows is based on the official Forestry Department guidelines for the hand-over of community forests (HMG 1991).
8. Indigenous Forest Management systems are 'rubber stamped' without careful appraisal for a number of reasons: it is a speedy short-cut method to handing over forests; project over-enthusiasm for anything indigenous; systems are assessed only on their ability to prevent environmental degradation/avert a Tragedy of the Commons scenario; ignorance within the expatriate community of the social structure of hill communities (often essentially feudal, based on control of forest and other lands).
9. Interest groups are not always defined by caste. Divisions can also be along administrative, political and occasionally gender lines. Often, however, interest groups have a socio-economic base determined by the caste system; for example, membership of charcoal burning and cattle grazing groups respectively.
10. Technically the Forest Department does not have the authority to intervene and the matter should be referred to the civil courts.

CHAPTER 12

1. The project work was expected to be undertaken in addition to standard workloads.
2. The difference between a care planner and a care manager is that the latter has access to a budget for the purchase of services.

CHAPTER 13

1. This is a much abbreviated version of an earlier paper, 'Community management and the rehabilitation of tank irrigation systems in Tamil Nadu: a research agenda' (Mosse 1994a). My interest in this subject arises from field and archival research carried out in a tank-irrigated area of southeastern Tamil Nadu between 1982 and 1984, and from the experience of developing participatory strategies for tank rehabilitation when working as Oxfam Representative in south India (1987–91). Further fieldwork and the writing of this paper have been supported by a Fellowship from the Economic and Social Research Council (L320273065) under the Global Environmental Change Programme, and with a grant from the Ford Foundation (New Delhi). I am grateful to the Centre for Water Resources (Anna University, Madras) for support in this and subsequent research, and to Nici Nelson for editorial work on earlier drafts. I remain solely responsible for the analysis provided and for any errors of fact or interpretation.
2. The historical perspective derives from work in progress in the southern districts of Tamil Nadu, in particular the former Zamindari estates of Sivagangai and Ramnathapuram.
3. It is not possible to summarize these complex changes here. For further detail see Mosse 1994a and forthcoming.
4. The way in which 'colonial sociology' invented other village-level institutions (e.g. the 'jajmani system') and the autonomous village republics of 'traditional India' more generally is the subject of several recent analyses (Dirks 1987; Fuller 1989; Mayer 1993; Ludden 1993; Mosse, forthcoming).
5. This contrasts with the system described by Leach (1961) which ensured a more or less equitable distribution of water to all landholders during times of scarcity (cf. Abeyratne 1990). Harriss reports a similar situation in a South Arcot village (1982: 126–30).

204

6. Two Institutional Organisers, two Technical Assistants and one Process Documentor.
7. For an account of the implementation of tank development work through the Nallaneri Society, based on detailed process documentation within the project and fieldwork undertaken after writing this paper, see Mosse forthcoming.
8. In fact, recent events in the village (1991–3) illustrate both these tendencies: on the one hand, Harijans withdrew labour from collective tank works or insisted on bargaining wages – in both cases rejecting inclusion in the 'moral economy' of the Mudaliar dominated Society; on the other hand, through land sales, Mudaliars began withdrawing from wet-land cultivation, shifting economic interests to nearby urban areas (Mosse forthcoming).
9. The recent experience of Nallaneri tank society illustrates precisely this scenario. The result was factional conflict and litigation which halted all project work for one and a half years (see Mosse, forthcoming).
10. The use of missionary support by low caste converts in south India to translate social gains obtained through conversion and expressed within the church to more widely acknowledged improvements in caste status provide examples of this (cf. Mosse 1994b).
11. Similarly, much is at stake in the public articulation of 'community' needs and priorities through increasingly popular methods of rapid and participatory appraisal and planning (Mosse 1994c).

CHAPTER 15

1. I am grateful to Harvest Help in London for supplying me with documents and for the comments on draft versions given by Dr Jock Stirrat, Ms Jackie Lane and Dr James Copestake.
2. See Chambers (1983 chapters 2 and 3) on the concept and description of rural development 'outsiders'. In this context it would include both GVAM and Harvest Help as both are from outside the local Tonga community.
3. My first contacts with Harvest Help/GVAM were in 1989 when I had applied to work for the project in Zambia. Although this post did not materialize, I kept contact with Harvest Help and they kindly allowed me to examine their files to produce this paper. The paper also benefited from detailed discussions with Dr James Copestake, erstwhile project officer in Zambia (1990–1) and currently a trustee for Harvest Help.
4. GVAM's name has since changed to 'Harvest Help/Zambia'. I will use the old designation, GVAM, to ease distinction between it and its English fund-raising counterpart: Harvest Help. Further, this study of GVAM pre-dates the name change. GVAM is a small NGO of Zambian origin, linked to Quaker Peace and Service.
5. On traditional Tonga lifestyle and culture prior to resettlement, see Scudder (1962 and 1971), Colson (1960). On the effects of resettlement on Tonga lifestyle, see Colson (1971).
6. This has been drawn principally from Uphoff, in Cernea (1985); Cohen and Uphoff (1980); Oakley and Marsden (1984); Oakley et al. (1991); Gezelius and Millwood (1988); with reference to Chambers (1983), Hedenquist (1989) and Topsoe-Jensen (1989).
7. See Topsoe-Jensen (1989) for the need for and approaches to meaningful participation in monitoring and evaluation. See Huizer (1989) on the need also for 'participatory action research'.

8. Indeed, especially powerful vapour lamps, powered by expensive generators, would increasingly have to be used on the cloudy waters of Kariba. See Ramberg *et al.* (1987: 320–1).
9. However, the co-operatives were adapted by their Tonga members to fit in with their own values i.e. they were based far more on the traditional mix of values of self-help/mutual aid than the western concept – with its socialist connotations – suggests. Traditional forms of participation can therefore survive in spite of an agency's top-down interventions.
10. Dr. Copestake has informed me that GVAM is now contracting out the rigs to a private company solely as an income generating activity for the NGO. This change was due to a combination of the following reasons: it was absorbing too much management time from GVAM staff; the overall macro-economic crisis in Zambia meant that the demand for kapenta collapsed in Lusaka; and after two years of negotiations between GVAM and Tonga village committees on how to transfer the business to co-operatives, Tonga communities decided themselves that the operation would be too difficult for them to manage. The aim of the fishery has reverted to a simple revenue-raising venture for the NGO.

CHAPTER 16

1. It should be noted however that many African NGOs have top-down, bureaucratic structures, so devolving power to local NGOs will not necessarily ensure participation of people at the grass-roots level.

CHAPTER 17

1. The present paper was written as a contribution to the GAPP Conference on Participatory Development (July, 1992) and solely represents the authors' personal views, not the official policy of the ODA.
2. See for example Mary Douglas's argument in *How Institutions Think* (1987) and compare this with the 'prisoner's dilemma' in which it is assumed that in many situations there will be a divergence between individual and collective rationality i.e. what is optimally good for the individual will be bad for the collectivity and vice-versa.

References

CHAPTER 1

Bachrach, P. and Baratz, M. (1970) *Power and Poverty. Theory and Practice*, Oxford: Oxford University Press.

Bryson, J. (1981) 'Women and agriculture in Sub-Saharan Africa: implications for development' in N. Nelson (ed.) *African Women in the Development Process*, London: Frank Cass.

Cernea, M. (1992) *The Building Blocks of Participation: Testing Bottom-up Planning*, World Bank Discussion Papers, no. 166, Washington: World Bank.

Chambers, R. (1984) 'Reflections on challenges and priority actions', presented to the World Bank Workshop on Participatory Development', unpublished, Washington, May.

Cornia, G., Jolly, R. and Stewart, F (eds) (1989) *Adjustment with a Human Face, a study for UNICEF*, Oxford: Clarendon Press.

Dahl, R. (1961) *Who Governs? Democracy and Power in an American City*, New Haven: Yale University Press.

Escobar, A. (1988) 'Power and visibility: development and the invention and management of the Third World, *Cultural Anthropology* vol. 3 pp. 428–443.

Fals Borda, O. (1988) *Knowledge and People's Power*, New Delhi: Indian Social Institute.

Ferguson, J. (1990) *The Anti-Politics Machine*, Cambridge: Cambridge University Press.

Fleming, S. (1993) 'Reconciling anthropologists' knowledge, policy and practice', *Anthropology in Action* no. 16 pp. 4–5.

Freire, P. (1972) *Pedagogy of the Oppressed*, Harmondsworth: Penguin.

Giddens, A. (1984) *The Constitution of Society*, Cambridge: Polity Press.

GTZ (1991) *Where There is No Participation*, Eschborn: Deutsche Gessellschaft fur Technische Zusammenarbeit.

Hancock, G. (1992) *Lords of Poverty*, London: Mandarin.

Hartsock, N. (1984) *Money, Sex, and Power: Toward a Feminist Historical Materialsm*, New York: Longman.

Hartsock, N. (1990) 'Foucault on power: a theory for women?' pp.157–175 in L. Nicholson (ed.) *Feminism/Postmodernism*, London and New York: Routledge.

Hymes, D. (1972) 'The use of anthropology: critical, political, personal' in D. Hymes (ed.) *Reinventing Anthropology*, New York: Random House.

Kieffer, C. H. (1984) 'Citizen empowerment, a developmental perspective', *Prevention in the Human Services* vol. 3 pp. 9–36.

Kochendörfer-Lucius, G. and Osner, K. (1991) *Development Has Got a Human Face*, Bonn: German Commission for Justice and Peace.

Lukes, S. (1974) *Power. A Radical View*, London and Basingstoke: Macmillan Press.

Lumb, R. (1980) 'Communicating with bureaucracy: the effects of perception on public participation in planning' pp.105–118 in R. Grillo (ed.) *'Nation' and 'State' in Europe*, London: Academic Press.

Marsden, D. and Oakley, P. (eds) (1990) *Evaluating Social Development Projects*, Oxford: Oxfam.

Moser, C. (1989) 'Gender planning in the Third World: meeting practical and strategic gender needs', *World Development* vol. 17 (11) pp. 1799–1825.

Nader, L. (1980) 'The vertical slice: hierarchies and children' pp. 31–44 in G. M. Brittan and R. Cohen (eds) *Hierarchy and Society*, Philadelphia: Institute for the Study of Human Issues.

Oakley, P. *et al* (1991) *Projects with People*, Geneva: International Labour Office.

ODA (1993) *Social Development Handbook*, London: Overseas Development Administration.

Organisation for Economic Co-operation and Development (1991) *Development Assistance Committee Chairman's Report*, Paris: OECD.

Parry, G. (ed.) (1972) *Participation in Politics*, Manchester: Manchester University Press.

Polsby, N. (1963) *Community Power and Political Theory*, New Haven: Yale University Press.

Rahnema, M. (1992) 'Participation', in W. Sachs (ed.) *The Developnment Dictionary*, London: Zed Press.

Rowlands, J. (1992) 'What is empowerment? The challenge of researching "Women, Empowerment and Development in Honduras" ', unpublished paper given to GAPP conference on Participatory Development, Goldsmiths' College London, July.

Skeffington, A. (1969) *People and Planning*, London: HMSO.

Turbyne, J. (1984) 'Participatory research into participatory development practice', paper to Anthropology in Action workshop on 'Participation in Social Development: Current Perceptions and Future Directions', Development Planning Unit, London, July.

Turbyne, J. (forthcoming) 'The enigma of empowerment: reflections on empowerment in Guatemalan development interventions' Ph.D. thesis, University of Bath.

United Nations Economic Commission for Africa (1990) *African Charter for Popular Participation in Development and Transformation*, Arusha.

Williams, R. (1976) *Keywords*, London: Fontana.

World Bank (1994) 'The World Bank and participation, fourth draft', Washington: World Bank.

Wright, S. (1990) 'Development theory and community development practice' pp. 41–64 in H. Buller and S. Wright (eds) *Rural Development: Problems and Practices*, Aldershot: Avebury.

Wright, S. (1994) 'Culture in anthropology and organizational studies' pp. 1–31 in S. Wright (ed.) *Anthropology of Organizations*, London: Routledge.

CHAPTER 2

Bell, D., Caplan, P. and Jahan Karim, W. (1993) *Gendered Fields. Women, Men and Ethnography*, London/ New York: Routledge.

Bowles, G. and Duelli Klein, R. (1983) *Theories of Women's Studies*, London/ Boston/Melbourne/Henley: Routledge and Kegan Paul.

Caplan, P. (1988) 'Engendering knowledge', *Anthropology Today* vol. 4 (5) pp. 8–12; vol. 4 (6) pp. 14–17.

Clifford, J. and Marcus, G. E. (1986) *Writing Culture: The Poetics and Politics of Ethnography*, Berkeley: University of California Press.

Gandhi, N. and Shah, N. (1992) *The Issues at Stake: Theory and Practice in the Contemporary Women's Movement in India*, New Delhi: Kali for Women.

Golde, P. (ed.) (1970) *Women in the Field. Anthropological Experiences*, Chicago: Aldine (1986 second enlarged and revised edition, Berkeley: University of California Press).

Haraway, D. (1990) *Simians, Cyborgs and Women*, London: Free Association Books.

Harding, S. (1987) 'Introduction: is there a feminist method?' in S. Harding (ed.) *Feminism and Methodology*, Bloomington/ Indianapolis: Indiana University Press.

Harding, S. (1992) 'Subjectivity, experience and knowledge: an epistemology from/ for rainbow coalition politics', *Development and Change* vol. 23 (3) pp. 175–93.

Hartsock, N. (1987) 'Rethinking modernism', *Cultural Critique* vol. 7 pp. 187–206.

Huizer, G. (1979) 'Anthropology and politics: from naiveté toward liberation?' in G. Huizer and B. Mannheim (ed.) *The Politics of Anthropology*, The Hague/ Paris: Mouton Publishers.

Hull, G., Bell Scott, P. and Smith, B. (1982) *But Some of Us Are Brave*, Old Westbury, N.Y.: The Feminist Press.

Jaquette, J. (ed.) (1989) *The Women's Movement in Latin America. Feminism and the Transition to Democracy*, London: Unwin Hyman.

Jayawardena, K. (1986) *Feminism and Nationalism in the Third World*, London: Zed Books/ New Delhi: Kali for Women.

Josselin de Jong, P. E. de (1977) 'The participants' view of their culture' in P. E. de Josselin de Jong (ed.) *Structural Anthropology in the Netherlands: Creature of Circumstance*, The Hague: Martinus Nijhoff.

Khasiani, S. A. (ed.) (1992) *Groundwork. African Women as Environmental Managers*, Nairobi: ACTS Press.

Marcus, J. (1992) 'Racism, terror and the production of Australian auto/ biographies' in J. Okely and H. Callaway (eds) *Anthropology and Autobiography*, London/ New York: Routledge.

Mascia-Lees, F., Sharpe, P. and Ballerino Cohen, C. (1989) 'The postmodernist turn in anthropology: cautions from a feminist perspective', *Signs: Journal of Women in Culture and Society* vol. 15 (1) pp. 7–33.

Mies, M. (1977) 'Methodische Postulate zur Frauenforschung' (Methodological Postulates for Women's Research), *Heksencollege: Verslagboek over Vrouwen, Wetenschap en Cultuur* vol. 1, Nijmegen.

Mies, M. (1983) 'Towards a methodology for feminist research' in G. Bowles and R. Duelli Klein (eds) *Theories of Women's Studies*, London: Routledge and Kegan Paul.

Mies, M. and Reddock, R. (eds) (1982) *National Liberation and Women's Liberation*, The Hague: Institute of Social Studies.

Mohanty, C. (1988) 'Under Western eyes: feminist scholarship and colonial discourses', *Feminist Review*, vol. 30 pp. 61–89. Reprinted and modified in C. Mohanty *et al.* (eds) (1991) *Third World Women and the Politics of Feminism*, Bloomington and Indianapolis: Indiana University Press.

Mohanty, C. (1991) 'Cartographies of struggle: Third World women and the politics of feminism' in C. Mohanty, A. Russo and L. Torres (eds) *Third World Women and the Politics of Feminism*, Bloomington and Indianapolis: Indiana University Press.

Mohanty, C., Russo, A. and Torres, L. (1991) *Third World Women and the Politics of Feminism*, Bloomington and Indianapolis: Indiana University Press.

Nencel, L. and Pels, P. (eds) (1991) *Constructing Knowledge. Authority and Critique in Social Science*, London/ Newbury Park/ New Delhi: Sage Publications.

Okely, J. (1992) 'Anthropology and autobiography: participatory experience and embodied knowledge' in J. Okely and H. Callaway (eds) *Anthropology and Autobiography*, London: Routledge.

Rohrlich-Leavitt, R., Sykes, B. and Weatherford, E. (1975) 'Aboriginal woman: male and female anthropological perspectives' in R. Rohrlich-Leavitt (ed.) *Women Cross-Culturally: Change and Challenge*, The Hague: Mouton.

Said, E. (1989) 'Representing the colonized: anthropology's interlocutors', *Critical Inquiry* vol. 15 pp. 205–25.

Schrijvers, J. (1979) 'Viricentrism and anthropology' in G. Huizer and B. Mannheim (ed.) *The Politics of Anthropology*, The Hague: Mouton.

Schrijvers, J. (1985) *Mothers for Life. Motherhood and Marginalization in the North Central Province of Sri Lanka*, Delft: EBURON.

Schrijvers, J. (1987) *Transformation in Feminist Perspective: Towards a New Epistemology*, Leiden: University of Leiden, Institute of Cultural and Social studies, Working Paper no. 76.

Schrijvers, J. (1991) 'Dialectics of a dialogical ideal; studying down, studying sideways and studying up' in L. Nencel and P. Pels (eds) *Constructing Knowledge: Authority and Critique in Social Science*, London/ Newbury Park/ New Delhi: Sage Publications.

Schrijvers, J. (1993) *The Violence of Development. A Choice for Intellectuals*, Utrecht: International Books/ New Delhi: Kali for Women.

Schrijvers, J. (1994) 'Towards increased autonomy? Peasant women's work in the North Central Province of Sri Lanka' in D. Bagchi and S. Raju (eds) *Women and Work in South Asia*, London: Routledge.

Sen, G. and Grown, C. (for DAWN, Development Alternatives with Women for a New Era) (1988) *Development, Crises and Alternative Visions. Third World Women's Perspectives*, London: Earthscan.

Shallat, L. (1990) 'Take back the earth: women, health and the environment', *Women's Health Journal* vol. 20, pp. 29–52. Latin American and Caribbean Women's Health Network, Chile.

Stacey, J. (1988) 'Can there be a feminist ethnography?', *Women's Studies International Forum* vol. 11 (1) pp. 21–27.

Steady, F. C. (ed.) (1981) *The Black Woman Cross-Culturally*, Cambridge (Mass.): Schenkmann Publishing Co.

Torres, G. (1992) 'Plunging into the garlic. Methodological issues' in N. and A. Long (eds) *Battlefields of Knowledge*, London/ New York: Routledge.

Watkins, B. (1983) 'Feminism: a last chance for the humanities?' in G. Bowles and R. Duelli Klein (eds) *Theories of Women's Studies*, London/ Boston/ Melbourne and Henley: Routledge and Kegan Paul.

Warren, C. A. B. (1988) *Gender Issues in Field Research*, Newbury Park, California: Sage Publications.

Wertheim, W. (1964) 'Society as a composite of conflicting value systems' in W. F. Wertheim *East-West Parallels; Sociological Approaches to Modern Asia*, The Hague: W. van Hoeve Ltd.

Whitehead, T. L. and Conaway, M. E. (eds) (1986) *Self, Sex and Gender in Cross-Cultural Fieldwork*, Urbana: University of Illinois Press.

CHAPTER 3

Agricultural Administration (1981) vol. 8 no. 6, Special Issue on Rapid Rural Appraisal.

Amanor, K. (1989) 'Abstracts on farmer participatory research', *Agricultural Administration (R&E) Network Paper* no. 5, London: Overseas Development Institute.

Bagadion, B. U. and Korten, F. F. (1991) 'Developing irrigators' organizations; a learning process approach' in M. M. Cernea (ed.) *Putting People First*, Oxford: Oxford University Press, 2nd Edition.

Burkey, S. (1993) *People First: a Guide to Self-Reliant Participatory Rural Development*, London: Zed Books Ltd.

Cernea, M. (ed.) (1991) *Putting People First: Sociological Variables in Rural Development* (second edition, first edition 1985), Oxford University Press for the World Bank.

Chambers, R. (1992a) 'The self-deceiving state', *IDS Bulletin* vol. 23 no. 4 pp. 31–42.

Chambers, R. (1992b) 'Rural appraisal: rapid, relaxed and participatory', *Discussion Paper* no. 311, Brighton: Institute of Development Studies.

Chambers, R. (1993) *Challenging the Professions: Frontiers for Rural Development*, London: Intermediate Technology Publications.

Chambers, R. (1994) 'All power deceives', *IDS Bulletin*, Vol. 25 no. 2 pp. 14–26.

Chambers, R., Pacey, A. and Thrupp, L. (1989) *Farmer First: Farmer Innovation and Agricultural Research*, London: Intermediate Technology Publications.

Conway, G. (1985) 'Agroecosystem analysis', *Agricultural Administration* vol. 20 pp. 31–55.

Cornwall, A., Guijt, I. and Welbourn, A. (1993) 'Acknowledging process: challenges for agricultural research and extension methodology', *Discussion Paper* no. 333, Brighton: Institute of Development Studies.

Farrington, J. and Martin, A. (1988) 'Farmer participation in agricultural research: a review of concepts and practices', *Agricultural Administration Occasional Paper* no. 9, London: Overseas Development Institute.

Farrington, J. and Bebbington, A. with Wellard, K. and Lewis, D. J. (1993) *Reluctant Partners? Non-Governmental Organizations, the State and Sustainable Agricultural Development*, London and New York: Routledge.

Fernandez, A. P. (1993) *The MYRADA Experience: the Interventions of a Voluntary Agency in the Emergence and Growth of People's Institutions for Sustained and Equitable Management of Micro-Watersheds*, MYRADA, No 2 Service Road, Domlur Layout, Bangalore 560 071, India, July.

FSSP (1987) *Diagnosis, Design and Analysis in Farming Systems Research and Extension, Volumes I, II and III, and Trainer's Manual*, Farming Systems Support Project, Institute of Food and Agricultural Sciences, University of Florida, Gainesville, Florida 32611, December.

Gilbert, E. H., Norman, W. and Winch, F. E. (1980) 'Farming Systems Research: a critical appraisal', *MSU Rural Development Paper no. 6*, Department of Agricultural Economics, Michigan State University, East Lansing, Michigan 48824.

ILEIA (1985 – present), *ILEIA Newsletter*, Information Centre for Low External Input and Sustainable Agriculture, Leusden, Netherlands.

KGVK (1991) *Management Training Manual*, Krishi Gram Vikas Kendra, Ranchi, Bihar, India.

KKU (1987) *Proceedings of the 1985 International Conference on Rapid Rural Appraisal*, Rural Systems Research and Farming Systems Research Projects, University of Khon Kaen, Thailand.

Longhurst, R. (ed.) (1981) 'Rapid Rural Appraisal', *IDS Bulletin*, vol. 12 no. 4.

Mascarenhas, J., Shah, P., Joseph, S., Devavaram, J., Jayakaran, R., Ramachandran, V., Fernandez, A., Chambers, R. and Pretty, J. (ed.) (1991) *Participatory Rural*

211

Appraisal: Proceedings of the February 1991 Bangalore PRA Trainers' Workshop, RRA Notes 13, IIED, London and MYRADA, Bangalore.

Mosse, D. (1993) 'Authority, gender and knowledge: theoretical reflections on the practice of participatory rural appraisal', *Agricultural Administration (Research and Extension) Network Paper* no. 44, London: Overseas Development Institute.

Poffenberger, M., McGean, B., Ravindarnath, N. H. and Gadgil, M. (eds.) (1992a) *Joint Forest Management Field Methods Manual Volume 1 Diagnostic Tools for Supporting Joint Forest Management Systems,* Society for the Promotion of Wastelands Development, 1 Copernicus Marg, New Delhi 110001.

Poffenberger, M., McGean, B., Khare, A. and Campbell, J. (ed.) (1992b) *Joint Forest Management Field Methods Manual Volume 2 Community Forest Economy and Use Patterns: Participatory Rural Appraisal (PRA) Methods in South Gujarat, India,* Society for the Promotion of Wastelands Development, 1 Copernicus Marg, New Delhi 110001.

Rhoades, R. (1982) *The Art of the Informal Agricultural Survey,* International Potato Center, Apartado 5969, Lima.

Scoones, I. and Thompson, J. (eds.) (1994) *Beyond Farmer First: Rural People's Knowledge, Agricultural Research and Extension Practice,* London: Intermediate Technology Publications.

Shah, P. (1993) 'Participatory Watershed Management Programmes in India: reversing our roles and revising our theories', *Rural People's Knowledge, Agricultural Research and Extension Practice, IIED Research Series* vol. 1 no. 3 pp. 38–67 London: International Institute for Environment and Development.

Shaner, W. W., Philipp, P. F. and Schmehl, W. R. (1982) *Farming Systems Research and Development: Guidelines for Developing Countries,* Boulder, Colorado: Westview Press.

Uphoff, N. (1992) *Learning from Gal Oya: Possibilities for Participatory Development and Post-Newtonian Social Science,* Ithaca: Cornell University Press.

Welbourn, A. (1991) 'RRA and the analysis of difference', *RRA Notes* vol. 14 pp. 14–23, London: International Institute for Environment and Development.

CHAPTER 4

Asad, T. (1973) *Anthropology and the Colonial Encounter,* London: Ithaca Press.

Boas, F. (1943) 'Recent anthropology', *Science* vol. 98 pp. 311–4; 334–7.

Caesara, M. (1982) *No Hiding Place. Reflections of a Woman Anthropologist,* London: Academic Press.

Cameron, D., Frazer, E., Harvey, P., Rampton, M. B. H., and Richardson, K. (1992) *Researching Language. Issues of Power and Method,* London: Routledge.

Chambers, R. (1983) *Rural Development. Putting the Last First,* London: Longman.

Chambers, R. (1992) 'Rural Appraisal: Rapid, Relaxed and Participatory', Institute of Development Studies Discussion Paper No. 311, Brighton, University of Sussex.

Cornwall, A. (1992) 'Tools for our trade? rapid or participatory rural appraisal and anthropology' *Anthropology in Action* no. 13 pp. 12–14.

Crapanzano, V. (1980) *Tuhami. Portrait of a Moroccan,* Chicago: University of Chicago Press.

Cresswell, T. (1992) 'Participatory Rapid Appraisal. An Investigation into the Health and Social Needs of People Living in Danesmoor,' Health Promotion Service. Chesterfield: North Derbyshire Health Authority.

Dumond, L. (1978) *The Headman and I,* Austin: University of Texas Press.

Dwyer, K. (1977) 'On the dialogue of fieldwork', *Dialectical Anthropology* vol. 2 pp. 143–151.

Dwyer, K. (1979) 'The dialogic of fieldwork', *Dialectical Anthropology* vol. 4 (3) pp. 205–24.

Fabian, J. (1983) *Time and the Other: How Anthropology Makes its Object*, New York: Columbia University Press.

Fals Borda, O. (1988) *Knowledge and People's Power*, New Delhi: Indian Social Institute.

Firth, R. (1939) 'An anthropologist's view of Mass-Observation', *Sociological Review* vol. 31 pp. 166–193.

Freire, P. (1972) *Pedagogy of the Oppressed*, Harmondsworth: Penguin.

Gaventa, J. (1980) *Power and Powerlessness. Quiescence and Rebellion in an Appalachian Valley*, Oxford: Clarendon.

Gedicks, A. (1979) 'Research from within and from below: reversing the machinery' pp. 461–480 in G. Huizer and B. Mannheim (eds) *The Politics of Anthropology*, The Hague: Mouton.

Gough, K. (1968) 'New proposals for anthropologists', *Current Anthropology* vol. 9 pp. 403–7.

Hall, B., Gillette, A. and Tandon, R. (eds) (1982) *Creating Knowledge: a Monopoly? Participatory Research in Development*, New Delhi: Society for Participatory Research in Asia.

Harrisson, T. (1937) 'Mass-Observation and the WEA', *The Highway* December, pp. 46–48.

Hobart, M. (ed.) (1993) 'Introduction: the growth of ignorance' pp. 1–30 in *An Anthropological Critique of Development. The Growth of Ignorance*, London: Routledge.

hooks, b. (1982) *Ain't I a Woman? Black Women and Feminism*, London: Pluto Press.

Huizer, G. (1979a) 'Anthropology and politics: from naivete toward liberation?', pp. 3–44 in G. Huizer and B. Mannheim (eds) *The Politics of Anthropology*, The Hague: Mouton.

Huizer, G. (1979b) 'Research through action: some practical experiences with peasant organization', pp. 395–420 in G. Huizer and B. Mannheim (eds) *The Politics of Anthropology*, The Hague: Mouton.

Jennings, H. and Madge, C. (eds) (1937) *May 12th: Mass-Observation Day Surveys*, London: Faber and Faber.

Jennings, H. (1985) *Pandaemonium*, London: Picador.

Kassam, Y. and Mustafa, K. (eds) (1982) *Participatory Research. An Emerging Alternative Methodology in Social Science Research*, New Delhi: Society for Participatory Research in Asia.

Kuper, A. (1983) *Anthropology and Anthropologists*, London: Routledge and Kegan Paul.

Lederman, R. (1986) 'The return of redwoman: fieldwork in Highland New Guinea', pp. 359–388 in P. Golde (ed.) *Women in the Field*, Berkeley: University of California Press.

Maguire, P. (1987) *Doing Participatory Research: A Feminist Approach*, Amherst, Mass.: Center for International Education.

Malinowski, B. (1922) *Argonauts of the Western Pacific*, London: Routledge.

Malinowski, B. (1938) 'A nation-wide intelligence service' pp. 83–121 in *Mass-Observation: First Year's Work 1937–8*, London: Lindsay Drummond.

Mani, L. (1990) 'Multiple mediations: feminist scholarship in the age of multinational reception' *Feminist Review* no. 35 pp. 24–41.

Marsden, D. and Oakley, P. (eds) (1990) *Evaluating Social Development Projects*, Oxford: Oxfam.

Marshall, T. H. (1937) 'Is Mass-Observation moonshine?', *The Highway* December, pp. 48–50.

Mohanty, C. (1988) 'Under Western eyes – feminist scholarship and colonial discourses', *Feminist Review* vol. 30 pp. 61–89.

Moore, H. (1988) *Feminism and Anthropology*, Cambridge: Polity Press.

Moors, A. (1991) 'Women and the orient: a note on difference' pp. 114–122 in L. Nencel and P. Pels (eds) *Constructing Knowledge*, London: Sage.

Moser, C. (1986) 'Approaches to community participation in urban development programmes in third world cities'. Unpublished paper for Economic Institute's International Workshop on Participation, September.

Oakley, P. and Marsden, D. (eds) (1984) *Approaches to Participation in Rural Development*, Geneva: International Labour Office.

Okely, J. (1975) 'The self and scientism', *Journal of the Anthropological Society of Oxford* Michaelmas, pp. 171–188.

Okely, J. (1992) 'Anthropology and autobiography: participatory experience and embodied knowledge' pp. 1–28 in J. Okely and H. Callaway (ed.) *Anthropology and Autobiography*, London: Routledge.

Pels, P. and Nencel, L. (1991) 'Introduction: critique and the deconstruction of anthropological authority' pp. 1–21 in L. Nencel and P. Pels (ed.) *Constructing Knowledge. Authority and Critique in Social Science*, London: Sage.

Said, E. (1978) *Orientalism*, London: Routledge and Kegan Paul.

Said, E. (1989) 'Representing the colonized: anthropology's interlocutors', *Critical Inquiry* vol. 15 pp. 205–25.

Scholte, B. (1974) 'Towards a reflexive and critical anthropology' pp. 430–57 in D. Hymes (ed.) *Reinventing Anthropology*, New York: Vintage Books.

Schrijvers, J. (1991) 'Dialectics of a dialogical ideal: studying down, studying sideways and studying up' pp. 162–179 in L. Nencel and P. Pels (ed.) *Constructing Knowledge: Authority and Critique in Social Science*, London: Sage.

Society for Participatory Research in Asia (1982) *Participatory Research. An Introduction*, New Delhi: Society for Participatory Research.

Stanley, L. (1990) 'The archaeology of a 1930s Mass-Observation project' University of Manchester, Department of Sociology, Occasional Paper no. 27.

Stocking, G. (1992) *The Ethnographer's Magic and Other Essays in the History of Anthropology*, Madison: University of Wisconsin Press.

Wright, S. (1992) 'Rural community development: what sort of social change?', *Journal of Rural Studies* vol. 8 pp. 15–28.

Wright, S. (forthcoming) 'Anthropology: still the 'uncomfortable discipline'?' in C. Shore and A. Ahmed (ed.) *The Future of Anthropology*, London: Athlone.

CHAPTER 5

Artaud, A. (1965) *Artaud Anthology*, London: City Lights Books or (1956, 1961) *Oeuvres Complètes, Vol I & II*, Paris: Editions Gallimard.

Boal, A. (1979) *Theatre of the Oppressed*, London: Pluto.

Freire, P. (1976) *Education: The Practice of Freedom*, London: Writers and Readers Publishing Cooperative.

Gubbels, P. and Kwene, N. (1993) *Rural Theatre for Integrated Development: Evaluation of SOS Sahel Drama Unit*, London: SOS Sahel.

Mlama, P. (1991) *Culture and Development: The Popular Theatre Approach in Africa*, Uppsala: The Scandinavian Institute of African Studies.

CHAPTER 6

Bahr, M. (1973) *Skid Row: An Introduction to Disaffiliation*, Oxford: Oxford University Press.

Bailey, K. D. (1987) *Methods of Social Research*, New York: Free Press.

Bogue, D. (1963) *Skid Row in American Cities*, Community and Family Centre, Chicago: University of Chicago Press.

Commission for Racial Equality (1984) *Race and Council Housing in Hackney*, London: Commission for Racial Equality.

Crano, W. D. and Brewer, M. B. (1973) *Principles of Research in Social Psychology*, New York: McGraw-Hill Inc.

Dean, J. P. (1967) 'Observation and interviewing' in J. P. Doby (ed.) *An Introduction to Social Research*, New York: Appleton Century Crofts.

Department of Psychology (1989) *The Faces of Homelessness: Interim Report to the Salvation Army*, Guildford: University of Surrey.

Drake, M., O'Brien, M. and Biebuyck, T. (1982) *Single and Homeless*, London: HMSO, Department of the Environment.

Finch, J. and Mason, J. (1990) 'Decision taking in the field process: theoretical sampling and collaborative working' in R. Burgess (ed.) *Studies in Qualitative Methodology: Reflections on Field Experience*, vol. 2, London: JAI Press.

Finch, P. J. and Breakey, W. R. (1986) 'Homelessness and mental health: An overview', *International Journal of Mental Health*, vol. 14 (4) pp. 6–41.

Greve, J., Page, D., and Greve, S. (1971) *Homelessness in London*, Edinburgh: Scottish Academic Press.

Henslin, J. M. (1990) 'It's not a lovely place to visit, and I wouldn't want to live there' in R. Burgess (ed.) *Reflections on Field Experience: Studies in Qualitative Methodology*, vol. 2, London: JAI Press Inc.

Housing Working Group of Reading and District Council of Churches. (1990) *Report on Homelessness*. Reading: The Sub-Committee of Reading and District Council of Churches.

London Housing Inquiry. (1988) *Speaking Out*, London: The London Housing Forum.

Orwell, G. (1949) *Down and Out in Paris and London*, London: Gollancz.

Randall, G. (1989) *Homeless and Hungry: A Sign of the Times*, London: Centrepoint Soho.

SHIL (1988) *Single Homelessness Among Black and Other Ethnic Minorities: Local Authority Policy and Practice*, London: Single Homeless in London.

Thomas, A. and Niner, P. (1989) *Living in Temporary Accommodation: A Survey of Homeless People*, London: HMSO.

Wallace, S. E. (1968) 'The road to Skid Row', *Social Problems* vol. 16 pp. 92–105.

Webb, E. J. Schwartz, R. D. and Sechrest, L. (1966) *Unobtrusive Measures: Nonreactive Research in the Social Sciences*, Chicago: Rand McNally.

CHAPTER 8

Alvarez-Buylla Roces, M. E., Lazos Chavero, E. and García-Barrios, J.R. (1989) 'Homegardens of a humid tropical region in Southeast Mexico: an example of an agroforestry cropping system in a recently established community', *Agroforestry Systems* vol. 8 pp. 133–56.

Arizpe, L. and Botey, C. (1987) 'Mexican agricultural development policy and its effects on rural women' in C. D. Deere and M. Leon (eds) *Rural Women and*

State Policy: Feminist Perspectives on Latin American Agricultural Development, Boulder, Colorado: Westview Press.

Benería, L. and Roldán, M. (1987) *The Crossroads of Class and Gender: Industrial Homework, Subcontracting and Household Dynamics in Mexico City*, Chicago: Chicago University Press.

Chambers, R. (1969) *Settlement Schemes in Tropical Africa*, London: Routledge.

Cresswell, T. (1992) 'Understanding some aspects of participatory rural appraisal', mimeo, GAPP Conference on Participatory Development July 1992.

Goetz, A. M. (1991) 'Feminism and the claim to know' in R. Grant and K. Newland (ed.) *Gender in International Relations*, Milton Keynes: Open University Press.

Greenberg, J. B. (1989) *Blood Ties: Life and Violence in Rural Mexico*, Tucson: University of Arizona Press.

Hawkesworth, M. (1989) 'Knowers, knowing, known: feminist theory and the claims of truth', *Signs* vol. 14 (3) pp. 533–57.

Hulme, D. (1987) 'State-sponsored land settlement policies: theory and practice', *Development and Change* vol. 18 pp. 418–36.

Lazos Chavero, E. and Alvarez-Buylla Roces, M. E. (1988) 'Ethnobotany in a tropical humid region: The home gardens of Balzapote, Veracruz, Mexico', *Journal of Ethnobiology*, vol. 8 (1) pp. 45–79.

Mohanty, C. T., Torres, L. and Russo, A. (ed.) (1991) *Third World Women and the Politics of Feminism*, Bloomington: Indiana University Press.

Moser, C. O. N. (1989) 'Gender planning in the Third World: meeting practical and strategic gender needs', *World Development* vol. 17(11) pp. 1799–1825.

Ong, A. (1988) 'Colonialism and modernity: Feminist re-presentations of women in non-western societies,' *Inscriptions*, vols. 3–4 pp. 79–93.

Rosaldo, G. (1990) 'De campesinos inmigrantes a obreras de la fresa en el Valle de Zamora, Michoacán' in G. Mummert (ed.) *Población y Trabajo en Contextos Regionales*, Zamora: El Colegio de Michoacán.

Rowlands, J. (1994) 'What is empowerment?', *Development in Practice*, in press.

Schrijvers, J. (1991) 'Dialectics of a dialogical ideal: studying down, studying sideways and studying up' in L. Nencel and P. Pels (ed.) *Constructing Knowledge: Authority and Critique in Social Science*, London: Sage.

Townsend, J. G. (1991) 'Geografía y género en la colonización agricola', *Documents d'Analisi Geográfica* vol. 18 pp. 89–99.

Townsend, J.G., Arrevillaga, U., Cancino, C., Pacheco, S. and Perez, E. (in press a) *Voces Femeninas de las Selvas*, Montecillo, Mexico: Colegio de Postgraduados.

Townsend, J. G., Arrevillaga, U., Bain, J., Cancino, C., Frenk, S. F. Pacheco, S. and Perez, E. (in press b) *Women's Voices from the Rainforest*, London: Routledge.

Townsend, J. G. with Bain de Corcuera, J. (1993) 'Feminists in the rainforest in Mexico', *Geoforum* vol. 24 (1) pp. 49–54.

Wilson, F. 1991 *Sweaters*, London: Macmillan.

Zapata, E. 1990 *Suenos y Realidades de la Mujer*, Montecillo: Colegio de Postgraduados.

CHAPTER 9

Cohen, A. (ed.) (1974) *Urban Ethnicity*, London: Tavistock.

Daniels, N. (1990) 'Orientalism again' in D. Hopwood (ed.) *Studies in Arab History*, New York: St. Martin's Press.

Eades, J. (1987) *Migrants, Workers and the Social Order*, London: Tavistock.

Eickelman, D. (1989) *The Middle East. An Anthropological Approach*, Englewood Cliffs: Prentice Hall.

IRES-Piemonte (ed.) (1991) *Uguali e Diversi: il Mondo Culturale, le Rete dei Rapporti, i Lavori degli Immigrati Non-Europei a Torino*, Turin: Rosenberg e Sellier.

IRES-Piemonte (ed.) (1992) *Rumore: Atteggiamenti Verso gli Immigrati Stranieri*, Turin: Rosenberg e Sellier.

Mayer P. (1962) 'Migrancy and the study of Africans in towns', *American Anthropologist* vol. 64 pp. 576–592.

Mitchell, C. (1969) *Social Networks in Urban Situations: Analysis of Personal Relationships in Central African Towns*, Manchester: Manchester University Press.

Mitchell, C. (1987) *Cities, Society and Social Perception: A Central African Perspective*, Oxford: Clarendon Press.

Reginato, M. (1990) *La Presenza Straniera in Italia; il Caso del Piemonte*, Milan: Franco Angelo.

Turner, V. (1968) *The Forest of Symbols. Aspects of Ndembu Ritual*, London and Ithaca: Cornell University Press.

Turner, V. (1969) *The Ritual Process. Structure and Anti-structure*, Chicago: Aldine Publishing.

Van Velsen, J. (1967) 'The extended case-method and situational analysis' in A. L. Epstein (ed.) *The Craft of Social Anthropology*, London: Tavistock.

CHAPTER 10

Batten, T. R. (1962) *Training for community development* Oxford: Oxford University Press.

Cairncross, S., Carruthers, I., Curtis, D. and Feachem, R. (1980) *Evaluation for Village Water Supply Planning*, London: Wiley.

Chambers, R. (1974) *Managing Rural Development*, Uppsala: Scandinavian Institute of African Studies.

Curtis, D. (1991a) *Beyond Government, Organisations for Common Benefit*, London: Macmillan.

Curtis, D. (1991b) 'Community development, problems and possibilities', mimeo, Development Administration Group, University of Birmingham.

Dube, S.C. (1958) *India's Changing Villages*, London: Routledge and Kegan Paul.

du Sautoy, P. (1958) *Community Development in Ghana*, London: Oxford University Press.

Feachem, R., Burns, E., Cairncross, S., Cronin, A., Cross, P., Curtis, D., Kalid Kahn, M., Lamb, D. and Southall, H. (1978) *Water, Health and Development*, London: Tri-Med.

Holmquist, F. (1970) 'Implementing rural development projects' in G. Hyden, R. Jackson and J. Okumu (ed.) *Development Administration, the Kenyan Experience*, Nairobi: OUP.

HSMO (1957) *Community Development: a Handbook*, London.

Kasfir, N. (1976) *The Shrinking Political Arena: Participation and Ethnicity in African Politics*, Berkley: University of California Press.

Korten, D. (1990) *Getting to the 21st Century: Voluntary Action and the Global Agenda*, West Hartford: CT. Kumarian Press.

O'Donovan, I. (1992) 'The role of the chairman in supporting community development', paper presented at the Workshop for Chairmen and Personnel Supervisors of Local Government, Institute of Administration, Ahmadu Bello University, 7th May 1992.

Schaffer, B. B. (1969) 'The deadlock in development administration' in C. Leys, (ed.) *Politics and Change in Developing Countries*, Cambridge: Cambridge University Press.

217

Toffler, A. (1990) *Power Shift, Knowledge, Wealth, and Violence at the Edge of the 21st Century*, New York: Bantam Books.

CHAPTER 11

Banko Janakari (1987) Editorial, *A Journal of Forest Information for Nepal. Community Forest Management*, vol. 1(4): pp.i-vi.

Bista, D. B. (1991) *Fatalism and Development: Nepal's Struggle for Modernization*, Calcutta: Orient Longman Ltd.

Gilmour, D. A. and Fisher, R. J. (1991) *Villagers, Forests and Foresters. The Philosophy, Process and Practice of Community Forestry in Nepal*, Nepal: Sahayogi Press.

Gronow, J. (1990) 'Forest user groups. Approaches to local forest management in the hills of Nepal', *AERDD Bulletin* no. 30, Reading.

HMG (1976) *Nepal's National Forestry Plan* (unofficial English translation, Nepal-Australia Forestry Project, Kathmandu 1979).

HMG (1990) *Master Plan for the Forestry Sector* (revised draft), His Majesty's Government of Nepal: Ministry of Forest and Soil Conservation.

HMG (1991) *Operational Guidelines if the Community Forestry Programme* (second edition), Kathmandu: Ministry of Forest and Environment (first edition 1990).

Midgley, J. Hall, A., Hardiman, M. and Narcine, D. (1986) *Community Participation, Social Development and the State*, London: Methuen.

Nadkarni, M.V., Syed Ajmal Pasha and Prabhakar, L.S. (1989) *The Political Economy of Forest Use and Management*, New Delhi: Sage.

CHAPTER 12

Allen, I; Hogg, D. and Peace, S. (1992) *Elderly People: Choice, Participation and Satisfaction*, London: Policy Studies Institute.

Audit Commission (1992) *Community Care: Managing the Cascade of Change*, London: HMSO.

Berman, Y. (1989) 'The structure of information in organizational frameworks: the social services department', *British Journal of Social Work* vol.19 pp.479–89.

Challis, L. (1990) *Organising Public Social Services*, Harlow: Longman.

Department of Health (1989) *Caring for People: Community Care in the Next Decade and Beyond*, London: HMSO.

Dill, A.E.P. (1990) 'Transformations of home: The formal and informal processes of home care planning' in J.F. Gubrium and A. Sankar (ed.) *The Home Care Experience: Ethnography and Policy*, Newbury Park, CA: Sage.

Freidson, E. (1984) 'The changing nature of professional control', *Annual Review of Sociology*, vol.10 pp.1–20.

Griffiths, R. (1988) *Community Care: Agenda for Action.*, London: HMSO.

Hugman, R. (1991) *Power in Caring Professions*, Basingstoke: Macmillan.

Hunter, D., McKegany, N. and MacPherson, I. (1988) *Care of the Elderly: Policy and Practice*, Aberdeen: Aberdeen University Press.

Lewis, J. and Meredith, B. (1988) *Daughters Who Care: Daughters Caring for Mothers at Home*, London: Routledge.

Lipsky, M. (1980) *Street-Level Bureaucracy: Dilemmas of the Individual in Public Services*, New York: Russell Sage Foundation.

Marsh, P. and Fisher, M. (1992) *Good Intentions: Developing Partnership in the Social Services*, London: Joseph Rowntree Foundation.

Mannion, R. (1991) *Quality in Community Care*, Social Policy Research Unit, York: University of York.

Meethan, K. F. and Thompson, C. (1993a) *In Their Own Homes: Incorporating Carers' and Users' Views in Care Management*, York: Social Policy Research Unit, University of York.

Meethan, K. F. and Thompson, C. (1993b) 'Negotiating community care: politics, locality and resources', *Policy and Politics* vol. 21 pp. 195–205.

Meethan, K. F., Thompson, C. and Parker, G. (1993) *Making it Happen? Care Management in Practice*, York: Social Policy Research Unit, University of York.

Nocon, A. (1989) 'Forms of ignorance and their role in the joint planning process' *Social Policy and Administration*, vol.23 (1) pp.31–47.

Parker, G. (1990) *With Due Care and Attention: A Review of Research on Informal Care*, London: Family Policy Studies Centre.

Reed. M. I. (1992) *The Sociology of Organizations: Themes, Perspectives and Problems*, Hemel Hempstead: Harvester Wheatsheaf.

Social Services Inspectorate/Social Work Services Group (1991a) *Care Management and Assessment: Managers' Guide*, London: HMSO.

Social Services Inspectorate/Social Work Services Group (1991b) *Care Management and Assessment: Practitioners' Guide*, London: HMSO.

Social Services Inspectorate/Social Work Services Group (1991c) *Training for Community Care: A Joint Approach*, London: HMSO.

Thornton, P. (1989) *Creating a Break: A Home Care Relief System for Elderly People and their Supporters*, Mitcham: Age Concern England.

Twigg, J. and Atkin, K. (1994) *Policy and Practice in Informal Care*, Milton Keynes: Open University Press.

Wistow, G. (1988) 'Beyond joint planning: managing community care' in G. Wistow and T. Brooks (ed.) *Joint Planning and Joint Management*, London: Royal Institute of Public Administration.

CHAPTER 13

Abeyratne, S. (1990) 'Rehabilitation of small-scale irrigation systems in Sri Lanka: state policy and practice in two systems'. IIMI Country Paper, Sri Lanka, No.6, Colombo: International Irrigation Management Institute.

Agarwal, A. and Narain, S. (1989) *Towards Green Villages: a Strategy for Environmentally-Sound and Participatory Rural Development*, Delhi: Centre for Science & Environment.

Ambler, J. (1992) 'Basic elements of an innovative tank rehabilitiation programme for sustained productivity,' unpublished paper, New Delhi: Ford Foundation.

Bagadion, B. U. and Korten, F. F. (1991) 'Developing Irrigators' Organizations: a Learning Process Approach' in M. Cernea (ed.) *Putting People First: Sociological Variables in Rural Development*, (second edition). Oxford: Oxford University Press; Washington D.C: The World Bank.

Chambers, R. Saxena, N. C. and Shah, T. (1989) *To the Hands of the Poor: Water and Trees*, New Delhi: Oxford and IBH Publishing.

Curtis, D. (1991) *Beyond Government: Organisations for Common Benefit*, London and Basingstoke: Macmillan.

CWR (1990) *Alternative Approaches to Tank Rehabilitation and Management – a Proposed Experiment: Annual Report 1988–89*, Centre for Water Resources, Anna University, Madras.

CWR (1991) *Alternative Approaches to Tank Rehabilitation and Management – a Proposed Experiment: Annual Report 1989–90*, Centre for Water Resources, Anna University, Madras.

Dirks, N. (1987) *The Hollow Crown: Ethnohistory of a South Indian Little Kingdom*, Cambridge: Cambridge University Press.

Douglas, M. (1986) *How Institutions Think*, London: Routledge & Kegan Paul

Fuller, C. (1989) 'Misconceiving the grain heap: a critique of the concept of the Indian Jajmani system' in J. Parry and M. Bloch (ed.) *Money and the Morality of Exchange*, Cambridge: Cambridge University Press.

Harriss, J. (1982) *Capitalism and Peasant Farming: Agrarian Structure and Ideology in Northern Tamil Nadu*, New Delhi: Oxford University Press.

Lardinois, R. (1989) 'Deserted villages and depopulation in rural Tamil Nadu c. 1780-c.1830' in T. Dyson (ed.) *India's Historical Demography*, London: Curzon Press.

Leach, E. R. (1961) *Pul Eliya*, Cambridge: Cambridge University Press.

Ludden, D. (1979) 'Patronage and irrigation in Tamil Nadu: a long-term view', *The Economic and Social History Review* vol. 16 (3) pp.347–365.

Ludden, D. (1985) *Peasant History in South India*, Princeton: Princeton University Press.

Ludden, D. (1993) 'Orientalist empiricism: transformations of colonial knowledge' in C. A. Breckenridge and P. van der Veer (eds) *Orientalism and the Post Colonial Predicament: Perspectives on South Asia*, Philadelphia: University of Pennsylvania Press.

Mayer, P. (1993) 'Inventing village tradition: the late 19th century origins of the north Indian 'jajmani system', *Modern Asian Studies* vol. 27 pp. 357–395.

Meinzen-Dick, R. (1984) *Local Management of Tank Irrigation in South India: Organisation and Operation*, Cornell Studies in Irrigation, No. 3. New York: Cornell University.

MIDS (1988) *Tamilnadu Economy: Performance and Issues*, Madras Institute of Development Studies. Delhi: Oxford and IBH Publishing.

Mosse, D. (1994a) 'Community management and the rehabilitation of tank irrigation systems in Tamil Nadu: a research agenda' *Papers in International Development*, Centre for Development Studies, Swansea, University of Wales (in press).

Mosse, D. (1994b) 'Idioms of subordination and styles of protest among Christian and Hindu Harijan (Untouchable) castes in Tamil Nadu', *Contributions to Indian Sociology* vol. 28 (2) (in press).

Mosse, D. (1994c) 'Authority, gender and knowledge: theoretical reflections on the practice of Participatory Rural Appraisal', *Development and Change* vol. 25 (3) pp. 497–525.

Mosse, D. (1994d) 'Global concepts and local contexts: anthropological knowledge in participatory rural development', paper presented at the Workshop on the research/Consultancy Interface, Centre for Development Studies, University of Wales, Swansea, 21–23 March 1994.

Mosse, D. (forthcoming) 'Village institutions, resources and power: the ideology and politics of tank irrigation development in south India' in R. L. Stirrat and R. Grillo (ed.) *The Anthropology of Development*.

Olson, M. (1971) *The Logic of Collective Action*, Cambridge, Mass.: Harvard University Press.

Ostrom, E. (1992) *Crafting Institutions for Self-Governing Irrigation Systems*, San Francisco: Institute for Contemporary Studies Press.

Reddy, S. T. (1989a) 'Declining groundwater levels in India', *Water Resources Development* vol. 5 (3) pp. 183–190.

Reddy, S. T. (1989b) *Status of Tanks in Karnataka: A Study*, Bangalore: Prarambha.

Reddy, V. R. (1990) 'Irrigation in colonial India: a study of Madras Presidency during 1860–1900', *Economic & Political Weekly* May 5–12 1990.

Shankari, U. and Shah, E. (1993) *Water Management Traditions in India*. Madras: PPST Foundation.

Singh, K. (1991) 'Managing common pool irrigation tanks: a case study in Andhra Pradesh and West Bengal' *Working Paper 14*, Institute of Rural Management, Anand.

Spencer, J. (1990) *A Sinhala Village in a Time of Trouble: Politics and Change in Rural Sri Lanka*, Oxford University Press: New Delhi.

Von Oppen, M. and Subba Rao, K. V. (1980) 'Tank irrigation in semi-arid tropical India', Economic Programme Progress Report, International Crops Research Institute for the Semi-Arid Tropics (ICRISAT), A.P., India.

Wade, R. (1987a) *Village Republics: Economic Conditions for Collective Action in South India*, Cambridge: Cambridge University Press.

Wade, R. (1987b) 'The management of common property resources: finding a co-operative solution', *Research Observer* vol. 2 (2) pp. 219–234.

CHAPTER 14

Adnan, S., Barrett, A., Nurul Alam, S. M. and Brustinow, A. (1992) *People's Participation. NGOs and the Flood Action Plan*, Dhaka: Research and Advisory Services.

Bebbington, A. (1991) 'Planning rural development in local organizations in the Andes: what role for regional and national scaling up?', *RRA Notes* vol. 11 pp.71–4.

Chambers, R. (1983) *Rural Development. Putting the Last First*, London: Longman.

Chambers, R. (1992) 'Rural appraisal: rapid, relaxed and participatory', *IDS Discussion Paper* 311, Institute of Development Studies, Sussex.

Cornwall, A., Guijt, I. and Welbourn, A. (1993). 'Acknowledging process: challenges for agricultural research and extension methodology', *Sustainable Agriculture Programme Research Series* vol. 1 pp. 21–47, London: International Institute for Environment and Development.

Dalal-Clayton, B. and Dent, D. (1994) *Surveys, Plans and People. A review of Land Resource Information and its Use in Developing Countries*, London: Environmental Planning Group, International Institute for Environment and Development.

Edwards, M. and Hulme, D. (1992) *Making a Difference? NGOs and Development in a Changing World*, London: Earthscan Publications Ltd.

Farrington, J., Bebbington, A. and Wellard, K. (1993) *Between the State and the Rural Poor: NGOs and Sustainable Agricultural Development*, London: Routledge.

Farrington, J. and Bebbington, A. (1994) 'From research to innovation: getting the most from interaction with NGOs in farming systems research and extension', *Sustainable Agriculture Programme Gatekeeper Series* SA43, London: International Institute for Environment and Development.

Fowler, A. (1991) 'What is different about managing non-government organizations (NGOs) involved in Third World development', *RRA Notes* vol. 11 pp.75–81.

Fowler, A. (1992) 'Prioritising institutional development: a new role for NGO centres for study and development', *Sustainable Agriculture Programme Gatekeeper Series* SA35, London: International Institute for Environment and Development.

Gibson, T. (1991) 'Planning for Real: the approach of the Neighbourhood Initiatives Foundation in the UK', *RRA Notes* vol. 11 pp. 29–30.

Gill, G. (1991) 'But what about the real data?', *RRA Notes* vol. 14 pp. 5–14.

Goethert, R. and Hamdi, N. (1988) *Making Microplans: A Community-Based Process in Programming and Development*, London: Intermediate Technology Publications.

Guijt, I. (1991) *Perspectives on Participation: Views from Africa*, London: International Institute for Environment and Development.

Inglis, A. (1991) 'Harvesting local forestry knowledge: a comparison of RRA and conventional surveys', *RRA Notes* vol. 12 pp. 32–40.

KKU (1987) *Rapid Rural Appraisal. Proceedings of the 1985 Conference on Rapid Rural Appraisal*, Khon Kaen: Farming Systems Research Project, Khon Kaen University.

Korten, D. (1980) 'The learning process approach', *Public Administration Review* vol. 40 pp.480–511.

Mascarenhas, J., Shah, P., Joseph, S., Devavaram, J., Jayakaran, R., Ramachandran, V., Fernandez, A., Chambers, R. and Pretty, J. (eds) (1991) 'Participatory rural appraisal in India', *RRA Notes* vol. 13 pp.10–48.

Mucai, G. M., Ndungu, M., Wanjiku, J., Thompson, J., Odeny, A. O. and Msumai, T.M. (1992) *Rapid Catchment Analysis of Ringuti Catchment, Kiambu*, Nairobi: Soil and Water Conservation Branch, Ministry of Agriculture.

Muya, F. S., Njoroge, M., Mwarasomba, L. A., Sillah, P. K., Kwedilima, I. and Pretty, J. (1992) *Rapid Catchment Analysis of Thigio Catchment, Kiambu*, Nairobi: Soil and Water Conservation Branch, Ministry of Agriculture.

Pretty, J. N. (1994) 'Alternative systems of inquiry for a sustainable agriculture' *IDS Bulletin* vol. 25 (2) pp.19–30.

Pretty, J. N. and Chambers, R. (1993) 'Towards a new learning paradigm: new professionalism and institutions for agriculture', *Sustainable Agriculture Programme Research Series* vol. 1 pp. 48–83, London: International Institute for Environment and Development.

Pretty, J. N., Guijt, I., Scoones, I. and Thompson, J. (1992) 'Regenerating agriculture: the agroecology of low-external input and community-based development' in J. Holmberg (ed.) *Policies for a Small Planet*, London: Earthscan Publications Ltd.

Pretty, J. N., Thompson, J. and Kiara, J. (1994) 'Agricultural regeneration in Kenya: the catchment approach to soil and water conservation', *Ambio* (forthcoming).

Roche, C. (1991) 'ACORD's experience in local planning in Mali and Burkina Faso', *RRA Notes* vol. 11 pp.33–41.

RRA Notes (1988–1994) vols. 1–20, Sustainable Agriculture Programme, London: International Institute for Environment and Development.

Shah, P. (1994) 'Village-managed extension systems: implications for policy and practice' in I. Scoones and J. Thompson (eds) *Beyond Farmer First: Rural People's Knowledge, Agricultural Research and Extension Practice*, London: Intermediate Technology Publications.

Uphoff, N. (1992) 'Local institutions and participation for sustainable development', *Sustainable Agriculture Programme Gatekeeper* SA31, London: International Institute for Environment and Development.

CHAPTER 15

Bourdillon, A. F. C., Cheater, A. P. and Murphree, M. W. (1985) *Studies of Fishing on Lake Kariba*, Mambo Occasional Papers, Socio-Economic Series No.20, Gweru (Zimbabwe).

Cernea, M. M. (ed.) (1985) *Putting People First: Sociological Variables in Rural Development*, World Bank, Oxford: Oxford University Press.

Chambers, R. (1983) *Rural Development: Putting the Last First*, London: Longman.
Cohen, J. M. and Uphoff N. T. (1980) 'Participation's place in rural development: seeking clarity through specificity', *World Development* vol.8 pp. 213–235.
Colson, E. (1960) *Social Organization of the Gwembe Tonga*, Human Problems in Kariba vol. 1, University of Zambia, Manchester: Manchester University Press.
Colson, E. (1971) *The Social Consequences of Resettlement: The Impact of the Kariba Resettlement upon the Gwembe Tonga* Kariba Studies IV, University of Zambia, Manchester: Manchester University Press.
Freire, P. (1972) *Pedagogy of the Oppressed* (M. Bergman Ramos trans.) Harmondsworth: Penguin.
Gezelius, H. and Millwood, D. (1988) 'N.G.O.s in development and participation in practice: an initial enquiry', Development Studies Unit, University of Stockholm, Popular Participation Programme, *PPP Working Paper* no. 3, July.
Harvest Help (1988) 'Detailed plan for kapenta fishing' prepared by GVAM.
Harvest Help (1990) 'Harvest Help. The Gwembe Valley past, present and future', London: Harvest Help/UK.
Harvest Help (undated) 'The Gwembe Project. Background information sheets 1–4', London: Harvest Help/UK.
Harvest Helper: Regular Reports from the Field of Progress: Gwembe Lakeside Project, Zambia Nos 1–21 (December 1985-December 1990) plus occasional supplements and reports by GVAM.
Hedenquist, J. A. (1989) *Popular Participation in Rural Development: the Masase Project in Zimbabwe*, Development Studies Unit, University of Stockholm, *PPP Working Paper* no. 5, January.
Huizer, G. (1989) 'Action research and people's participation: an introduction and some case studies', Third World Center, Catholic University of Nijmegen. *Occasional Paper* 19, November.
Mabaye, A. (1987) 'Some management aspects and constraints in the Lake Kariba fishery', *Naga, the ICLARM Quarterly* October 1987.
Oakley, P. and Marsden, D. (1984) *Approaches to Participation in Rural Development*, Geneva: International Labour Organization.
Oakley, P. *et al.* (1991) *Projects with People: The Practice of Participation in Rural Development*, Geneva: International Labour Organization.
Poulton, R. and Harris, M. (ed.) (1988) *Putting People First: Voluntary Organisations and Third World Development*, London and Basingstoke: Pitman.
Ramberg, L., Bjork-Ramberg, S., Kautsky, N. and Machena, C. (1987) 'Development and biological status of Lake Kariba – a man-made tropical lake', *AMBIO* vol. 16 no. 6.
Scudder, T. (1962) *The Ecology of the Gwembe Tonga*, Northern Rhodesia: The Rhodes-Livingstone Institute.
Scudder, T. (1971) 'Gathering among African woodland savannah cultivators. A case study: The Gwembe Tonga', University of Zambia, *Zambian Papers* No.5.
Scudder, T. (1982) 'Eight ways in which to raise living standards in Gwembe District and to reduce agricultural shortfalls', California Institute of Technology, October, mimeo.
Scudder, T. (1985) 'A history of development in the Twentieth Century: the Zambian portion of the Middle Zambezi Valley and the Lake Kariba Basin', Co-operative Agreement on Human Settlements and Natural Resource Systems Analysis, Institute for Development Anthropology *Working Paper* no. 22. New York, August.
Scudder, T. (1990) '1990 evaluation of the Gwembe Valley Agricultural Mission (Harvest Help/Zambia)', Harvest Help/U.K., December.

Scudder, T. (1993) 'Development-induced relocation and refugee studies: 37 years of change and continuity among Zambia's Gwembe Tonga', *Journal of Refugee Studies* vol. 6 no. 2, pp. 123–52.

Scudder, T., Colson, E. and Scudder, M. E. D. (1982) 'An evaluation of the Gwembe South Development Project', Zambia' Institute for Development Anthropology *Working Paper* No.5. New York, August.

Topsoe-Jensen, B. (1989) 'Popular participation, monitoring and evaluation in integrated rural development. The case of PDRI in Guinea-Bissau', University of Stockholm, Development Studies Unit, *PPP Working Paper* no. 6 December.

UNRISD (1975) *Rural Institutions and Planned Change vol. VIII. Rural Co-operatives as Agents of Change: a Research Report and a Debate*, Geneva 1975.

Uphoff, N. (1985) 'Fitting projects to people', pp. 359–395 in M. Cernea (ed.) *Putting People First: Sociological Variables in Rural Development*, Oxford: Oxford University Press.

Wood, A. (1987) 'Report to the trustees of Voluntary and Christian Service on a visit in July 1987 to the Gwembe Valley Agricultural Mission', London: Harvest Help/UK.

CHAPTER 16

Bratton, M. (1989) 'The politics of government-NGO relations in Africa', *World Development* vol. 17 (4) pp. 569–87.

Brodhead, T. (1988) *Bridges of Hope?*, Ottawa: The North South Institute.

Gorman, R. F. (1984) *Private Voluntary Organisations as Agents of Development*, Boulder, Colorado: Westview Press.

Korten, D. C. (1990) *Getting to the 21st Century*, Connecticut, USA: Kumarian Press.

Paul, S. (1987) *Community Participation in Development Projects*, World Bank Discussion Paper no. 6, Washington DC: World Bank.

Poulton, R. and Harris, M. (ed.) (1988) *Putting People First*, London: Macmillan.

Smith, B. (1984) 'U.S. and Canadian PVOs as transnational development institutions' in R. F. Gorman (ed.) *Private Voluntary Organisations as Agents for Development*, Boulder, Colorado: Westview Press.

Smith, B. (1987) 'An agenda of future tasks for international and indigenous NGOs: views from the North', *World Development* vol. 15 Supplement pp. 87–93.

Tendler, J. (1982) *Turning PVO's into Development Agencies: Questions for Evaluation*, USAID Program Evaluation Discussion Paper No. 12, Washington DC: USAID.

Wangola, P. (1990) *'On the African Crisis and People's Participation and the Indigenous Non-Governmental Organisations in Africa's Recovery asnd Development'*, Addis Ababa: UN Economic Commission for Africa.

CHAPTER 17

Askew, I. (1988) 'Community participation in family planning: a comparative analysis of community participation projects in the South with social policy and programme recommendations for Family Planning Associations', Occasional Series on Community Participation, London: International Planned Parenthood Federation.

Chambers, R., Saxena, N. C. and Shah, T. (1989) *To the Hands of the Poor*, London: Intermediate Technology Publications.

Douglas, M. (1987) *How Institutions Think*, London: Routledge.

Kanbur, R. (1992) *Heterogeneity, Distribution and Cooperation in Common Property Resource Management,* Policy Research Working for the World Development Report, Washington DC: World Bank.

Moser, C. (1989) 'Gender planning in the Third World: meeting practical and strategic gender needs', *World Development* vol. 17 (2) pp. 1799-1825.

Paul, S. (1986) 'Community participation in development projects. The World Bank experience', paper presented at Economic Development Institute Workshop on Community Participation, Washington DC.

Platteau, P. (1991) 'The free market is not readily transferable: reflections on the links between market, social relations and moral norms', paper for the 25th Jubilee of the IDS, University of Sussex.

Sachs, I. (1987) *Development and Planning,* Cambridge: Cambridge University Press.

World Health Organization (1988) *The Challenge of Implementation: District Health Systems for Primary Health Care,* Geneva: World Health Organization.

World Bank (11991) *A Common Vocabulary: Popular Participation Learning Group,* Washington DC: World Bank.

225